NEW STUDIES IN BIBLICAL THEOLOGY 58

THE GLORY OF GOD
AND PAUL

T0311325

NEW STUDIES IN BIBLICAL THEOLOGY 58

Series editor: D. A. Carson

THE GLORY OF GOD AND PAUL

Texts, themes and theology

Christopher W. Morgan
and Robert A. Peterson

APOLLOS

Academic
An imprint of InterVarsity Press
Downers Grove, Illinois

APOLLOS (an imprint of Inter-Varsity Press, England)
36 Causton Street, London SW1P 4ST, England
Website: www.ivpbooks.com
Email: ivp@ivpbooks.com

InterVarsity Press, USA
P.O. Box 1400, Downers Grove, IL 60515, USA
Website: www.ivpress.com
Email: email@ivpress.com

Inter-Varsity Press, England, publishes Christian books that are true to the Bible and that
communicate the gospel, develop discipleship and strengthen the church for its mission in the world.

IVP originated within the Inter-Varsity Fellowship, now the Universities and Colleges Christian
Fellowship, a student movement connecting Christian Unions in universities and colleges
throughout Great Britain, and a member movement of the International Fellowship of Evangelical
Students. That historic association is maintained, and all senior IVP staff and committee members
subscribe to the UCCF Basis of Faith. Website: www.uccf.org.uk.

InterVarsity Press®, USA, is the book-publishing division of InterVarsity Christian Fellowship/USA®
and a member movement of the International Fellowship of Evangelical Students.
Website: www.intervarsity.org.

First published 2022

Set in 10/13.25pt Minion Pro and Gill Sans Nova
Typeset in Great Britain by CRB Associates, Potterhanworth, Lincolnshire
Printed and bound in Great Britain by Ashford Colour Press Ltd, Gosport, Hampshire

Produced on paper from sustainable sources.

UK ISBN: 978–1–78974–281–7 (print)
UK ISBN: 978–1–78974–282–4 (digital)

US ISBN: 978–1–5140–0447–0 (print)
US ISBN: 978–1–5140–0448–7 (digital)

British Library Cataloguing-in-Publication Data
A catalogue record for this book is available from the British Library.

Library of Congress Cataloging-in-Publication Data
A catalog record for this book is available from the Library of Congress.

Contents

Series preface

New Studies in Biblical Theology is a series of monographs that address key issues in the discipline of biblical theology. Contributions to the series focus on one or more of three areas: (1) the nature and status of biblical theology, including its relations with other disciplines (e.g. historical theology, exegesis, systematic theology, historical criticism, narrative theology); (2) the articulation and exposition of the structure of thought of a particular biblical writer or corpus; and (3) the delineation of a biblical theme across all or part of the biblical corpora.

Above all, these monographs are creative attempts to help thinking Christians understand their Bibles better. The series aims simultaneously to instruct and to edify, to interact with the current literature and to point the way ahead. In God's universe mind and heart should not be divorced: in this series we will try not to separate what God has joined together. While the notes interact with the best of scholarly literature, the text is uncluttered with untransliterated Greek and Hebrew, and tries to avoid too much technical jargon. The volumes are written within the framework of confessional evangelicalism, but there is always an attempt at thoughtful engagement with the sweep of the relevant literature.

Some topics are so ubiquitous in Scripture that it is difficult to treat them in a succinct and penetrating way. One is reduced to sweeping generalities. This book by Chris Morgan and Robert Peterson, *The Glory of God and Paul*, is the exception. After cautiously surveying the use of 'the glory of God' in Scripture, Morgan and Peterson embark on a careful inductive analysis of the use of the expression in Paul, book by book – the most controlled form of biblical theology – before attempting a thoughtful synthesis. Before taking up this topic in the future, the wisest preachers and teachers will want to consult this book.

D. A. Carson
Trinity Evangelical Divinity School

Authors' preface

> The design of the ensuing discourse is to declare some part of that glory of our Lord Jesus Christ which is revealed in the Scripture, and proposed as the principal object of our faith, love, delight, and admiration. But, alas! After our utmost and most diligent inquiries, we must say, How little a portion is it of him that we can understand! His glory is incomprehensible, and his praises unutterable.
> (John Owen)

Like Owen we are both drawn to and humbled by this magnificent theme. We are attracted to the glory of God as iron shavings are drawn to a magnet. It exerts a strong pull on our minds and hearts! It is the grandest of themes, and we want to behold and enjoy it. But immediately we identify with David's words:

> Such knowledge is too wonderful for me;
> it is high; I cannot attain it.
> (Ps. 139:6)

Who is qualified to write on the glory of God? If that were the question, we would never have undertaken such a fool's errand. No one is qualified. Certainly not us. So, both compelled and humbled, we write with zeal to promote God's glory and with awareness that this noble theme puts us in our place.

Studying and teaching various theology classes and lectures led us to ask how glory is the ultimate end of God, but in such a way as not to negate that his goals flow out of his very nature/attributes. How can God's acting out of love, justice, grace, mercy, and so on, all be summarized by biblical writers as God's acting for his glory? How does God's glory as his ultimate end relate to his multiple purposes? How does God's acting to glorify himself cohere with his self-giving love? How does God seek both his glory and our good, and how do these work hand in hand? How does being made in the image of God relate to the glory of God?

So about ten years ago, we contributed to and edited the volume *The Glory of God*, volume two in our Theology in Community series. In it, we assembled an all-star team: Stephen J. Nichols, Tremper Longman III, Richard R. Melick Jr, Andreas J. Köstenberger, Richard B. Gaffin Jr, Bryan Chapell and J. Nelson Jennings. Together they explored the biblical data, systematic implications and pastoral missional themes concerning God's glory.

Other projects in our series all shed light on glory, and God's glory shed light on them: suffering and God's goodness, the deity of Christ, the kingdom of God, sin, heaven, the love of God and biblical spirituality. Other projects kept revealing glory's interconnectedness with other themes: hell, the theology of James, Christ and his saving work, the Spirit and union with Christ, evangelical unity, assurance of salvation, the church, and so on.

Studying and writing on the church particularly extended our questions. Careful reading on the church in Ephesians made our hearts sing and our minds wonder in what sense the church is the fullness of him who fills all in all (Eph. 1:21–23). What does it mean for the church to be the one new humanity and how does that relate to the image of God? How is it possible that Paul writes: 'to him be glory *in the church*' (3:21)?[1] If Christ will present the church to himself as glorious (5:22–33), in what sense is the church glorious now?

Writing a systematic theology textbook together also led us to notice central motifs of various theologians. But what motifs are really worthy of such a role in one's theology? The glory of God surely emerges as one of the strongest candidates. How does glory shape and correlate with the major theological loci – God and his revelation, humanity, sin, Christ, Christ's saving work, the Holy Spirit, salvation, the church and the future? And so on.

This NSBT volume does not attempt to answer all these questions. Instead, it reflects another step on our journey in theology, and another step in our longing to better understand God and his glory. While some of the above questions are treated here, this book is not macrocosmic but focused. After one chapter introducing the glory of God in a panoramic way and another chapter relating the glory of God in the biblical story, we ask what Paul teaches about the glory of God. What are his key passages? What themes are most linked to glory in his teachings? What is his overall

---

[1] All emphasis in Scripture quotations throughout the book has been added by the authors.

theology of the glory of God? And how does his theology of glory shape the Christian life?

It has been a privilege and a delight to write this together – there is something special about studying together, working through questions together, sharing applications together, and refining one another along the way.

We thank Don Carson for his warm invitation, superb scholarship and editorial insights. We thank Philip Duce at Inter-Varsity Press for his editorial guidance. We thank Eldo Barkhuizen for his outstanding work as our IVP copy editor.

We are also grateful for the copy-editing of Elliott Pinegar, the research assistance of Kevin Hall, and the wide-ranging adeptness of Maigen Turner. We thank Gary McDonald and SoCal Baptist Ministries. We also feel blessed to serve alongside our friends at California Baptist University, Immanuel Baptist Church in California and Covenant of Grace Church in St. Charles, Missouri.

Abbreviations

ABG	Arbeiten zur Bibel und ihrer Geschichte
ANE	Ancient Near East
BECNT	Baker Exegetical Commentary on the New Testament
BRF	Basics of the Reformed Faith
BST	The Bible Speaks Today
BTB	*Biblical Theology Bulletin*
CCT	Contours of Christian Theology
CNTC	Calvin's New Testament Commentaries
DJG	*Dictionary of Jesus and the Gospels*, ed. J. B. Green, J. K. Brown and N. Perrin, 2nd edn, Downers Grove: InterVarsity Press; Nottingham: Inter-Varsity Press, 2013
DLNTD	*Dictionary of the Later New Testament and Its Developments*, ed. R. P. Martin and P. H. Davids, Downers Grove: InterVarsity Press; Leicester: Inter-Varsity Press, 1997
DOTP	*Dictionary of the Old Testament: Pentateuch*, ed. T. D. Alexander and D. W. Baker, Downers Grove: InterVarsity Press; Leicester: Inter-Varsity Press, 2003
DPL	*Dictionary of Paul and His Letters*, ed. G. F. Hawthorne and R. P. Martin, Downers Grove: InterVarsity Press; Leicester: Inter-Varsity Press, 1993
EBC	Expositor's Bible Commentary
EBT	Explorations in Biblical Theology
EDBT	*Evangelical Dictionary of Biblical Theology*, ed. W. A. Elwell, Grand Rapids: Baker, 1996
EEC	Evangelical Exegetical Commentary
ESV	English Standard Version
FOET	Foundations of Evangelical Theology
FTB	Focus on the Bible
HBT	*Horizons in Biblical Theology*
ICC	International Critical Commentary

IDB	*Interpreter's Dictionary of the Bible*, ed. G. A. Buttrick, New York: Abingdon, 1962
ISBE	*International Standard Bible Encyclopedia*, ed. G. W. Bromiley, rev. edn, Grand Rapids: Eerdmans, 1979–95
IVPNTC	IVP New Testament Commentary Series
JBPR	*Journal of Biblical and Pneumatological Research*
JETS	*Journal of the Evangelical Theological Society*
JSNT	*Journal for the Study of the New Testament*
JSNTSup	Journal for the Study of the New Testament Supplement Series
LXX	Septuagint
MT	Masoretic Text
NAC	New American Commentary
NACSBT	NAC Studies in Bible and Theology
NASB	New American Standard Bible
NCBC	New Century Bible Commentary
NDBT	*New Dictionary of Biblical Theology*, ed. T. D. Alexander, B. S. Rosner, D. A. Carson and G. Goldsworthy, Leicester: Inter-Varsity Press; Downers Grove: InterVarsity Press, 2000
NDSB	New Daily Study Bible
NDT	*New Dictionary of Theology*, ed. S. B. Ferguson, D. F. Wright and J. I. Packer, Downers Grove: InterVarsity Press; Leicester: Inter-Varsity Press, 1988
NIBC	New International Biblical Commentary
NICNT	New International Commentary on the New Testament
NICOT	New International Commentary on the Old Testament
NIDB	*New Interpreter's Dictionary of the Bible*, ed. K. D. Sakenfeld, 5 vols., Nashville: Abingdon, 2006–9
NIDNTTE	*New International Dictionary of New Testament Theology and Exegesis*, ed. M. S. Silva, 2nd edn, Grand Rapids: Zondervan, 2014
NIDOTTE	*New International Dictionary of Old Testament Theology and Exegesis*, ed. W. A. VanGemeren, Grand Rapids: Zondervan, 1997
NIGTC	New International Greek Testament Commentary
NIV	New International Version
NovTSup	Supplements to Novum Testamentum

NRSVA	New Revised Standard Version, Anglicized
NSBT	New Studies in Biblical Theology
NT	New Testament
NT	*Novum Testamentum*
NTS	*New Testament Studies*
OT	Old Testament
OTL	Old Testament Library
PNTC	Pillar New Testament Commentary
PTW	Preaching the Word
SBJT	*Southern Baptist Journal of Theology*
SBL	Studies in Biblical Literature
SHST	Studies in Historical and Systematic Theology
SNTSMS	Society for New Testament Studies Monograph Series
TDNT	*Theological Dictionary of the New Testament*, ed. G. Kittel and G. Friedrich, tr. G. W. Bromiley, 10 vols., Grand Rapids: Eerdmans, 1964–76
TDOT	*Theological Dictionary of the Old Testament*, ed. J. G. Botterweck, H.-J. Fabry and H. Ringgren, tr. D. E. Green and D. W. Scott, 10 vols., Grand Rapids: Eerdmans, 1975–2005
THNTC	Two Horizons New Testament Commentary
TIC	Theology in Community
TNTC	Tyndale New Testament Commentaries
TPG	Theology for the People of God
tr.	translated, translation
TrinJ	*Trinity Journal*
TS	*Theological Studies*
TWOT	*Theological Wordbook of the Old Testament*, ed. R. L. Harris and G. L. Archer Jr, 2 vols., Chicago: Moody, 1980
TynB	*Tyndale Bulletin*
WBC	Word Biblical Commentary
WC	Westminster Commentaries
WJE	Works of Jonathan Edwards
WTJ	*Westminster Theological Journal*
WUNT	Wissenschaftliche Untersuchungen zum Neuen Testament
ZA	*Zeitschrift für Assyriologie*
ZECNT	Zondervan Exegetical Commentary on the New Testament

Introduction

There is something exceedingly improving to the mind in a contemplation of the Divinity. It is a subject so vast, that all our thoughts are lost in its immensity; so deep, that our pride is drowned in its infinity . . . But when we come to this master science, finding that our plumbline cannot sound its depth, and that our eagle eye cannot see its height, we turn away with the thought that . . . 'I am but of yesterday, and know nothing.' No subject of contemplation will tend more to humble the mind, than thoughts of God. But while the subject humbles the mind, it also expands it . . . The most excellent study for expanding the soul, is the science of Christ, and Him crucified, and the knowledge of the Godhead in the glorious Trinity.[1]
(C. H. Spurgeon)

As clowns yearn to play Hamlet, so I have wanted to write a treatise on God.[2]
(J. I. Packer)

Charles Haddon Spurgeon and J. I. Packer are perceptive: studying wonderful truths about our God both humbles the mind and expands it. We do not know of a more mind-humbling and soul-expanding truth than the glory of God, the subject of this volume.

This book specifically treats the glory of God in the epistles of the apostle Paul. The first two chapters lay the groundwork for what follows. The first chapter offers a panorama of God's intrinsic and extrinsic glory in Scripture and its theology. The second chapter looks at the prominent place of glory in the biblical story of creation, fall, redemption and consummation.

---

[1] Quoted in Packer (1993: 17–18).
[2] Ibid. 11.

Chapters 3–7 provide exegesis of the major Pauline doctrinal loci of God's glory. We consider the glory of God and the following:

- Salvation in Romans
- The resurrection in 1 Corinthians
- The new covenant in 2 Corinthians
- The church in Ephesians
- Eschatology in 2 Thessalonians

The final two chapters build on the exegesis to round out the volume with synthesis. Chapter 8 provides a systematic theology of the glory of God in Paul. And the last chapter treats the Christian life and God's glory. In a heartfelt manner we invite readers to join us with a view toward learning more about this grand theme and saying sincerely *soli Deo gloria*.

1

A panorama of God's glory[1]

Soli Deo gloria – to God alone be the glory! Sinclair Ferguson captures the spirit in which this book is written:

> The truth is that we are prone to looking through the wrong end of the telescope. We move from man to God. But true thinking – thinking that recognizes the real distinction between the Creator and the creature, between the Infinite and the finite, must always begin with God. It is not so much that we describe God in *anthropomorphic* terms; it is that He has created us in a *theomorphic* way. We are the miniatures. In us – created, finite people – are embedded microcosmic reflections of realities that are true of God Himself in a macrocosmic, uncreated, infinite way.[2]

This book attempts the audacious task of setting forth the immense glory of the infinite Creator as it permeates Holy Scripture. God's glory appears in the following:

- In major sections of Scripture
- In relation to key doctrines
- At turning points in the biblical story
- In different senses in Scripture
- As intrinsic and extrinsic
- In biblical tensions
- In redemptive history

---

[1] This chapter is an adaptation of Morgan and Peterson 2010: 153–187.
[2] Ferguson 2014: 32; emphases original.

God's glory appears in major sections of Scripture

In a way that is consistent but by no means uniform,[3] every major section of Scripture addresses the subject of the glory of God:

Law: 'I will get glory over Pharaoh and all his host, and the Egyptians shall know that I am the LORD.' (Exod. 14:4)

Prophets: 'I am the LORD; that is my name; / my glory I give to no other, / nor my praise to carved idols.' (Isa. 42:8)

Writings: 'The LORD of hosts, / he is the King of glory!' (Ps. 24:10)

Gospels: 'And now, Father, glorify me in your own presence with the glory that I had with you before the world existed.' (John 17:5)

Acts: '[Stephen], full of the Holy Spirit, gazed into heaven and saw the glory of God, and Jesus standing at the right hand of God.' (Acts 7:55)

Pauline Epistles: 'waiting for our blessed hope, the appearing of the glory of our great God and Saviour Jesus Christ'. (Titus 2:13)

General Epistles: 'He is the radiance of the glory of God and the exact imprint of his nature, and he upholds the universe by the word of his power.' (Heb. 1:3)

Revelation: 'The city has no need of sun or moon to shine on it, for the glory of God gives it light, and its lamp is the Lamb.' (Rev. 21:23)

God's glory appears in relation to key doctrines

Every major doctrine is also significantly related to the glory of God:

Revelation: 'All the promises of God find their Yes in [Christ]. That is why it is through him that we utter our Amen to God for his glory.' (2 Cor. 1:20)

God: 'To the only God, our Saviour, through Jesus Christ our Lord, be glory, majesty, dominion, and authority, before all time and now and for ever. Amen.' (Jude 25)

---

[3] Note the distinctions and subtleties to the presentations of God's glory when comparing e.g. Exodus to Isaiah, Psalms to Ezekiel, Luke to John or any of the above to Paul.

Humanity: 'You have made [man] a little lower than the heavenly beings / and crowned him with glory and honour.' (Ps. 8:5)

Sin: 'Whoever is ashamed of me and of my words in this adulterous and sinful generation, of him will the Son of Man also be ashamed when he comes in the glory of his Father with the holy angels.' (Mark 8:38)

Christ: 'My brothers, show no partiality as you hold the faith in our Lord Jesus Christ, the Lord of glory.' (Jas 2:1)

Salvation: 'I heard what seemed to be the loud voice of a great multitude in heaven, crying out, "Hallelujah! / Salvation and glory and power belong to our God."' (Rev. 19:1)

The Holy Spirit: 'If you are insulted for the name of Christ, you are blessed, because the Spirit of glory and of God rests upon you.' (1 Peter 4:14)

The church: 'Let us rejoice and exult / and give him the glory, / for the marriage of the Lamb has come, / and his Bride has made herself ready.' (Rev. 19:7)

Last things: 'After you have suffered a little while, the God of all grace, who has called you to his eternal glory in Christ, will himself restore, confirm, strengthen, and establish you.' (1 Peter 5:10)

God's glory appears at turning points in the biblical story

Key turning points in the biblical story emphasize God's glory and attest to its varied manifestations:[4]

1 God's glory is revealed through creation (Gen. 1 – 2; Ps. 19:1–2; Rom. 1:18–25).
2 God's glory is identified with humans created in the image of God, crowned with glory (Gen. 1:26–31; 2:4–24; Ps. 8:3–5; 1 Cor. 11:7).
3 God's glory is linked to the exodus (Exod. 16:10; 24:9–18; 34:29).
4 God's glory is linked to fire/bright light/shining (Exod. 3:2–6; Isa. 60:1–3; Rev. 21:11, 23).
5 God's glory is linked to a cloud (Exod. 24:16; 2 Chr. 5:13–14; Luke 9:26–36).

---

[4] Everett F. Harrison highlights several of these manifestations in Harrison 1982.

6 God's glory is linked to the Sabbath (Exod. 24:15–18).[5]

7 God's glory manifested to Moses (Exod. 33:18–23), when he described his experience of God's glory in something resembling physical form.

8 God's glory fills the tabernacle (Exod. 40:34; Lev. 9:6, 23; Num. 16:19, 42; 20:6).

9 God's glory fills the earth (Num. 14:20–23; Ps. 19:1–6; Isa. 6:3).

10 God's glory fills the temple (1 Kgs 8:10–11).

11 God's glory is above the heavens (Pss 8:1; 113:4).

12 God's glory is revealed in a vision to Isaiah (Isa. 6:1–5).

13 God's glory is revealed in visions to Ezekiel (Ezek. 1:28; 3:12; 10:4, 18; 11:22).

14 God's glory is identified with his people (Isa. 40:5; 43:6–7; 60:1).

15 God's glory is identified with Christ, including his incarnation (John 1:1–18); birth narratives (Luke 2:9, 14, 32); miracles (John 2:11; 11:38–44); transfiguration (Luke 9:28–36; 2 Peter 1:16–21); suffering and crucifixion (John 13:31–32; 17:1–5; Luke 24:26; 1 Peter 1:10–11); resurrection/exaltation (Acts 3:13–15; Rom. 6:4; Heb. 2:5–9); ascension (Acts 1:6–11; 1 Tim. 3:16); session/reign (Heb. 1:3; 1 Peter 3:21–22); and coming/victory/judgment (Matt. 24:30; Titus 2:13; 2 Thess. 1:6–9).

16 God's glory is identified with the Holy Spirit (John 16:14; Eph. 1:13–14; 1 Peter 4:14).

17 God's glory is identified with the church (Eph. 1:22–23; 3:20–21; 5:22–29).

18 God's glory is shown in the new creation (Isa. 66:15–24; Rom. 8:18–27; Rev. 21 – 22).[6]

God's glory appears in different senses in Scripture

Because the glory of God is so woven into the fabric of the biblical story, Scripture speaks of the glory of God in different senses. This is partly why

---

[5] Kline 1980; cf. Horton 2008: 14: 'Creation and new creation are interdependent themes, especially with the unifying theme of the procession of creation into the "seventh-day" consummation led by the creature bearing the Creator's image and likeness.'

[6] Rev. 21 – 22 evinces many of these themes, including Eden, temple, ark, light, creation, Israel, church and Christ.

God's glory is, as John Frame acknowledges, one of the hardest Christian terms to define.[7] For this reason we must exercise care as we construct definitions that faithfully represent biblical usage.

At a basic level, we note that the glory of God is sometimes used in the Bible as an adjective, sometimes as a noun and sometimes as a verb. God is *glorious* (adjective), reveals his *glory* (noun) and *is to be glorified* (verb).

More particularly, 'glory' translates the Hebrew *kābôd* and the Greek *doxa*.[8] *Kābôd* stems from a root that means 'weight' or 'heaviness'. Depending on its form, it could have the sense of honourable, dignified, exalted or revered. C. John Collins explains that it became 'a technical term for God's manifest presence'. It is similar in many respects to the concept of God's name in the Old Testament.[9]

According to Sverre Aalen, *doxa* in secular Greek refers to an opinion, a conjecture, repute, praise or fame. He maintains that these concepts were transformed by the Septuagint. Aalen also maintains that *doxa* translated *kābôd* and took on its same meaning, referring to God's manifestation of his person, presence and/or works, especially his power, judgment and salvation.[10]

Using these terms, the Bible speaks of the glory of God in several distinct senses. First, *glory is used as a designation for God himself.* For example, Peter refers to God the Father as the 'Majestic Glory' (2 Peter 1:17). This rare phrase is apparently a Hebrew way of referring to God without stating his name (a circumlocution).

Second, *glory sometimes refers to an internal characteristic, an attribute or a summary of attributes of God.* This is similar to saying that glory is occasionally used as an adjective. God is intrinsically glorious in the sense of fullness, sufficiency, majesty, beauty and splendour. Examples of this usage abound. Psalms refer to God as 'the King of glory' (24:7–10) and 'the God of glory' (29:3). Stephen speaks of 'the God of glory' (Acts 7:2), and the apostle Paul prays to the 'Father of glory' (Eph. 1:17). Displaying a remarkably high Christology, James refers to Jesus as the 'Lord of glory' or the 'glorious Lord', depending on how one translates the phrase.[11] Either way, the point is the same: like the Father, Jesus is characterized by

---

7 Frame 2002: 592.
8 See Longman 2010: 47–78; Kittel 1967: 2.252–255.
9 Collins 1997; cf. von Rad 1962: 1.238–241.
10 Aalen 1971: 2.44–48; cf. Kittel 1967: 2.252–255.
11 See Morgan 2010: 151.

glory. The Spirit, too, is identified with glory (1 Peter 4:14; cf. John 16:14; Eph. 1:13–14), especially through the language of presence, indwelling and temple (John 14:15–17, 26; 15:26; 16:7–15; Rom. 8:9–11; 1 Cor. 3:16; 6:19–20; Eph. 2:19–22).

Third, the Bible speaks of *glory as God's presence.* As we noted, Collins and Aalen both underscore this in their respective explanations of the Hebrew and Greek terms for glory. This understanding of glory is emphatic in the events surrounding the exodus. The glory cloud (Exod. 13 – 14; 16:7; 20; 24; cf. Rev. 15:8), the manifestations to Moses (Exod. 3 – 4; 32 – 34) and God's presence in the tabernacle (Exod. 29:43; 40:34–38) all highlight God's covenantal presence.[12] Walter Kaiser puts it simply: 'Glory, then, is a special term that depicts God's visible and active presence.'[13] This connotation of God's glory also emerges in passages related to the ark of the covenant (1 Sam. 4 – 5), the temple (1 Kgs 8:10–11; 2 Chr. 5 – 7), the eschatological temple in Ezekiel (43:1–5), the person of Christ (John 1:1–18; Col. 1:15–20, 27; 2:1–3, 13–15; Heb. 1), the Holy Spirit (John 14 – 16) and even heaven itself (Rev. 21 – 22).

Fourth, the Bible often depicts *glory as the display of God's attributes, perfections or person.* John's Gospel speaks of glory in this way, as Jesus performs 'signs' that manifest his glory (2:11). The Bible uses various terms for this concept, but the idea is clear: as God puts his works on display, he glorifies himself. He displays his mercy, grace, justice and wrath in salvation and judgment (cf. Rom. 9:20–23; Eph. 2:4–10).

A fifth connotation is of *glory as the ultimate goal of the display of God's attributes, perfections or person.* Exodus and Ezekiel are replete with passages that unfold God's actions for the sake of his name, or in order that people will know he is the Lord.[14] Jesus instructs that Lazarus' death and subsequent resurrection had an ultimate purpose: they were for the glory of God (John 11:4, 40). Peter's death also shared this purpose (21:19). Paul points out that God chooses, adopts, redeems and seals us 'to the praise of his glorious grace' (Eph. 1:6, 12, 14). That is, in saving us, God displays his grace; and in displaying his grace, he brings glory to himself. Further, the whole trinitarian plan of redemption displays this goal, as seen in the mutual glorification of each person of the Trinity. The glorious Father

---

[12] See Longman 2010.
[13] Kaiser 2007: 120.
[14] See Edwards 1998: 237–239. For texts that declare that people or other things will *know that I am Yahweh* (and related expressions) see Hamilton 2006a: 64.

sends the glorious Son, who voluntarily humbles himself and glorifies the Father through his incarnation, obedient life and substitutionary death (Phil. 2:5–11). In response the Father glorifies the Son, resurrecting him from the dead and exalting him to the highest place (Acts 3:13–15; Rom. 6:4; Phil. 2:9–11). The Father sends the glorious Spirit, who glorifies the Son (John 16:14). And this all redounds to the glory of the Father (Phil. 2:11).[15]

Sixth, *glory sometimes connotes heaven, the heavenly or the eschatological consummation of the full experience of the presence of God.* Hebrews 2:10 speaks of 'bringing many sons to glory'; Philippians 4:19 offers the covenant promise 'My God will supply every need of yours according to his riches in glory in Christ Jesus' (cf. Eph. 3:16, 'according to the riches of his glory'). The people of God will ultimately receive glory, honour, immortality and eternal life, which are used somewhat synonymously (Rom. 2:7). Such glory was prepared for them in eternity (9:23). Jesus is also said to be 'taken up in glory' (1 Tim. 3:16), which could be understood as in heaven, gloriously or a combination of the two. The bodies of believers, too, will be raised 'in glory' (1 Cor. 15:43), and faithful elders will receive an unfading crown of glory (1 Peter 5:4).

Seventh, *giving glory to God may also refer to appropriate response to God in the form of worship, exaltation or exultation.*[16] Psalm 29:2 urges, 'Ascribe to the LORD the glory due his name.' At Jesus' birth, after God's glory shines (Luke 2:9), the heavenly host resounds with 'glory to God in the highest' (Luke 2:14), and the shepherds are 'glorifying and praising God' (Luke 2:20). Further, the Bible is filled with doxologies, such as Romans 16:27, that accentuate our need to give glory to God: 'To the only wise God be glory for evermore through Jesus Christ!' (cf. Rom. 11:36; Gal. 1:5; Eph. 3:20–21; Phil. 4:20; 2 Tim. 4:18; Jude 24–25; Rev. 1:5–6). Some doxologies are directed toward Christ (2 Peter 3:18; Heb. 13:21). Similarly, other passages instruct God's people to glory in Christ (2 Cor. 10:17), in his cross (Gal. 6:14) and in our suffering by virtue of our union with Christ (2 Cor. 11 – 12). Glorifying God is an expected and appropriate response of God's people (Matt. 5:13–16; 15:31; Mark 2:12; Luke 4:15; John 15:8). We are even commanded to glorify God in our bodies (1 Cor. 6:20), in our food and drink choices along with their corresponding relationships (1 Cor. 10:31) and in the proper exercise of spiritual

---

15 See Köstenberger 2010.
16 For a more detailed list of passages see Newman 1997: 395–396.

gifts (1 Peter 4:11). Romans 14 – 15 underlines the importance of the church's glorifying God with a unified voice; as the church displays unity to the glory of God (15:6–7), the Gentiles will glorify God (vv. 8–9; cf. Rev. 4 – 5).

It is important to notice that these multiple meanings are distinct but related. We might think of it this way: *The triune God who is glorious displays his glory, largely through his creation, image-bearers, providence and redemptive acts. God's people respond by glorifying him. God receives glory and, through uniting his people to Christ, shares his glory with them – all to his glory.* The divinely initiated and sovereignly guided interaction spirals forward to the consummation and throughout eternity. Though a chart cannot fully capture these ideas, it may help:

Internal glory → external glory → response to glory → receives glory → shares glory → unto glory

Scripture, then, speaks of various nuances of God's glory, all central in the biblical story:

- Glory possessed
- Glory purposed
- Glory displayed
- Glory ascribed
- Glory received
- Glory shared

To restate, God, who is intrinsically glorious (glory possessed), graciously and joyfully displays his glory (glory displayed), largely through his creation, image-bearers, providence and redemptive acts. God's people respond by glorifying him (glory ascribed). God receives glory (glory received) and, through uniting his people to the glorious Christ, shares his glory with them (glory shared) – all to his glory (glory purposed, displayed, ascribed, received and graciously shared throughout eternity). The next chapter will attempt to show that the entire biblical plotline of creation, fall, redemption and consummation is the story of God's glory.

At the ground of all this is the fact that the intrinsically glorious God extrinsically displays his glory, a theme to which we now turn.

God's glory appears as intrinsic and extrinsic

Fundamentally, the glory of the triune God is both intrinsic and extrinsic. God is intrinsically glorious, in the sense of fullness, sufficiency, majesty, honour, worth, beauty, weight and splendour. God's glory is then extrinsically set forth, as John Calvin memorably put it: 'The world was no doubt made, that it might be a theatre of the divine glory.'[17] Because of God's gracious communication, his glory is something that may be seen, marvelled at and rejoiced in.

Jonathan Edwards saw this and referred to God's glory as internal and also as a communication of himself.[18] More recently, David Huttar has observed that God's glory is intrinsic, 'prior to any external manifestation of it' and 'fundamentally independent of external manifestation'. He adds, 'Yet it is also true that God's glory is also manifest.'[19]

While most theologians grant that the glory of God is in some sense intrinsic and extrinsic, they vary in how they categorize it and especially in how they understand what we label here 'intrinsic'. For example, in his *New Testament Theology* Donald Guthrie lists glory first in his discussion of God's attributes.[20] Walter Elwell references 'God's glory as his being'.[21] R. Albert Mohler Jr asserts, 'God's glory is best understood as the intrinsic beauty and external manifestation of God's being and character.'[22] John Piper exults that 'the glory of God is the infinite beauty and greatness of his manifold perfections'.[23] J. I. Packer designates it as 'fundamental to God' and refers to God's glory as his 'excellence and praiseworthiness set forth in display'.[24]

---

[17] Calvin 2003: 266 (on Heb. 11:3).

[18] Edwards 1998: 230–241.

[19] Huttar 1996: 287–288.

[20] Guthrie 1981: 90–94; cf. George 2007: 222.

[21] Elwell 1991: 41.

[22] R. Albert Mohler Jr, 'In the Beginning: The Glory of God from Eternity', sermon preached at Ligonier Ministries' 2003 National Conference. In this sermon Mohler suggests a tension between God's internal glory, which is unchanging, and its external manifestation, which varies.

[23] John Piper, 'To Him Be Glory Forevermore (Romans 16:25–27)', sermon delivered 17 December 2006.

[24] Packer 1988: 271–272. Packer refers to this as 'glory shown' and distinguishes it from his other category, 'glory given', which is 'honor and adoration expressed in response to this display'.

In his treatment of the theology of Jonathan Edwards, John Gerstner places God's glory at the end of the natural attributes of God and at the beginning of the moral attributes because, according to Gerstner, Edwards viewed the glory of God as belonging to both and as expressing infinite knowledge, holiness and happiness.[25] Gerstner explains:

> In the sermon on Psalm 89:6 Edwards had the glory of God consisting in God's greatness (natural attribute) and goodness (moral attribute). *So glory is another word used for the sum total of all divine excellencies. It refers to the internal as well as manifestative glory. The latter amounts to a setting forth of the attributes in their reality and fullness.*[26]

These helpful definitions and descriptions reveal an inherent challenge related to speaking of God's glory. Biblical and systematic theologians struggle to answer the question 'Is God's glory an attribute, a summary attribute, his being or the outward expression of his being?'

Old Testament scholars tend to come at all this differently. Some, such as John Collins, underscore God's glory as his manifest presence.[27] Raymond Ortlund speaks similarly, but also ties glory to God's nature and beauty:

> What is the glory of the Lord? His glory is the fiery radiance of his very nature. It is his blazing beauty . . . The glory of the Lord . . . is God himself becoming visible, God bringing his presence down to us, God displaying his beauty before us.[28]

Others, such as John Hartley, view God's glory as the manifestation of his essence, which is often linked to God's holiness.[29] Hartley follows

---

[25] Gerstner 1993: 2.33–34.

[26] Ibid. 2:34; emphasis added.

[27] Collins 1997.

[28] Ortlund 2005: 237.

[29] More work is needed on the relationship between God's holiness and his glory. Hartley (2003: 420–422) is helpful: 'Holiness, being the quintessential character of God, is the center of divine motivation. It affects everything God does. Moreover, the adjectives attached to holiness, such as majestic, glorious, and awesome, inform us that the essence of beauty is holiness . . . Holiness is powerfully manifested in God's revelations: God's commission of Moses at the burning bush (Ex 3:1–4:17), God's deliverance of Israel at the sea (Ex 15:2–18), the theophany at Sinai (Ex 19:1–24:18) and Moses's special vision of God (Ex 33:18–34:9) . . .

C. Vriezen here, who defines glory as 'the radiant power of [God's] Being, as it were the external manifestation of [God's] mysterious holiness'.[30]

We make progress if we perceive what lies behind both approaches. Despite the initial differences, there is a shared understanding of the glory of God as the extrinsic manifestation of the intrinsic. While some highlight God's presence,[31] others see the intrinsic glory as an attribute, or as some sort of summary of his attributes, or even more broadly as God's essence, or nature. Some sort of holistic or macro approach to understanding the intrinsic nature of God's glory becomes necessary, however, because Scripture plainly links the extrinsic display of God's glory to a variety of his attributes and works, as well as to terms that stress his very person and nature.

Further, it seems best to understand God's extrinsic glory as the communication of his intrinsic fullness and sufficiency. In Romans 11:36, for example, Paul concludes, 'From him and through him and to him are all things. To him be glory for ever.' God's self-sufficiency and glory are intricately linked: God is the Creator ('from him'), sustainer ('through him') and goal ('to him') of all things. The self-sufficient and independent God creates out of fullness, guides out of fullness and receives back glory according to his communicated fullness.[32]

Before we proceed, we should pause and recognize that if God's intrinsic glory were not displayed extrinsically, we would be unable to know any of this. All we know about God's intrinsic glory is through God's self-revelation, particularly Scripture, which records and interprets the extrinsic display of God's intrinsic glory. Further, since the infinite God does not communicate himself exhaustively to finite creatures, the extrinsic display is less than the intrinsic. As awe-inspiring as the extrinsic glory is, it never fully expresses the fullness of God's intrinsic glory that

---

The holy God often manifested his presence as a glowing brightness comparable to a fire . . . This glory-holiness juxtaposition is very similar to that found in Isaiah 6:3 . . . [Exod. 40:34–35] is the denouement of the book of Exodus. The glory that had led Israel out of Egypt and had appeared on Mount Sinai now came and occupied the newly built tabernacle. The holy God had come to dwell among the covenant people. This powerful manifestation of God's glory communicated to the Israelites the power, dignity, and splendor of God's holiness.'

[30] Vriezen 1966: 150; cited in Hartley (2003: 422).

[31] In such discussions it is important to remember God's unity/simplicity. See Berkhof 1941: 62; Grudem 2020: 211–214.

[32] Frame 2002: 607; Edwards 1998: 150–161. We thank Steve Wellum for his ideas related to this point.

it communicates. That being so, even to begin to understand God's intrinsic glory we must examine his extrinsic displays.

Scripture connects the display of the glory of God to a variety of his attributes: holiness (Lev. 11:44; Isa. 6:1–8; Rev. 4 – 5; 21 – 22), uniqueness (Isa. 42:8), power (Exod. 13:21–22; 16:10–11; John 11:40; Rom. 6:4; 2 Thess. 1:8–9), beauty, majesty and goodness.[33] God's glory is also tied to his works: creation (Gen. 1 – 2; Ps. 19:1–6), salvation (Exod. 13:21–22; Eph. 1:3–14), providence (Exod. 16:10–12; 40:36–38), judgment (Num. 14:10–23; 16:41–45; Ezek. 39:21–29; Matt. 16:27–28; 2 Thess. 1:8–9) and victory (Exod. 16:7–12; Ps. 57:5–11; Isa. 2:10–21). Even more astounding is that Scripture links our triune God's glory with more holistic ideas that stress his very nature: God's presence (Exod. 33:13–18; 40:34; 1 Sam. 4:21–22; Ps. 84:11; 2 Thess. 1:8–10; Jude 24; Rev. 21 – 22),[34] name,[35] holiness (which many Old Testament scholars see as his essence; Lev. 11:44; Isa. 6:1–8; Rev. 4 – 5; 21 – 22), face, Spirit, fullness and honour (1 Tim. 1:17; cf. 2 Peter 1:17).

Since God's glory is the extrinsic display of so many attributes, of a panorama of God's works and of holistic terms related to God's very nature, it is clear that God's intrinsic glory must be viewed holistically. Put differently, if the display of God's power is a display of his glory, and if his presence is a central meaning of his glory, then glory must be something broad enough to cover such wide-ranging depictions.

This also makes sense of other biblical data, those that relate to the ultimate end of all things. The Bible repeatedly affirms that God's activities of creation, providence, salvation and judgment are all for his glory. Yet the Bible offers various attributes that will be set forth in display to be marvelled at, and displays of those attributes are not subsumed under a primary attribute but are depicted as ultimate. For example, in Exodus God acts so that others will recognize his utter uniqueness and power. In Romans God's saving action is to display his righteousness, justice, wrath,

---

[33] A. H. McNeile (1908: 215) defines glory as 'a spectacle of outward beauty as a visible sign of His moral perfection'.

[34] Newman (1997: 396) suggests that, along with wisdom, spirit, image, word, name and power, glory 'formed part of the semantic-filled words that could sign God's revealed presence'.

[35] See Waltke (2007: 474), who suggests that the glory and name theologies complement each other: 'The glory of God is unapproachable and dangerous, but the name of God is something with which his worshippers are permitted to become familiar. God's glory is preferred when the context is that of the dramatic, exceptional manifestations of God, but "name" is used in contexts where the kind of revelation of and the people's response is more intimate.' Waltke bases some of this on McConville 1979: 156–157; cf. Edwards 1998: 239; Piper 1991.

power and mercy and the riches of his glory (Rom. 3:21–26; 9:20–23). In Ephesians God acts for the ultimate display of at least three attributes: grace (1:6, 12, 14), kindness (2:4–10) and wisdom (3:10–11).

Such biblical data suggest that God's intrinsic glory is broader than a single attribute. It corresponds to his very being and sometimes functions as a sort of summation of his attributes. Edwards is again helpful:

> The thing signified by that name, the glory of God, when spoken of as the supreme and ultimate end of all God's works, is the emanation and true external expression of God's internal glory and fullness; . . . or, in other words, God's internal glory, in a true and just exhibition, or external existence of it.[36]

We turn now to see how various truths related to God's intrinsic and extrinsic glory emerge. Each pair initially appears to be in tension but actually coheres.

God's glory appears in biblical tensions

The fundamental distinction between God's intrinsic and extrinsic glory manifests itself in various biblical expressions. Surprisingly, Scripture presents these expressions in tension:

- God's glory is transcendent and immanent
- God's glory is full and received
- God's glory is unique and shared

God's glory is transcendent and immanent

Since God's glory is both intrinsic and extrinsic, it makes sense that it would also be both transcendent and immanent, which we consider in reverse order. God has chosen to display his glory among his people in various ways, and many of the more familiar ones are immanent. Such an instance is the familiar encounter of Moses with God and the glory cloud on Mount Sinai, in which it is said, 'The glory of the LORD dwelt on Mount Sinai' (Exod. 24:16; cf. Deut. 5:22–27). Such an immanent view of God's glory is found also in narratives concerning the ark of the covenant:

---

[36] Edwards 1998: 243.

There was nothing in the ark except the two tablets of stone that Moses put there at Horeb, where the LORD made a covenant with the people of Israel, when they came out of the land of Egypt. And when the priests came out of the Holy Place, a cloud filled the house of the LORD, so that the priests could not stand to minister because of the cloud, for the glory of the LORD filled the house of the LORD.

Then Solomon said, 'The LORD has said that he would dwell in thick darkness. I have indeed built you an exalted house, a place for you to dwell in for ever.'

(1 Kgs 8:9–13; cf. 2 Chr. 5:13 – 6:2)

God's glory is said to fill the temple and the earth, as Psalm 19 and Isaiah 6 attest. This immanence is seen most clearly in the incarnation of Jesus, as the eternal Son of God dwells among us and displays his unique glory (John 1:1–18).

However, all these passages assume that God's glory is intrinsically transcendent. Paul House's comments on Exodus show how God graciously displays his transcendent glory immanently:

At last Yahweh's intention to dwell among the nations is fulfilled. Moses erects the edifice as he has been commanded (40:1–33). The result is stunning. God's 'glory,' literally 'God's heaviness,' fills the tabernacle (40:34). Such is the heaviness of God's presence that not even Moses can enter (40:35). This glory eventually subsides, but not totally, since God does remain in the people's midst. Evidence of this ongoing presence leads Israel to break camp and travel when necessary (40:36–38). Thus, Yahweh not only dwells with the people; Yahweh also keeps the promise to go with Israel and eventually give them the promised land (cf. 33:14; 34:1–14).[37]

That God's glory is immanent and transcendent is also evident in the temple narratives of 1 Kings. We saw that 1 Kings 8:11 discloses this immanence here: '[T]he glory of the LORD filled the house of the LORD.' And Solomon's prayer of dedication of the temple, recorded in 1 Kings 8, acknowledges the transcendence of God's glory: '[W]ill God indeed dwell

---

[37] House 1998: 125.

on the earth? Behold, heaven and the highest heaven cannot contain you; how much less this house that I have built!' (v. 27).

Isaiah 6 also makes this clear. Geoffrey Grogan explains:

> The language of fullness . . . occurs three times in these verses (6:1, 3, 4), twice in application to the temple and once to the whole earth. So this passage, insisting as it does on the awesome transcendence of the sovereign God, also emphatically teaches his immanence. His transcendence is not remoteness or aloofness but is known through his presence in his created world and temple.[38]

Psalmists frequently express God's glory as transcendent. It is 'above the heavens'. For example, Psalm 8:1 declares:

> O LORD, our Lord,
>> how majestic is your name in all the earth!
> You have set your glory above the heavens.

Willem VanGemeren lauds how God's transcendent glory is also immanent:

> The Redeemer-King of Israel is the creator! His name (Yahweh) is glorious over all the earth, by virtue of his creative activities (cf. Gen 1:1–31). What is marvelous is the Great King's revelation of his glory in, and thereby his self-involvement with, his creation. He, the glorious One, has endowed the earth with glory! . . . The 'majesty' of Yahweh's name radiates from his work on earth and heaven . . . All creation reveals the power and glory of God's name.[39]

Psalm 113:4 also resounds with exalted language to stress the transcendent glory of God:

> The LORD is high above all nations,
>> and his glory above the heavens!
> (Cf. 57:5, 11)

---

[38] Grogan 1986: 55–56.
[39] VanGemeren 1991: 110.

This idea of God's glory as above the heavens underlines his transcendence and gives a rhetorical effect, making the reality of his immanence even more striking.[40]

Observing the transcendent and immanent nature of God's glory, Walther Eichrodt concluded:

> The sense that Yahweh's majesty was exalted far above all created things . . . asserted itself. This came about in various ways; either by stressing the absolute transcendence of the *kabod*, so that mortal man had always to be kept apart from it, or by reducing it to a spatially and temporarily limited medium of Yahweh's self-manifestation, a means by which the transcendent God made his personal presence visible to his own.[41]

God's glory is full and received

Another expression of God's intrinsic and extrinsic glory is the dual reality of the fullness of his glory and his genuine reception of glory. To be sure, God is self-sufficient, independent, lacks nothing and does not need our faith, worship or ascription of honour (Isa. 42 – 66; Acts 17:16–34). Yet the God who is all-glorious displays his glory, his people respond by glorifying him and in turn God receives glory.

God's reception of glory does not imply that he does not already have intrinsic glory in all its fullness, as John Owen forcefully reminds us:

> All things that are, make no addition to God, no change in his state. His blessedness, happiness, self-satisfaction, as well as all other his infinite perfections, were absolutely the same before the creation of anything, whilst there was nothing but himself, as they are since he has made all things: for the blessedness of God consists in the ineffable mutual in-being of the three holy persons in the same nature, with the immanent reciprocal actings of the Father and the Son in the eternal love and complacency of the Spirit.[42]

God creates and acts out of his fullness *and* is pleased to manifest his glory to his creatures. Completely sufficient, God is pleased to receive

---

40 Ibid. 714.
41 Eichrodt 1967: 31.
42 Owen 1684: 160.

glory from them, but not in the sense that they add something to him. Rather, they acknowledge, enjoy, love and delight in God and his glory.[43] As the Westminster Shorter Catechism states, 'Man's chief end is to glorify God, and to enjoy him for ever.' We extol God, reflect God and find ourselves satisfied in him by having the manifestation of his fullness communicated to us and by our appropriate response of dependent faith and awe-inspired worship.[44] In this way our faith acknowledges our insufficiency and depends on his sufficiency. This glorifies God as we recognize our creaturely dependence and his infinite independence. Similarly, our worship is triggered by our awareness of his infinite worthiness. All this glorifies him as it manifests his fullness, self-sufficiency and glory as the beginning, middle and end of this process (cf. Rom. 11:33–36).

That God's glory is both full and received is articulated marvellously in Revelation 4:8–11:

[T]he four living creatures, each of them with six wings, are full of eyes all round and within, and day and night they never cease to say,

'Holy, holy, holy, is the Lord God Almighty,
    who was and is and is to come!'

And whenever the living creatures give glory and honour and thanks to him who is seated on the throne, who lives for ever and ever, the twenty-four elders fall down before him who is seated on the throne and worship him who lives for ever and ever. They cast their crowns before the throne, saying,

'Worthy are you, our Lord and God,
    to receive glory and honour and power,
for you created all things,
    and by your will they existed and were created.'

In the form of a prayer, Owen also portrays our appropriate response to these truths:

---

[43] Cf. Ps. 29:1–3; Isa. 41:16; 42:1; 43:21; 46:13; Matt. 5:16; John 15:8; Rom. 15:6–9; 1 Cor. 6:20; 10:31.

[44] See Edwards 1998: 154–168.

Blessed Jesus! We can add nothing to you, nothing to your glory; but it is a joy of heart to us that you are what you are, that you are so gloriously exalted at the right hand of God; and we do long more fully and clearly to behold that glory, according to your prayer and promise.[45]

God's glory is unique and shared

Another expression of God's intrinsic and extrinsic glory is that his glory is both unique and shared. God alone is intrinsically glorious. He is uniquely and incomparably glorious. As Richard Gaffin points out, glory is pre-eminently a divine quality; ultimately only God has glory.[46] And according to Isaiah 42:8, God jealously guards his glory:

I am the LORD; that is my name;
> my glory I give to no other,
> nor my praise to carved idols.

In the intrinsic sense, God's glory is unique. No one and nothing else is glorious. All idols are unworthy of comparison.

But, amazingly, the glorious God extrinsically manifests his glory and communicates his fullness. In so doing he remains ontologically unique and distinct from his creatures[47] and graciously shares his glory and makes glorious many things.

For example, the Bible makes it clear that humans are created in God's image with glory, honour and dominion. Psalm 8:4–8 is instructive. Though humans are minute in comparison to God or the heavens, he remembers and has special concern for them. Indeed, God has even 'crowned' humans 'with glory and honour' (8:5), which connotes kingship (cf. 29:1; 104:1).[48]

Further, God shares his glory with Israel (cf. Rom. 9:4). In the same section of Isaiah appear statements such as 'My glory I will not give to another' (42:8; 48:11) and those that refer to God's calling and putting his

---

[45] Owen 1684: 128.
[46] Gaffin 2000: 508; 2010.
[47] Horton (2008: 62): 'Even those rendered one in Christ by the gospel become brothers and sisters, not a fusion of persons.'
[48] VanGemeren 1991: 112–114. Heb. 2:7–8 (quoting Ps. 8) ascribes 'glory/honour' and dominion to Adam and Eve before the fall. V. 8 says these were lost; v. 9 says Christ, the second Adam, recovered them; v. 10 speaks of Christ's people being led to glory as a result.

name on Israel (43:1–6; 44:1–5), glorying in Israel (46:13) and, yes, even making Israel glorious. 'My glory I will not give to another' refers in context to God's unique glory and his warnings to Israel that he allows no idols and brooks no rivals (cf. 48:11–12). Nevertheless, Isaiah declares to the people of God that the Lord 'has glorified you' (55:5). Even more, Isaiah 60 shows that God's glory will rise upon them (60:1) and will be seen on them (v. 2) and that other nations will see their radiance and glory, for God has made them beautiful (vv. 3–9; 62:2). God says to his people, 'I will make you majestic for ever, / a joy from age to age' (60:15), and in turn God himself will be glorified (v. 21).

This hope of the glorious God's not only manifesting his glory to the people of Israel but also sharing it with them is echoed in Simeon's blessing of Jesus:

> Lord, now you are letting your servant depart in peace,
>   according to your word;
> for my eyes have seen your salvation
>   that you have prepared in the presence of all peoples,
> a light for revelation to the Gentiles,
>   and for glory to your people Israel.
> (Luke 2:29–32)

This idea of the uniquely glorious God's sharing his glory with his people would appear bizarre, except for the fact that it is such a prominent theme. The breadth of the New Testament teaching on this is astounding.

In his high priestly prayer Jesus reveals, 'The glory that you have given me I have given to them, that they may be one as we are one' (John 17:22). Peter refers to himself as a partaker in the glory that will be revealed (1 Peter 5:1) and encourages suffering believers that 'the God of all grace, who has called you to his eternal glory in Christ, will himself restore, confirm, strengthen and establish you' (v. 10).

But it is the apostle Paul who most develops this idea that we share in God's glory. Because of our union with Christ, we, in some sense and to the extent it could be true of creatures, participate and share in his glory.[49] As Michael Horton ably puts it, 'What happens for us is the basis for what

---

[49] See Ferguson 1996: 91–189; cf. Horton 2008: 27: 'Only the Spirit can keep us aware simultaneously of the otherness of Jesus and our communion with and in him.' Cf. Horton's helpful critique of Eastern Christendom's approach to deification (2007: 267–307).

happens to us and in us.'[50] Paul instructs the Thessalonian believers that God calls us into his own kingdom and glory (1 Thess. 2:12). He also prays for their faith, 'so that the name of our Lord Jesus may be glorified in you, and you in him' (2 Thess. 1:12). Paul encourages the Thessalonians to gratitude because God called them so that they 'may obtain the glory of our Lord Jesus Christ' (2 Thess. 2:14; cf. Col. 1:27; 3:4).

To the Corinthians Paul also highlights the shared nature of this glory in conjunction with Jesus' identity as the new Adam and his saving work, particularly in the cross and resurrection: '[W]e impart a secret and hidden wisdom of God, which God decreed before the ages for our glory. None of the rulers of this age understood this, for if they had, they would not have crucified the Lord of glory' (1 Cor. 2:7–8). Because of our union with Christ and his resurrection, our bodies too will be raised in glory (15:42–58). Later, in one of the most penetrating Christological and soteriological statements in all of Scripture, Paul explains, '[W]e all, with unveiled face, beholding the glory of the Lord, are being transformed into the same image from one degree of glory to another' (2 Cor. 3:18).[51] He develops this more in chapter 4, where he culminates his argument by stating that 'this light momentary affliction is preparing for us an eternal weight of glory beyond all comparison' (4:17). Related truths about sharing in glory appear throughout Paul's writings, especially in Romans and Ephesians, which we will examine in more detail later.

God's glory appears in redemptive history

Thus far we have studied God's intrinsic and extrinsic glory and their multiple expressions, including his glory as transcendent and immanent, full and received and unique and shared. We still must survey some other important expressions of God's extrinsic glory. These redemptive-historical expressions of God's extrinsic glory are helpfully viewed from the following vantage points:

- Particularity and universality
- Already and not yet

---

[50] Horton 2007: 307.
[51] See Gaffin 2010.

- Divine sovereignty and human responsibility
- God's ultimate end and other ends

Particularity and universality

God has extrinsically displayed his glory both particularly and universally. Exodus portrays the particularity of God's glory:

- Pillar of cloud and fire (Exod. 14 – 15)
- God's glory displayed in judgment of Israel (16:7–10)
- Glory in cloud (19:9)
- Cloud, thunder, lightning, mountain, trumpet blast, smoke and fire (19:16–17; 20:18–19)
- Sinai, cloud, mountain, fire, and so on (24:15–17)
- Ark of the covenant, court of tabernacle, presence, power and covenant (Exod. 24 – 27; 29:43–46)
- Moses' encounter with God (Exod. 33 – 34)
- God withdraws his presence in the wilderness due to sin (33:3–5)
- Glory filled the tabernacle, cloud covered tent of meeting (40:34)

The particularity of the revelation of God's glory is also found throughout Scripture, as God manifests himself particularly in the temple (1 Kgs 8:11), Israel, the church, heaven, and so forth. We recognize these covenantal and particular expressions and are inclined to focus on them – and rightly so.

We should not fail, however, to notice that God's glory is also universal. Interestingly, the familiar story of Isaiah's encounter with God in Isaiah 6 reveals that God's glory is both particular and universal. It is particular in that the vision is of God's glory filling the temple, with all the accompanying shakes, sounds and smoke. Yet God's glory is also depicted as universal: '[T]he whole earth is full of his glory!' (Isa. 6:3). 'YHWH's abundant glory presses . . . beyond the sphere of the heavenly-earthly temple and the royal palace into the world.'[52] Particularity and universality are frequent in Isaiah, especially in chapters 40–66. For instance, Isaiah 66:18 states, 'I know their works and their thoughts, and the time is coming to gather all nations and tongues. And they shall come and see my glory.'

---

[52] Preuss 1995: 167.

The Psalms also convey God's glory as both particular and universal. Psalm 26:8 stresses particularity:

> O LORD, I love the habitation of your house,
>   and the place where your glory dwells.
> (Cf. Exod. 40:34–35; 1 Kgs 8:11)

And Psalm 19 emphasizes universality: the glory of God is communicated to all people at all times in all places through the witness of creation (cf. Pss 8; 72:19). Indeed, creation witnesses universally to God's glory.

Already and not yet

Another redemptive-historical expression of God's extrinsic glory can be viewed from the vantage point of the already-and-not-yet tension.

God is glorious. His glory has been and is presently being displayed. That is clear from many of the texts and topics already referenced:

- Creation (Ps. 19:1–6)
- Humans being created in the image of God (Gen. 1:26–28; Ps. 8; Jas 3:9–12)
- Particular manifestations (Isa. 6:3)
- Christ (John 1:14–18)
- Salvation (Eph. 1 – 2)

However, history still awaits God's ultimate display of himself.[53] Commenting on Isaiah, Ortlund puts it passionately: 'His glory will be admired and delighted in and trembled at everywhere.'[54] Later he adds, 'God is moving toward the new heavens and the new earth. He has promised the full display of his glory.'[55]

At the consummation, Jesus' return will be glorious (Matt. 16:27–28; 24:30; Mark 13:26; Luke 21:27; 2 Thess. 1:6–11; Titus 2:13). Further, his victory will be glorious, his judgment will be glorious and his punishment of the wicked in hell will be glorious (Rom. 9:20–23; Rev. 20:11–15). Most

---

[53] See Isa. 4:2–6; 40:5; 48:5; 55:5; 59:19; 60:1, 19; 62; 66:12, 18–20, 21–24; Hab. 2:14; Luke 2:25–32; Rom. 5:2; 2 Cor. 4:17; Phil. 2:10–11; 1 Peter 4:13; Rev. 4 – 5; 21 – 22; Edwards 1998: 155; Beale 2004.
[54] Ortlund 2005: 236.
[55] Ibid. 385.

of all, Jesus' revelation of himself in the new creation will be glorious (Rev. 21 – 22). And, as previously noted, through his saving work and our union with him the church will be presented as glorious (Eph. 5:27; cf. Rom. 8:18–30; 2 Cor. 4:17–18).

Since the glory of God is extrinsic, it is closely related to the biblical story and thus tied to the already-and-not-yet tension. As such, the glory of God is now being displayed, but its ultimate display is still future (1 John 3:2).

Divine sovereignty and human responsibility

Another vantage point from which to examine the redemptive-historical expressions of God's extrinsic glory is that of the truths of divine sovereignty and human responsibility. God is glorious, manifests his infinite glory and will receive the glory he is due. As we have seen, the not yet is coming. Nothing can thwart it. It is the goal of God's cosmic redemptive history, and God will sovereignly bring it to pass (Rom. 8:18–30; 9:20–23; 11:33–36; Eph. 1:3–14, esp. v. 11; Phil. 2:5–11).

But it is also clear that humans are responsible to glorify God as God and worship him.[56] Indeed, Isaiah chastises the people of Judah for their defiance of God's glory (Isa. 3:8). Israel was often encouraged to obedience for the sake of God's name (Isa. 52:3–6; Rom. 2:24). The people also prayed to that end (Pss 57:5, 11; 108:5).

Jesus similarly urges his followers, '[L]et your light shine before others, so that they may see your good works and give glory to your Father who is in heaven' (Matt. 5:16). He later reminds them, 'By this my Father is glorified, that you bear much fruit and so prove to be my disciples' (John 15:8).

In Romans Paul stresses that our refusal to glorify God as God and our subsequent foolish exchange of his glory for that of the creature is the basis of our guilt (1:18–32; cf. 5:12–21; Eph. 2:1–3). Paul later underlines human responsibility as he urges the church to be united for the glory of God:

> that together you may with one voice glorify the God and Father of our Lord Jesus Christ. Therefore welcome one another as Christ has welcomed you, for the glory of God.
>
> For I tell you that Christ became a servant to the circumcised to show God's truthfulness, in order to confirm the promises given

---

[56] See Edwards 1998: 155–156.

to the patriarchs, and in order that the Gentiles might glorify God for his mercy. As it is written,

'Therefore I will praise you among the Gentiles,
and sing to your name.'
(Rom. 15:6–9, citing Ps. 18:49)

Paul also reminds the Corinthians of their responsibility to glorify God in all their actions: '[Y]ou were bought with a price. So glorify God in your body' (1 Cor. 6:20); '[D]o all to the glory of God' (10:31). Our responsibility to glorify God is profound, as it shapes every aspect of our lives. Paul likewise prays that the Philippians would 'approve what is excellent, and so be pure and blameless for the day of Christ, filled with the fruit of righteousness that comes through Jesus Christ, to the glory and praise of God' (Phil. 1:10–11).

The apostle Peter also stresses our responsibility to glorify God, linking it to the nature and mission of the church:

you are a chosen race, a royal priesthood, a holy nation, a people for his own possession, that you may proclaim the excellencies of him who called you out of darkness into his marvellous light. Once you were not a people, but now you are God's people; once you had not received mercy, but now you have received mercy.

Beloved, I urge you as sojourners and exiles to abstain from the passions of the flesh, which wage war against your soul. Keep your conduct among the Gentiles honourable, so that when they speak against you as evildoers, they may see your good deeds and glorify God on the day of visitation.
(1 Peter 2:9–12)

Peter later instructs:

whoever speaks, as one who speaks oracles of God; whoever serves, as one who serves by the strength that God supplies – in order that in everything God may be glorified through Jesus Christ. To him belong glory and dominion for ever and ever.
(1 Peter 4:11)

Thus God is already intrinsically glorious, and will sovereignly bring about the consummation and receive ultimate glory. At the same time, we are responsible to glorify him.

God's ultimate end and other ends

A fourth helpful way of viewing the redemptive-historical expressions of God's extrinsic glory is that of his ultimate and multiple ends. That God's ultimate purpose is his glory is clear enough in Scripture and standard in Reformed theology.[57] It is the goal of creation; the exodus; Israel; Jesus' ministry, life, death, resurrection and reign; our salvation; the church; the consummation and all of salvation history. Paul often highlights this cosmic goal: '[T]hose whom he foreknew he also predestined to be conformed to the image of his Son, in order that he might be the firstborn among many brothers' (Rom. 8:29); '[A]ll things were created through him and for him' (Col. 1:16; cf. Rom. 11:33–36; Heb. 2:10).[58]

While the Bible teaches that God's glory is his ultimate end, it also shows that God often acts with multiple ends in mind. Regarding the exodus, for instance, why did God redeem his people from slavery in Egypt? One might quickly reply, 'For his glory.' Certainly, God redeems his people from slavery to glorify himself. But many other goals also play a part in this. The book of Exodus presents God's reasons for deliverance as multifaceted:

- His concern for his oppressed people (Exod. 3 – 4)
- His faithfulness to the covenant promises made to Abraham, Isaac and Jacob (3:15; 4:5; 6:8; 32:13; 34:6; cf. Deut. 7:6–10)
- That Israel would serve the LORD (Exod. 4:23; 6:5; etc.)
- That Israel would know that he is the LORD (6:7; 10:2)
- To give Israel the Promised Land (6:8)
- That the Egyptians would know that he is the LORD[59] (7:5; 14:3–4, 15–18)
- That Pharaoh would know the LORD is incomparable (7:17; 8:10–18)

---

[57] See Berkhof 1941: 136; Edwards 1998: 125–136; Hodge 2003: 1.535–536, 566–567; Shedd 2003: 344, 364.

[58] See Edwards 1998: 210–220; Piper: 2003a: 250–266, 306.

[59] Pharaoh arrogantly questions God in Exod. 5:2, 'Who is the LORD, that I should obey his voice and let Israel go?' Hamilton (2006a: 72) observes that 'the narrative recounts Yahweh's campaign to remedy Pharaoh's ignorance'; cf. House 1998: 87–125.

- To display his power (9:16)
- That his name might be proclaimed in all the earth (9:16)
- To pass down a heritage to the children (10:1–2)
- That his wonders might be multiplied (11:9)
- To get glory over Pharaoh and his army (14:3–18)
- For Israel's sake (18:8)

God delivered his people for a variety of reasons, not merely one. The incomparable God acts out of love, covenant faithfulness and jealousy (notice the emphasis on uniqueness). He does so for his glory, for Israel's good, for judgment on Egypt and for the continuance of his covenant people. Recognizing these multiple ends does not detract from an emphasis on God's glory but underscores it. Indeed, in the exodus God displays his love, covenant faithfulness, jealousy, providence and power through his wonders, salvation and judgment, in which he manifests himself and thus glorifies himself.

Or we can consider the doctrine of salvation and ask why God saves us. One might hastily retort, 'For his glory.' Again, that is a correct answer. But the Bible provides a wide range of reasons. That God's motive in saving us is his love is set forth powerfully and regularly: John 3:16 states, 'For God so loved the world, that he gave' (cf. 1 John 4:9–10). Ephesians 1:4–5 extols that 'in love' God predestined us (cf. Deut. 7:6–8), and Ephesians 2:4 ties our salvation to God's love, mercy and grace (cf. Titus 3:4–5). John 17 records Jesus' high priestly prayer, interweaving God's glory and the good of his people, praying and acting in part 'for their sake' (17:19). Romans 8:28 also makes it clear that redemptive history is, in large part, for the good of God's people. So why does God save? For many reasons, as noted above, but in and through all of them God displays who he is and thus glorifies himself. God manifests his glory because in saving us he displays his wisdom (Rom. 11:33–36; 1 Cor. 1:18–31; Eph. 3:10–11), righteousness, justice (Rom. 3:25–26), love, mercy, kindness (Rom. 9:20–23; Eph. 2:4–7), freedom, wrath and power (Rom. 9:20–23). Texts such as Ephesians 2:4–10 set this forth with clarity and force:

> God, being rich in mercy, because of the great love with which he loved us, even when we were dead in our trespasses, made us alive together with Christ – by grace you have been saved – and raised us

up with him and seated us with him in the heavenly places in Christ
Jesus, so that in the coming ages he might show the immeasurable
riches of his grace in kindness towards us in Christ Jesus. For by
grace you have been saved through faith. And this is not your own
doing; it is the gift of God, not a result of works, so that no one may
boast. For we are his workmanship, created in Christ Jesus for
good works, which God prepared beforehand, that we should walk
in them.

Understanding this is significant, as it helps us address a common
question concerning God's glory: If God seeks his own glory above all
things, does this mean he is selfish? After all, if we seek our own glory, we
are deemed selfish. The standard answer to that line of enquiry is that God
is the ultimate being and the highest end, and we are not. Good behaviour
seeks the highest end, so God's making himself his own ultimate end is
appropriate. If we make ourselves the highest end, however, we are acting
inappropriately because we treat ourselves as the highest end when we are
not. Such argumentation is correct and beneficial but fails to do justice to
much of the biblical emphasis concerning God's goodness and love. The
argument understates God's genuine desire for the good of his creatures,
and fails to show how God's love and glory are united. Passages such as
the ones just quoted emphasize how God saves us out of love, displays his
kindness toward us for all eternity and is glorified through the entire
display. In this way God is self-giving and self-exalting, saving us for our
good and his glory. He gives himself to us, which simultaneously meets
our needs and demonstrates his sufficiency. Thus his love and glory
cohere.[60]

That God is simultaneously self-giving and self-exalting is displayed
also in the mutual glorification of the persons of the Trinity. The glorious
Father sends the glorious Son, who voluntarily humbles himself and
glorifies the Father through his incarnation, obedient life and substitutionary death (Phil. 2:5–11; cf. John 1:18; 7:18; 10:1–30; 14:13; 17). In
response the Father glorifies the Son, resurrecting him from the dead and
exalting him to the highest place (Acts 3:13–15; Rom. 6:4; Phil. 2:9–11).
The Father sends the glorious Spirit, who glorifies the Son (John 16:14).
And this all takes place to the glory of the Father (Phil. 2:11).

---

[60] Edwards 1998: 248–249.

Each member of the Trinity gives to the others as a display of love and as a way of accomplishing cosmic redemption. The Son says to the Father, 'I love you and the people you have given me, so I will undergo humiliation and suffering for you and them.' And then the Father responds to the Son, 'I love you and these people, so for your sake and theirs I desire to raise and exalt you to the highest place and reputation.' Amazingly, through serving the Father, the Son is glorified, and, through blessing the Son, the Father is glorified (John 17:1–5; Phil. 2:5–11). Further, the Father blesses the Son with people to save, depicted as love gifts from the Father. The Son, in turn, saves and keeps all of these love gifts, giving them back to the Father (John 6; 10; 17). The Father blesses the Son with gifts (us!), and the Son blesses the Father by giving gifts in return. In addition, the Spirit communicates the gifts, disclosing to believers what belongs to the Father and the Son (John 16:14–15).

Jesus' high priestly prayer also reveals that the self-giving and self-exalting triune God draws his redeemed people into the circle of fellowship, mutual blessing and shared glory. Jesus begins his prayer, 'Father, the hour has come; glorify your Son that the Son may glorify you' (John 17:1). Jesus longs to be glorified not for his own benefit but for the glory of the Father and of his people (17:20–24). Owen underscores this:

> It is evident that in this prayer the Lord Christ has respect to his own glory and the manifestation of it, which he had in the entrance asked of the Father (John 17:4–5). But in this place he has not so much respect to it as his own, as to the advantage, benefit, satisfaction, and blessedness of his disciples in the beholding of it.[61]

Such is the peculiar nature of Christ: he is the loving Lord who gives and serves (Matt. 20:26–28; John 13:1–17; Phil. 2:5–11). From John 17 we also learn that the Father grants glory to the Son because of his eternal love for the Son (17:24). Does any of this sound selfish? Not at all! The Father is determined to bless the Son, and the Son is determined to bless the Father! The mutuality and reciprocating love of God displayed within the Trinity flows outward even to bless us. By union with Christ we are recipients of God's love and its corresponding blessings, including forgiveness of

---

[61] Owen 1684: 42.

our sins, adoption into his family and final glorification (17:22). And because it is God who accomplishes all of this, it is for our good *and* his glory!

The panorama of the glory of God is greater than words can express. The same is true for the biblical narrative of God's glory, to which we now turn. The words of Herman Bavinck, late-nineteenth- and early-twentieth-century Dutch Reformed theologian, form a nice bridge between this chapter and the next:

> The 'glory of the Lord' is the splendor and brilliance that is insepar-
> ably associated with all of God's attributes and his self-revelation in
> nature and grace, the glorious form in which he everywhere appears
> to his creatures. This glory and majesty . . . appeared to Israel . . . It
> filled the tabernacle and temple . . . This glory is above all manifested
> in Christ, the only-begotten Son (John 1:14) and through him in the
> church (Rom. 15:7; 2 Cor. 3:18), which is looking for 'the blessed
> hope and the manifestation of the glory of our great God and
> Saviour, Jesus Christ' (Titus 2:13).[62]

---

62 Bavinck 2003–8: 2.252.

2
The drama of God's glory

Is there a grander and yet more overlooked biblical theme than the glory of God? Other themes, it is true, are equally overlooked. But no theme is grander than that of God's glory. The biblical story is, in large part, the drama of God's glory:

> The triune God who is glorious displays his glory, largely through his creation, image-bearers, providence, and redemptive acts. God's people respond by glorifying him. God receives glory and, through uniting his people to Christ, shares his glory with them – all to his glory.[1]

We will trace this drama of the glory of God through the Bible's storyline:

- God's glory and creation
- God's glory and the fall
- God's glory and redemption
- God's glory and the consummation
- The drama of God's glory

God's glory and creation

In creation God reveals his glory in the things he has made, especially in humanity, his image-bearers. But even before creation the eternal Trinity exists, glorious in perfections, needing nothing. As we saw in chapter 1, theologians make a key distinction between God's *intrinsic* and *extrinsic* glory. God's intrinsic glory is the inherent glory that belongs to him alone

---

[1] Morgan and Peterson 2010: 159.

as God, independent of his works. God's extrinsic glory is his intrinsic glory partially unveiled in his works of creation, providence, redemption and consummation.

Scripture revels in God's intrinsic glory:

[W]ill God indeed dwell on the earth? Behold, heaven and the highest heaven cannot contain you; how much less this house that I have built!
(1 Kgs 8:27)

The LORD is high above all nations,
    and his glory above the heavens!
Who is like the LORD our God,
    who is seated on high,
who looks far down
    on the heavens and the earth?
(Ps. 113:4–6)

I am the LORD; that is my name;
    my glory I give to no other,
    nor my praise to carved idols.
(Isa. 42:8)

the blessed and only Sovereign, the King of kings and Lord of lords, who alone has immortality, who dwells in unapproachable light, whom no one has ever seen or can see. To him be honour and eternal dominion. Amen.
(1 Tim. 6:15–16)

God discloses a portion of his intrinsic glory extrinsically in creation. God is central in Genesis 1 – 2, for he is the Creator, not a creature. The creation is neither God nor a part of God. God is absolute and has independent existence, whereas creation derives its existence from him and continually depends on him as its sustainer (Col. 1:17; Heb. 1:3). 'The heavens declare the glory of God' (Ps. 19:1). Humans have seen God's 'eternal power and divine nature . . . ever since the creation of the world' in the things he has made (Rom. 1:20). The transcendent Creator shows his sovereignty in creation, for as divine King he effects his will by his mere word (Gen. 1:3). God also reveals his goodness in creation, as the steady refrain testifies: 'And God saw that it was good' (Gen. 1:4, 10, 12, 18, 21, 25). Creation's inherent goodness precludes a fundamental dualism between spirit and matter, in which spirit is good and matter bad. Instead, material creation reflects God's goodness, wisdom and glory, evident in his provision of light, land, vegetation and animals. In creation God reveals his glory in the things he has made.

When God forms man from the dust of the ground, man is more than dust, for God personally breathes into him the breath of life (Gen. 2:7). Most importantly, God, the divine Person, especially reveals his glory in his creation of humans as persons made in his image (1:26–28). In doing so God invests his image-bearers with glory, honour and dominion. David is amazed at how God made man:

> you have . . .
>   crowned him with glory and honour.
> You have given him dominion over the works of your hands.
> (Ps. 8:5–6)

When Paul speaks of humans as divine image-bearers, he implies the idea of God's glory. While all creation testifies to God's glory, humans are unique as they bear God's image and glory to the world, serving as his representatives and stewards over the land, plants and animals.

In Genesis 1 – 2 God blesses Adam and Eve with an unhindered relationship with him, intimate enjoyment of each other and delegated authority over creation. God gives only one prohibition: not to eat of the tree of the knowledge of good and evil.

God's glory and the fall

Sadly, Adam and Eve disobey God's command (Gen. 3) and tarnish God's glory-image. As a result of their sin, they and their descendants fall short of God's glory and even exchange it for idols. A 'crafty' tempter questions God and deflects the woman's attention from the covenantal relationship with God (3:1–5). The woman's inflated expectations in eating (the fruit is edible and attractive and promises to give insight) are dashed, for the first pair's eyes are opened; they know they are naked and hide (vv. 7–8). The contrast arrests us: the forbidden fruit does not deliver what the tempter had promised but brings dark realities of which their good and truthful Lord had warned them.

Their rebellion brings God's justice, as Allen Ross observes:

> They sinned by eating, and so would suffer to eat; she led her husband to sin, and so would be mastered by him; they brought pain into the world by their disobedience, and so would have painful toil in their respective lives.[2]

The couple feel shame (v. 7), and estrangement from and fear toward God, and try to hide from him (vv. 8–10). They are alienated from each other, as the woman blames the serpent and the man blames the woman and even God! (vv. 10–13). Pain and sorrow follow. The woman will experience greater pain in childbirth; the man will toil trying to grow food in a land with pests and weeds. And worse, God banishes the couple from his glorious presence in Eden (vv. 22–24).

The man and woman ignore God's warning (2:17) and, after eating the forbidden fruit, die. Though they do not yet die physically, they do so spiritually, and their bodies begin to experience decay leading to physical death (3:19). Most disturbing, although sin originated in the garden, it did not stay there. It brings forth spiritual death, more sin and condemnation for all those whom Scripture describes as 'in Adam' (Rom. 5:12–21; Eph. 2:1–3).

Sin devastates God's image-bearers, whom he made to reflect his glory. The Bible describes sin as a 'falling short'. Thus sin is a failure to keep God's law (1 John 3:4), an absence of his righteousness (Rom. 1:18), a lack of reverence for God (Jude 15) and, most notably, a falling 'short of the glory of God' (Rom. 3:23). Thus sin is the quality of human actions that causes them to fail to glorify the Lord and brings disrepute on his name.[3]

The storyline of Genesis 4 – 11 reinforces this conclusion, for Cain kills Abel (4:8) and sin proves to be massive and continual (6:5–11), prompting God to bring the flood (Gen. 6 – 9). The tower of Babel episode portrays God as judging proud, self-seeking humans who attempt to advance their name rather than, as God's image-bearers, to advance his name and glory (11:1–9). This illustrates another terrible effect of sin on God's glory: idolatry. Paul's words pertain to all humans since the fall, although not

---

[2] Ross 1997: 148.
[3] Morgan with Peterson 2020.

all worship physical images: they 'exchanged the glory of the immortal God' for an image (Rom. 1:23; cf. 1 John 5:21). Sin is our failure to image our Creator to the world. Sin is trading the glory of the incorruptible God for something less (Ps. 106:20; Jer. 2:11–12). Affirming that 'sin came into the world through one man' (Rom. 5:12) and that though humans 'knew God, they did not honour him as God or give thanks to him' (1:21), Richard Gaffin captures the sad condition of image-bearers since the fall:

> They have withheld worship and adoration, their due response to the divine glory reflected in the creation around them and in themselves as God's image bearers. Instead, with futile minds and foolish, darkened hearts (cf. 1 Cor. 1:18–25), they have idolatrously exchanged God's glory for creaturely images, human and otherwise (Rom. 1:21–23). Having so drastically defaced the divine image, they have, without exception, forfeited the privilege of reflecting his glory (Rom. 3:23). This *doxa*-less condition, resulting in unrelieved futility, corruption and death, permeates the entire created order (Rom. 8:20–22).[4]

God's glory and redemption

Thankfully, God does not eradicate humanity for cosmic treason but graciously works to redeem it and the cosmos. In redemption God begins to restore his glory in his image-bearers. He intends to restore humans as full image-bearers who will reflect his glory.

The patriarchs to the exile

God calls Abraham from idolatry and enters into covenant with him, promising to be God to him and his descendants (Gen. 12:1–3; 17:7). God promises to give Abraham a land, to make him into a great nation and through him to bless all peoples (12:3). From Abraham come Isaac and Jacob, whose name God changes to Israel and from whom God brings twelve tribes and a nation.

God identifies his glory with his people Israel (Isa. 40:5; 43:6–7; 60:1). He promises to bless them so that they will bless the nations, who will glorify him. When Egypt enslaves the covenant people, God redeems them through Moses, showing his glory in plagues and exodus so all will know he is

---

4 Gaffin 1993: 348.

incomparable (Exod. 9:16). He also displays his glory through theophanies, the giving of the law and chiefly through the tabernacle and the temple. God's presence guides his people as they occupy the Promised Land under Joshua. God gives Israel kings. Under David the kingdom grows and God renews his covenant with his people. He promises to make David's descendants into a dynasty and to establish the throne of one of them for ever (2 Sam. 7:16). Solomon builds a temple to manifest God's presence. Solomon does much right, but his disobedience leads to the kingdom's split into the northern kingdom of Israel and the southern kingdom of Judah.

God sends prophets to turn his sinful people away from worthless idols and back to himself, the uniquely glorious God. These prophets call the people to covenant faithfulness and warn of the judgment that will come if they fail to repent. Nevertheless, the people repeatedly rebel. In response God sends the northern kingdom into captivity to Assyria in 722 BC and the southern kingdom into captivity to Babylon in 586 BC. Through the prophets God also promises to send a deliverer (Isa. 9:6–7; 52:13 – 53:12). The prophets yearn for Israel to become what God intended – glorious (Isa. 60 – 66) – when the Messiah arrives. God promises to restore his people to their land from Babylonian captivity after seventy years (Jer. 25:11–12), and does so under Ezra and Nehemiah. The people rebuild the walls of Jerusalem and build a second temple. Yet the Old Testament ends with God's people continuing to turn away from him (Malachi).

Jesus and the church

Four hundred years later God sends his Son as the promised Messiah, Suffering Servant, King of Israel and Saviour of the world. As the Messiah, Jesus is glorious, but not as expected. The Jews hope for a political leader to restore Israel to its former glory. But Jesus' redemption and his glory are deeper than anticipated, for he is the Lord of glory, the radiance of God's glory, even Yahweh himself (Dan. 7:13–14; Heb. 1:3; Jas 2:1). Jesus the Messiah is the eternal Son, intrinsically glorious, who humbles himself to become a man (John 1:1–18; Phil. 2:5–11). Both lowly shepherds and glorious angelic hosts mark his birth (Luke 2:1–20). His signs witness to his glorious identity and the presence of God's kingdom (Matt. 12:28; John 2:11; 11:38–44). In the transfiguration Jesus' glory shines brightly (Mark 9:2–13; 2 Peter 1:16–21).

Jesus chooses twelve disciples to lead his messianic community. He brings God's kingdom by casting out demons, performing miracles and preaching good news. The Jewish leaders oppose him for opposing their traditions. The Sanhedrin condemns Jesus in an illegal trial, and Pontius Pilate, against his will and pressured by Jewish leaders, crucifies him. Humanly speaking, Jesus dies as a victim in a despicably evil act. Yet his death fulfils God's eternal plan, and Jesus succeeds in his mission to seek and save the lost. His glory is linked with his suffering and death (John 17:1–5). The cross is also Jesus' path to more glory (1 Peter 1:10–11). And the cross also displays God's glory by showing his righteousness and love (Rom. 3:25–26). Jesus not only bears the world's sin in death but is also raised from the dead. His resurrection confirms his identity, defeats sin and death, gives new life to believers and promises their future resurrection. He is raised by the glory of the Father to glory and exalted to the highest status (Rom. 6:4; Phil. 2:9–11; Heb. 2:9). He ascends gloriously and reigns in the same manner (Acts 7:55–56; 1 Tim. 3:16).

Jesus tells his disciples to take the gospel to all nations, fulfilling God's promise to bless all peoples through Abraham. They are to disciple others, who will do the same. On Pentecost Jesus sends his Spirit, who forms the church as the New Testament people of God. The early church is committed to evangelism (Acts 2:38–41), fellowship (vv. 42–47), ministry (vv. 42–46) and worship (v. 47). The church faces persecution, but some Jews and many Gentiles trust Christ and churches are planted. The apostles teach sound doctrine, correct error and call believers to live for God. They teach that the Father plans salvation, the Son accomplishes it and the Spirit applies it. God calls, regenerates, declares righteous and adopts into his family all who trust Christ. God makes his people increasingly holy and glorious in Christ (2 Cor. 3:17–18).

The glorious triune God manifests his glory and, through union with Christ, shares it with his people. Paul praises God's mighty power that produces 'glory in the church and in Christ Jesus' (Eph. 3:20–21). Paul depicts the church in glorious language: it is 'the fullness of him who fills all in all' and 'a dwelling place for God' (1:23; 2:22). Even more so than creation, the church is the theatre of and witness to God's glory (3:10–11). As God's people love and seek him, he gives them joy, which in turn brings him glory (as Mary exemplifies; Luke 1:46–47).[5] The church is now being sanctified, and one day Christ will present it 'to himself in splendour,

---

[5] As John Piper has argued at length, 'God is most glorified in us when we are most satisfied in him.' See e.g. Piper 2003a.

without spot or wrinkle or any such thing, that she might be holy and without blemish' (Eph. 5:27). Indeed, the church is a new humanity, a display people, testifying that God's mission of cosmic reconciliation is well underway and heading toward the grand finale of history (1:10–11; 2:14–16; 3:10–11). In the meantime, the church glorifies God through its worship and character, which has been transformed by the Spirit to communicate God's communicable attributes. As the church is marked by love, holiness, goodness, justice and faithfulness, God is reflected and thus glorified.[6]

God's glory and the consummation

The biblical drama of God's glory culminates in the consummation, which is also characterized by glory. Jesus will finish what he has started, and his return will be glorious (Matt. 16:27; Luke 21:27; Titus 2:13), as will his victory, judgment and punishment of the wicked (2 Thess. 1:6–11; Rev. 20:11–15). Most of all, Jesus' revelation of himself in the new creation will be glorious in the church and the cosmos (Rom. 8:21; Eph. 5:27; Rev. 21 – 22).

Having been justified by faith, then, believers 'rejoice in hope of the glory of God' (Rom. 5:2). Because we have been united to Christ, whom the Father raised from the dead by his glory (6:4), we too have new life. Though we may suffer now, God guides history to his intended goals, including glorifying us with Christ (8:17). This entails 'the glory that is to be revealed in us' (v. 18), 'the freedom of the glory' of God's children (v. 21), our ultimate conformity to Christ's image (v. 29) and our glorification (v. 30).

Moreover, God will bring 'many sons to glory' (Heb. 2:10). God prepared such glory for us 'beforehand' (Rom. 9:23), and, because of our union with Christ and his resurrection, our bodies will likewise be raised in glory (1 Cor. 15:42–58).

Paul shows that our union with Christ is 'to the praise of his glorious grace' and 'glory' (Eph. 1:6, 12, 14) and results in personal and cosmic redemption (vv. 3–14), even our 'glorious inheritance' from 'the Father of glory' (vv. 17–18). The landmark consummation passage is Revelation 21 – 22. Just as Genesis 1 – 2 shows that the biblical story begins with

---

[6] For more on how the church relates to God's glory see Morgan 2013.

God's creation of the heavens and earth, Revelation 21 – 22 shows that it ends with God's creation of a new heaven and earth. The story begins with the goodness of creation and ends with the goodness of the new creation. The story begins with God's dwelling with his people in a garden-temple and ends with God's dwelling with his people in heaven, a new earth-city-garden-temple.

The glory of God is manifested in the new creation (Isa. 66:22–23; Rom. 8:18–27; Rev. 21:9 – 22:5). And since God's extrinsic glory is communicated to his people in salvation history, it relates to the already-and-not-yet tension. God's glory is now being displayed, and yet its ultimate display is still future (1 John 3:2). Gregory Beale's insights into the central theological theme of Revelation are helpful: 'The sovereignty of God and Christ in redeeming and judging brings them glory, which is intended to motivate saints to worship God and reflect his glorious attributes through obedience to his word.'[7] Further, 'nothing from the old world will be able to hinder God's glorious presence from completely filling the new cosmos' or to 'hinder the saints from unceasing access to that divine presence'.[8]

Once and for all God's victory is consummated. God's judgment is final, sin is vanquished, justice prevails, holiness predominates and God's glory is unobstructed. God's eternal plan of cosmic reconciliation in Christ is actualized, and God is 'all in all' (1 Cor. 15:28). As a part of his victory, God casts the devil and his demons into the lake of fire, where they are not annihilated but rather 'tormented day and night for ever and ever' (Rev. 20:10). Then God judges everyone: the powerbrokers, those deemed nobodies and everyone in between. '[I]f anyone's name was not found written in the book of life, he was thrown into the lake of fire' (v. 15). God consigns to hell all who do not belong to the people of Jesus (cf. Dan. 12:1; Rev. 13:8; 21:8, 27).

Magnificently, the new heaven and new earth arrive, and God dwells with his covenant people (Rev. 21:3, 7), comforts them (v. 4) and renews all things (v. 5). John depicts heaven as a glorious temple, multinational and holy (vv. 9–27). God's people rightly bear his image: serving and worshipping him, reigning with him, knowing him directly (22:1–5). God receives the worship he is due and blesses humans beyond measure so that

---

they finally live to the fullest the realities of being created in his image and showing his glory. And throughout it all God is glorified.

The drama of God's glory

As humans, we refused to acknowledge God's glory and instead sought our own, forfeiting the glory he intended for us as his image-bearers. By his grace, however, through union with Christ, God restores believing image-bearers to participate in and reflect his glory. We are recipients of glory, are being transformed in glory and will one day be sharers of glory. Our salvation is from sin to glory. We have received great grace: we who exchanged the glory of God for idols and rebelled against his glory have been, are being and will be transformed by the very glory we despised and rejected! Even more, through union with Christ together we are the church, the new humanity, the firstfruits of the new creation, bearing God's image, displaying how life ought to be and making known the wisdom of God to the angels in heaven.

All of this redounds to his glory, as God in his manifold perfections is exhibited, known, rejoiced in and prized. In this sense, the entire biblical plotline – creation, fall, redemption and consummation – is the drama of God's glory. Jonathan Edwards captured it well: 'The whole is *of* God, and *in* God, and *to* God; and he is the beginning, middle, and end.'[9]

---

[9] Edwards 1998: 247; emphases original.

3
The glory of God and salvation: Romans

Paul's masterful epistle to the Romans, his 'grandest exposition of the gospel',[1] says much about the glory of God. Although it seems overreaching to regard God's glory as *the* major theme of this epistle,[2] it is *a* major theme, affecting many doctrinal emphases of the letter. Romans lends itself, therefore, to an outline of God's glory in terms of those doctrines, especially those related to salvation:

- God's glory and the gospel
- God's glory and the image of God
- God's glory and sin
- God's glory and the work of Christ
- God's glory, faith and justification
- God's glory and sanctification
- God's glory and suffering
- God's glory and heaven
- God's glory and Israel
- God's glory and election
- God's glory and church unity
- God's glory and worship

God's glory and the gospel

Paul's concern for the glory of God is evident from the beginning of his most famous epistle. He alludes to God's glory in both the salutation and the thematic statement.

---

[1] Moo 1996: 744.
[2] So Schreiner (1998: 22–23).

The salutation (Rom. 1:5)

Paul includes key themes already within the letter's salutation: the gospel and Christ, its focus. God called Paul to be an apostle and set him apart 'for the gospel of God' (v. 1). This gospel is all about God's Son, who is both human and divine (vv. 2–4). God gave Paul and others grace and the apostolic office to preach the gospel 'among all the nations', including in Rome (vv. 5–6). God did this 'for the sake of his name' (v. 5). It is well known that 'name' signifies person, and here it signifies the person of Jesus. Paul's ministry to Gentiles lay heavily upon his heart. Although he spent himself to bring salvation to them, an even higher motive drove him – the exaltation of Jesus' name. Schreiner comments aptly, 'What was fundamental for Paul was the glory and praise of Jesus Christ.'[3] Paul sought to accomplish this goal through gospel proclamation to Jews and Gentiles alike.

The theme (Rom. 1:16–17)

Paul affirms that he is proud of the message of salvation: 'I am not ashamed of the gospel' (Rom. 1:16). The reason? Because it is God's power to save believers. This is an amazing statement, too easily passed over. Paul is identifying the gospel with an attribute of God, specifically his power. God has so associated his power with the gospel message that the apostle could speak like this.

Although there is no explicit mention of God's glory, the idea is implied. This is clarified by a summary of Paul's teaching on salvation, as Moo shows. The Old Testament uses the word 'salvation' with a wide range of meaning. This is also true of the New Testament as a whole. Paul, however, uses the word of spiritual deliverance. His focus, in line with the New Testament's, includes present participation of blessings belonging in full to the age to come. Moreover, 'particularly, in light of Rom. 3:23 and the use of "save" in 8:24 (cf. vv. 18–23), "salvation" here must include the restoration of the sinner to a share of the "glory of God"'.[4]

It is true that 'glory' and 'glorious' most often refer to final salvation after Christ's return (Phil. 3:20–21). Cranfield, however, urges us to view present salvation in terms of future glory: 'Future eschatological salvation

---

[3] Ibid. 35–36.
[4] Moo 1996: 66–67.

reflects its glory back into the present for those who confidently hope for it.'[5]

Paul continues his thematic statement: 'For in it [the gospel] the righteousness of God is revealed from faith for faith, as it is written, "The righteous shall live by faith"' (Rom. 1:17). Romans is about God's making his righteousness known in the gospel. Romans 1:18 – 4:25 highlights justification by faith. And justification highlights God's glory, for its focus is 'Jesus Christ and him crucified' (1 Cor. 2:2). The cross reveals God's redeeming and judging righteousness and thereby displays his glory.

God's glory and the image of God

Paul's thematic statement deals with the gospel and God's righteousness broadcast in the apostolic preaching (Rom. 1:16–17). But the very next verse changes the subject from God's saving righteousness to his condemning righteousness: 'For the wrath of God is revealed from heaven against all ungodliness and unrighteousness of men, who by their unrighteousness suppress the truth' (v. 18). Here Paul begins a section that ends in 3:20 to explain why humans need the gospel. He explains that sinners push away the truth of God, especially of his great power and divinity, that he has revealed in creation.

Ungrateful hearts (Rom. 1:19–21)

Ever since the beginning of the world God's creation has borne witness to him, so that people are inexcusable for rejecting him.[6] Though knowledge of God got through to them, 'they did not honour him as God or give thanks to him, but they became futile in their thinking, and their foolish hearts were darkened' (v. 21). The NIV helps us understand verse 21: 'For although they knew God, they neither *glorified* him as God nor gave thanks to him.' Humans failed to give the Supreme Being and their Maker the glory that was his due. The verb 'glorify' (*doxazein*) appears five times in Romans and here (and in 15:6, 9) refers to what human beings 'owe to God's glory of recognizing Him as God, as their Creator and the Lord of their life, in humble trust and obedience', as Cranfield says (cf. 4:20; 15:7).[7]

---

[5] Cranfield 2004: 530.
[6] See Morgan and Peterson 2008a.
[7] Cranfield 2004: 117.

A terrible exchange (Rom. 1:22–23)

All humans owe God glory, but, rather than worshipping their Creator, rebels spurned him, as their hearts and minds rejected the knowledge of God. Worst of all, 'Claiming to be wise, they became fools, and exchanged the glory of the immortal God for images resembling mortal man and birds and animals and creeping things' (vv. 22–23). To understand the folly and heinousness of this exchange, we must consider the meaning of the words 'the glory [*doxa*] of the immortal God'. Cranfield comes to our aid:

> In extra-biblical Greek the primary meaning of δόξα is 'opinion', its secondary meaning 'the opinion which others have of one', so 'repute', 'good repute', 'glory'. But in the Bible the meaning 'opinion' has almost completely disappeared, and δόξα has acquired a new meaning as a result of its being used to translate the Hebrew *kābôd*, namely, 'glory', 'splendour', 'majesty', with reference to external appearance. So it is used to denote the manifest majesty of God (e.g. LXX Ps 96[MT 97]:6; Exod 40:35; Isa 6:3; 40:5). In the NT it can further denote the divine quality of life. But in this verse it is best understood as referring to that self-manifestation of the true God spoken of in vv. 19 and 20.[8]

This is the worst exchange ever – sinners exchanged God's great glory, his divine splendour and majesty, for idols! Richard Gaffin profoundly connects God's glory and the image of God in humans:

> For Paul the essence of human sin is the rebellion of the creature against the Creator in whose image he has been made, a renouncing of the truth of the creaturely dependence that divine image-bearing entails, for the lie of human self-sufficiency and independence from God. This deeply rooted revolt is such that human beings refuse to acknowledge God's glory evident in the entire creation and evident particularly in and to themselves because they, uniquely as creatures, are God's image. The creaturely capacities given, with being that image, capacities to be for God, for doing his will and obeying

---

8 Ibid. 119–120.

his law, are instead directed against him in devoting to self or some other creature the worship and service due to him alone. The result of sin is not the loss of the divine image but its defacement or distortion, the loss of image-bearing integrity.[9]

God's glory and sin

Sin is universal (Rom. 1:18 – 3:20)

From Romans 1:18 to 3:20 Paul pounds away to convict stubborn human beings, including those who give sin free rein in their lives (1:32), hypocrites (2:1–5), pagans (2:12–16) and Jews (2:17–24). Finally, in 3:9–20 Paul brings the whole world to its knees before a holy God. His indictments include the following:

> [W]e have already charged that all, both Jews and Greeks, are under sin.
> (v. 9)

> None is righteous, no, not one;
>> no one understands;
>> no one seeks for God.
> (vv. 10–11)

> Now we know that whatever the law says it speaks to those who are under the law, so that every mouth may be stopped, and the whole world may be held accountable to God.
> (v. 19)

In 3:21 Paul returns to his announced theme – the revelation of God's saving righteousness. He has stressed that salvation is not gained by law-keeping (3:19–20). And now he qualifies. He does not separate salvation entirely from the law; on the contrary, 'the Law and the Prophets bear witness to' free justification (v. 21). God's saving righteousness is received through faith in Christ by every believer, 'For there is no distinction: for all have sinned and fall short of the glory of God' (vv. 22–23). While Paul

---

[9] Gaffin 2010: 147.

has moved past his major treatment of sin to that of justification by faith, here he summarizes humankind's sinful position before a holy God. '[A]ll have sinned and fall short of the glory of God'. Paul underscores the universality of sin. When he shifts from the aorist tense ('all have sinned') to the present tense ('fall short'), he moves from treating Adam's original sin to every human's actual sins.

Sin is failure to glorify God (Rom. 3:23)

The key issue is that Paul depicts continuing human iniquity as falling short 'of *the glory of God*' (3:23). Moo helpfully links sharing in God's glory as final salvation and the image of God. Just as 'sharing in God's "glory" involves conformity to the "image of Christ" (Rom. 8:29–30; Phil. 3:21), so the absence of glory involves a declension from the "image of God" in which human beings were first made'.[10]

Sin is complex (Rom. 1:25)

'[A]ll have sinned and fall short of the glory of God'. These memorable words encapsulate Paul's doctrine of sin. They point back to Adam's primal transgression and at the same time draw attention to our present rebellion against God. Scripture describes sin in many ways, including the following:

Sin is a failure to glorify God and rebellion against him.
Sin is offence against God and violation of his law.
Sin is a wilful act and the present state of human existence.
Sin is personal and social.
Sin involves commission, omission and imperfection.
Sin is a rogue element in creation.
Sin is a failure to image the Creator to the world.
Sin includes guilt and pollution.
Sin includes thoughts, words and actions.
Sin is deceitful.
Sin has a beginning in history and will have an end.[11]

---

[10] Moo 1996: 226–227.
[11] These headings are taken from Morgan with Peterson 2020: 194–200. For biblical exposition see those pages as well as Mahony 2013.

Sin is thus a huge and complex topic in Scripture. Even the long list above is not comprehensive. But it is very helpful and puts first things first, as Schreiner cogently argues from Romans 1. Though verses 24–32 rightly point to sin as the trespass of the law, sin goes deeper:

> Failing to glorify God is the root sin . . . Sin does not consist first and foremost in acts that transgress God's law . . . These particular acts are all rooted in a rejection of God as God, a failure to give him honor and glory.[12]

Sin leads to God's glory (Rom. 3:5, 7)

Ironically, although God is holy and hates sin, ultimately sin leads to his glory, because 'our unrighteousness serves to show the righteousness of God' (3:5), and 'through my lie God's truth abounds to his glory' (v. 7). Both of these texts refer to the fact that God's judgment results in his being glorified. 'God's name and honor are cleared in his judgment of Jewish sinners.'[13] Actually, God will be glorified in the judgment and condemnation of all sinners, as Peterson shows:

> God is majestic beyond all our imagining. He, therefore, deserves the eternal praise of every one of his creatures. Many human beings, however, refuse to bow before him as Lord, and because God is holy and righteous he must punish their rebellion . . . Lest we think that somehow God is defeated by his enemies, Revelation assures us that, because God is infinitely majestic, his glory is the supreme good in the universe. God will manifest his glory in the eternal salvation of his people and in the eternal damnation of his foes.[14]

God will display his glory in the condemnation of the lost. Our next topic is God's basis for saving lost humans.

God's glory and the work of Christ

God glorifies himself through the saving work of his beloved Son. God displays his glory in Christ's death and resurrection that accomplish

---

[12] Schreiner 1998: 88.
[13] Ibid. 157.
[14] R. A. Peterson 1995: 207–208.

propitiation, reconciliation and obedience as the basis for justification and inaugurate the new creation.[15]

God's glory in propitiation (Rom. 3:25–26)

Cranfield rightly calls Romans 3:21–26 'the centre and heart of the whole of Rom 1:16b–15:13'.[16] This is because it solves the problem caused by human rebellion (treated in 1:18 – 3:20) and returns to the epistle's theme of the revelation of God's saving righteousness in the gospel (1:16–17). But 1:18 – 3:20 developed a different theme: the revelation of God's wrath toward Jews and Gentiles who dishonour God's holy name.

Christ lovingly bears the full cost of forgiveness by his sacrifice on the cross (his 'blood'), which propitiates God's wrath, enabling him to maintain his righteous character and to justify everyone who trusts his Son as Lord and Saviour. The cross thus displays God's love and righteousness simultaneously. Christ gives himself for us in love and, by bearing God's punishment against sin, enables God to acquit believing sinners without compromising his moral integrity.

Schreiner agrees with John Piper, who considers God's glory the primary issue. However, Schreiner disagrees with Piper when he defines righteousness as God's desire for his glory. God's desire to promote his name drives his desire to show his righteousness in salvation and judgment. 'By demonstrating his saving and judging righteousness, God has vindicated his name before the world.'[17]

God's glory in reconciliation (Rom. 5:6–11)

In Romans 5:1–11 Paul expands his vision, adding to justification reconciliation, God's making peace through Christ's death and resurrection. He begins in this way: 'Therefore, since we have been justified by faith, we have peace with God through our Lord Jesus Christ' (Rom. 5:1). Humans' need for reconciliation is alienation: '[Y]ou, who once were alienated and hostile in mind, doing evil deeds, he has now reconciled in his body of flesh by his death' (Col. 1:21–22). By God's amazing grace, 'while we were enemies we were reconciled to God by the death of his Son' (Rom. 5:10), so that now we are God's friends.

---

[15] For a treatment of Christ's saving events and the biblical pictures that interpret them see Peterson 2012.

[16] Cranfield 2004: 199.

[17] Schreiner 1998: 198–199; referring to Piper 1983: 127–130.

After stating that Christ's death and resurrection will preserve us, Paul concludes Romans 5:1–11 by rejoicing in reconciliation: '[N]ow that we are reconciled, [we shall] be saved by his life. More than that, we also rejoice in God through our Lord Jesus Christ, through whom we have now received reconciliation' (vv. 10–11).

God's glory in Christ's obedience (Rom. 5:18–19)

Romans 4 is Paul's great treatment of saving faith. Before and after that chapter the apostle focuses on Christ's atonement. In 3:25–26 Paul presents Christ as a propitiation, as we have seen. This is the atonement in 'negative' terms, as Christ's propitiation turns away God's wrath. Paul presents Christ's atonement in 'positive' terms in 5:18–19:

> as one trespass led to condemnation for all men, so one act of right-eousness leads to justification and life for all men. For as by the one man's disobedience the many were made sinners, so by the one man's obedience the many will be made righteous.

Here Paul contrasts the acts of Adam and Christ, the second Adam, and their enormous effects on their respective peoples. Adam's sin plunged the human race into sin and condemnation. Christ's work gained justification and eternal life for all believers.

Paul labels Christ's saving accomplishment 'one act of righteousness' and 'obedience'. Jesus' 'one act of righteousness' is his crucifixion in the place of sinners. His 'obedience' is his obedience 'to the point of death, even death on a cross' (Phil. 2:8). Believers' confidence of acceptance by God now and at the final judgment lies not in their faith but in the faithful Christ's atoning work and resurrection. Referring to Romans 5:12–21, Moo elucidates:

> The passage shows why those who have been justified and reconciled can be so certain that they will be saved from wrath and share in 'the glory of God': it is because Christ's act of obedience ensures eternal life for all those who are 'in Christ.'[18]

---

[18] Moo 1996: 316.

Christians look forward to a glorious future because Jesus loved them and gave himself for them (Gal. 2:20).

God's glory in the new creation (Rom. 6:4)

Paul exhorts his readers to a godly lifestyle by reminding them of their union with Christ in his death and resurrection. They are joined to Christ in his death, and therefore sin's power over them is broken. They no longer need to live under its tyranny. They also are joined to Christ in his resurrection and therefore are to live new lives characterized by holiness and love. Paul is compelled to remind the Roman Christians that baptism signifies believers' dying with Christ to sin and living with him for God (Rom. 6:1–4).

'We were buried therefore with him by baptism into death, in order that, just as Christ was raised from the dead by the glory of the Father, we too might walk in newness of life' (Rom. 6:4). We died with Christ to sin's power, and it has no right to lord over us. We were raised with Christ; when Paul speaks of 'newness of life', he refers to the new age, inaugurated by Jesus' resurrection and reaching fulfilment in bodily resurrection at the end of this age.

God's work in Christ includes both his atoning death and his triumphant resurrection. Key for us is Paul's reference to Christ's being 'raised from the dead by the glory of the Father'. This is a unique use of 'glory' for the apostle. It here stands for the Father's power that raised Jesus from the dead. Cranfield helps us: 'God's use of His power is always glorious, and His use of it to raise the dead is a specially clear manifestation of His glory.'[19]

Because Jesus is alive and has sent the Spirit, believers already are 'beholding the glory of the Lord' in the gospel and 'being transformed . . . from one degree of glory to another' (2 Cor. 3:18). And they anticipate the risen Christ's transforming their lowly bodies to be 'like his glorious body' (Phil 3:21). Moo links Christ's resurrection both to the Christian life and to future glory. The apostle bases Christians' present possession of eternal life on Christ's powerful resurrection. 'Even now believers participate in this glory (cf. 2 Cor. 3:16) as they look toward the final manifestation of glory in connection with the transformation of the body (Phil. 3:21).'[20]

---

19 Cranfield 2004: 304.
20 Moo 1996: 366–367.

God's glory, faith and justification

God's glory and faith (Rom. 4:20)

Curiously, Paul has a doctrine of boasting, and it sheds light on our understanding of glory. On the one hand, he boasts in the Lord (1 Cor. 1:31; 2 Cor. 10:17; both from Jer. 9:23–24), his weaknesses (2 Cor. 12:9) and the cross: '[F]ar be it from me to boast except in the cross of our Lord Jesus Christ' (Gal. 6:14). On the other hand, Paul most definitely does *not* boast in the law (Rom. 2:23), humans (1 Cor. 3:21), the flesh (Gal. 6:13), outward appearance (2 Cor. 5:12) or especially works, for salvation is by grace through faith – 'not a result of works, so that no one may boast' (Eph. 2:9).

Father Abraham is the prime example of someone justified by faith, not works: '[I]f Abraham was justified by works, he has something to boast about, but not before God', for he was justified by faith, not works (Rom. 4:1–5). In fact, grace and faith are correlative: we cannot have one without the other (v. 16). Schreiner is correct: 'Boasting and any sense of earning eternal life are eliminated.'[21] Boasting is thus another way of speaking of giving glory to God, to whom it belongs.

Romans 4:20 reinforces this point with reference to Abraham: 'No distrust made him waver concerning the promise of God, but he grew strong in his faith as he gave glory to God' (Rom. 4:20). Humanly speaking, Abraham knew it was impossible for him and Sarah to bear children, for they were too old (vv. 18–19). Moo explains that Abraham's faith gained the victory and glorified God: 'Abraham's faith gained strength from its victory over the hindrance created by the conflict between God's promise and the physical evidence. And in this strengthening of his faith, Abraham gave "glory to God."'[22]

The contrast between Romans 1:20–21 and 4:20–21 is stark, as a comparison shows:

> they are without excuse. For although they knew God, they did not honour ['glorify', NIV] him as God or give thanks to him, but they became futile in their thinking, and their foolish hearts were darkened. (Rom. 1:20–21)

---

[21] Schreiner 1998: 220–221.
[22] Moo 1996: 285–286.

No distrust made him waver concerning the promise of God, but he grew strong in his faith as he gave glory to God, fully convinced that God was able to do what he had promised.
(Rom. 4:20–21)

Despite the evidence of God in creation, in Romans 1 unbelievers failed to glorify God when they disbelieved, but in Romans 4 Abraham, the father of the faithful, glorified him when he believed God's promise in spite of the physical evidence. What does it mean in general to give God glory? Morris answers clearly:

Giving glory to God means ascribing to God what is due to him . . . It is, of course, impossible to increase God's glory; 'giving glory to God' means recognizing the glory he has and taking the place appropriate to the creature over against the Creator.[23]

Which is precisely what the rebels in 1:21 did not do.

What does it mean specifically to give God glory as Abraham did? Cranfield answers with help from Calvin:

A man gives glory to God when he acknowledges God's truthfulness and goodness and submits to His authority. '. . . no greater honour can be given to God than by sealing His truth by our faith' is Calvin's comment. By embracing His promise and believing it faith does that which the men, of whom 1:21–23 speaks, failed to do.[24]

Paul speaks of faith again in chapter 14 in the context of 'the strong' and 'the weak'. 'The strong' are free to disregard annulled Old Testament dietary restrictions, while 'the weak' sin against their consciences if they ignore those restrictions. Paul tells the strong to respect the weak in the name of love, and he tells the weak not to sin against their consciences. Paul concludes:

Blessed is the one who has no reason to pass judgement on himself for what he approves. But whoever has doubts is condemned if he

---

[23] Morris 1988: 212–213.
[24] Cranfield 2004: 249.

eats, because the eating is not from faith. For whatever does not proceed from faith is sin.
(Rom. 14:22–23)

Schreiner correlates 14:23 with 1:18–25: 'Idolatry is the fundamental sin because self rather than God becomes the center of one's affections and reliance. Faith is the only way to please God because it looks to him as the all-sufficient one.'[25]

God's glory and justification (Rom. 3:25b–26)

God's act of declaring believing sinners righteous also manifests his great glory. Schreiner tells how God's desire for his glory lies behind his showing both his saving and judging righteousness in Christ's cross. Christ's propitiatory death satisfies God's justice. At the same time Christ's atonement extends God's mercy to all believers, as Schreiner contends: 'The desire for his glory undergirds his desire to demonstrate his righteousness . . . By demonstrating his saving and judging righteousness, God has vindicated his name before the world.'[26]

In addition, as Schreiner explains, God's zeal for his glory shines in his declaring righteous all who trust Jesus. God is glorified in justifying lost persons who believe in Jesus, because so doing magnifies his grace. 'The vilest offender who truly believes / That moment from Jesus a pardon receives.'[27] How could this be? God glorifies himself in Christ's death (and resurrection) and in accepting as sons or daughters all the wayward who turn from sin and embrace God's Son. This is the grace and wonder of the gospel.

God's glory and assurance (Rom. 8)

God's amazing grace extends to his granting assurance of salvation to his people. He does not keep his children in line by threatening to disown them if they are disobedient. Instead, he motivates them to love and holiness by assuring them of final glory. He assures believers in three main ways: through the promises of his Word, the inner testimony of the Holy Spirit and working in their lives:[28]

---

[25] Schreiner 1998: 739.
[26] Ibid. 198–199.
[27] Fanny Crosby, 'To God Be the Glory', 1875.
[28] See Peterson 2019.

Word: 'I am sure that neither death nor life, nor angels nor rulers, nor things present nor things to come, nor powers, nor height nor depth, nor anything else in all creation, will be able to separate us from the love of God in Christ Jesus our Lord.'
(Rom. 8:38–39)

Spirit: 'The Spirit himself bears witness with our spirit that we are children of God.'
(Rom. 8:16)

Changed lives: '[A]ll who are led by the Spirit of God are sons of God.'
(Rom. 8:14)

Because he loves them so, God gives his children confidence that they will 'obtain the glory of our Lord Jesus Christ' (2 Thess. 2:14). Romans 5 – 8 is bordered by 5:1–11 and 8:18–39, which both teach that God preserves his saints amid suffering. Moo rightly asserts concerning Romans 5 – 8, 'Assurance of glory is, then, the overarching theme in this second major section of Romans.'[29]

Both 5:1–11 and 8:18–39 affirm, against the threat of tribulation and suffering, the certainty of the Christian's final salvation because of God's love, the work of Christ, and the ministry of the Holy Spirit. This theme, the 'hope of sharing in God's glory' (cf. 5:2 and 8:18, 30), 'brackets' all of chaps. 5–8.[30]

God's glory and sanctification

Paul is concerned not only with people's getting right with God (justification). He is concerned also about people's living for God (via progressive sanctification). In various places throughout Romans Paul connects Christian living with God's glory.

Grace is not licence (Rom. 3:8)

At points Paul defends himself against accusations that his message of God's free grace promotes sinful living. He shudders at the thought of

---

[29] Moo 1996: 293.
[30] Ibid.

God's not judging sin (Rom. 3:5–6). In fact, for the apostle it is axiomatic that God will 'judge the world' (v. 6). Enemies have charged that when Paul says things such as '[W]here sin increased, grace abounded all the more' (5:20), he teaches that our continuing to sin 'abounds to [God's] glory' (3:7). Paul is offended at those who claim that he teaches, 'Why not do evil that good may come? – as some people slanderously charge us with saying.' His response? 'Their condemnation is just' (v. 8).

At times Paul presents the Christian life as a battle against the world, the flesh and the devil. He speaks of battles within himself: 'I see in my members another law waging war against the law of my mind' (Rom. 7:23). He also envisions the Christian life in cosmic terms: '[W]e do not wrestle against flesh and blood, but against the rulers, against the author-ities, against the cosmic powers over this present darkness, against the spiritual forces of evil in the heavenly places' (Eph. 6:12). And he charges his disciple Timothy, 'This charge I entrust to you, Timothy, my child, in accordance with the prophecies previously made about you, that by them you may wage the good warfare' (1 Tim. 1:18).

Does this use of martial language mean that Paul believes that Chris-tians are consigned to defeat in this life? Not at all, for Christ our Victor has overcome in his death and resurrection. Believers must continue to fight the good fight (as Paul did, 2 Tim. 4:7), but they will overcome, as Morris makes plain:

> Christians do not lead defeated lives, constantly at the mercy of every temptation. They are liberated, triumphant. But that does not mean a life of ease, free from all temptation. The decisive victory has been won, but the war still drags on. Temptations still come, and evil must be defeated every day. Yet Paul sees final victory as assured and knows that in due course the fulness of glory will be revealed (8:18, 30). But for now the Christian must be on guard, knowing what victory is like but still waging the war.[31]

Grace triumphs over sin's power (Rom. 6 – 7)

Romans 6 and 7 are Paul's most famous chapters on the Christian life, and rightly so. In the previous chapters the apostle has condemned the world before a holy God, who in amazing grace delivers all who believe in Christ

---

[31] Morris 1988: 191.

from the penalty of sin. Now Paul turns from sin's penalty to its power. Romans 6 deals with overcoming sin's power. God in Christ has set believers free from sin's domination. Its two paragraphs treat this theme, but the first (vv. 1–14) treats it negatively, turning from sin, while the second (vv. 15–23) does so positively, pursuing godliness.[32]

Paul begins the chapter by revisiting Jewish attacks on his gospel: 'Are we to continue in sin that grace may abound?' (Rom. 6:1). He recoils from such an idea, and proceeds to teach that God's grace powerfully breaks sin's tyranny. Paul points believers to union with Christ for the power to defeat sin's dominion. We died with Christ to sin's power and were raised with him to newness of life (vv. 3–11).

Romans 6:12–23 treats the bondage of all humans and freedom in Christ. Although Cranfield finds the image of slavery 'inappropriate', he admits its value:

> [This passage] underlines the fact that the question of a man's being free in the sense of having no master, of not being a slave at all, simply does not arise. Only two alternatives present themselves, to have sin for one's master or to have God . . . ; there is no third possibility.[33]

God in Christ has liberated from sin's tyranny all who believe the gospel:

> thanks be to God, that you who were once slaves of sin have become obedient from the heart to the standard of teaching to which you were committed, and, having been set free from sin, have become slaves of righteousness.
> (vv. 17–18)

As usual, Paul moves from the indicative of God's mighty deeds to the imperatives of Christian obedience. Because God has set them free, Christians are to live as men and women free from sin: '[J]ust as you once presented your members as slaves to impurity and to lawlessness leading to more lawlessness, so now present your members as slaves to righteousness leading to sanctification' (v. 19).

---

[32] Moo 1996: 350–351.
[33] Cranfield 2004: 321.

Romans 7:7–25 is one of the most difficult passages in all of Paul's letters. As Schreiner shows, the debate as to whether Paul is speaking of an unregenerate person or a Christian struggling with sin has remarkably strong arguments on both sides. His solution? The passage's main focus is not on the identity of the speaker but on the law and its inability to produce righteousness. Although he concludes Paul speaks autobiographically, Schreiner is convinced that is not his main point:

> Paul's personal history is paradigmatic because it is the story of all people who live under the law ... The arguments are so finely balanced because Paul does not intend to distinguish believers from unbelievers in this text.[34]

Paul concludes that the law lacks the ability to sanctify humans.

Paul does not want us to misunderstand. The fault does not lie in the law itself, for 'the law is holy, and the commandment is holy and righteous and good' (7:12). The fault lies in human beings, who rebel against their Maker and break his commandments with impunity. Certainly, that is true for unbelievers, who cannot please God (8:7–8). Although believers have been saved from sin's penalty, they still struggle to overcome its power. They obey God and his moral commandments, but not perfectly (cf. Gal. 5:16–17). Schreiner strikes the balance shown by Paul, taking all his epistles into account: believers fight against sin and lose some battles, but Paul's accent on the Christian life is true victory over sin.

Grace and renewed minds (Rom. 12:1–2)

Paul tells how God's redeemed people relying on the Spirit's power can counter the ugly lifestyle described in the last half of Romans 1:

> I appeal to you therefore, brothers, by the mercies of God, to present your bodies as a living sacrifice, holy and acceptable to God, which is your spiritual worship. Do not be conformed to this world, but be transformed by the renewal of your mind, that by testing you may discern what is the will of God, what is good and acceptable and perfect.

---

[34] Schreiner 1998: 371, 390.

Schreiner tells how God reverses the downward spiral of thinking that appears in Romans 1:18–32. He renews believers' minds so that they believe in and love the truth. Moreover, God gradually transforms them 'from glory to glory' as they 'contemplate the Lord's glory' (2 Cor. 3:18).[35] Moo sums up the Christian life and God's glory: 'Our new relationship with Christ enables us – and requires us – to produce those character traits, thoughts, and actions that will be "for God's glory."'[36]

God's glory and suffering

Suffering and hope (Rom. 5:2–4)

With other New Testament writers, Paul teaches that God uses suffering to build character. He begins chapter 5 by telling his readers that reconciliation accompanies justification (Rom. 5:1). Reconciliation is God's making peace between him and us and us and him based on his Son's death and resurrection (vv. 9–10). Through the Mediator believers not only have been saved by grace through faith but also now live by faith in the realm of grace: '[W]e have also obtained access by faith into this grace in which we stand' (v. 2). Further, they 'rejoice in hope of the glory of God' (v. 2); that is, the hope of eschatological glory.

The hope of resurrected life on the new earth under the new heavens gives God's people great joy as they walk with him. It also motivates us to persevere amid trials and temptations, for they too are a cause of joy: 'We rejoice in hope of the glory of God. Not only that, but we rejoice in our sufferings, knowing that suffering produces endurance, and endurance produces character, and character produces hope' (vv. 2–4). Paul sets up a chain of causes and effects that results in believers' increased hope of heavenly glory. All people experience sufferings, including Christians. If we respond in faith and obedience to sufferings, God uses them to help us endure. As we endure, God changes our character so that we become steady people on whom he can rely. And when we see God at work improving our character, this increases our hope of heaven. Seeing God at work in this life strengthens our hope of glory in the next life.

---

[35] Ibid. 647–648.
[36] Moo 1996: 418.

Schreiner traces Paul's train of thought:

> The reason believers exult in afflictions, then, is that they conspire to produce greater hope . . . Those who undergo troubles are toughened up, so that they are able to withstand the storms of life . . . Such tested character in turn generates hope . . . because moral transformation constitutes evidence that one has really been changed by God. Thus it assures believers that the hope of future glory is not an illusion.[37]

Suffering with Christ (Rom. 8:16–17)

Paul treats adoption, God the Father's adopting as his children all who trust Christ as Redeemer. Adoption pertains to the present, in which the Spirit directs Christians, frees them from sin's bondage and testifies to their hearts that they belong to the Father (Rom. 8:14–16). Adoption also pertains to the future, for 'we wait eagerly for adoption as sons, the redemption of our bodies' (v. 23). In verse 17 Paul links the present and future: the Spirit testifies within that we are God's children, 'and if children, then heirs – heirs of God and fellow heirs with Christ'.

Paul speaks of the future inheritance of God's children and then adds a qualification: we are children and heirs 'provided we suffer with him in order that we may also be glorified with him' (Rom. 8:16–17). God saves believers by uniting them to Christ in salvation. This includes union with him in his death, which entails present suffering, and also includes union with him in his resurrection, which entails future glory.

Suffering and glory (Rom. 8:18)

As we have just seen, Paul acknowledges that God calls his people to lives that involve suffering. Indeed, Paul himself was well acquainted with suffering (cf. 2 Cor. 11:23–29). However, in more than one passage he contrasts present suffering with future glory in order to give Christians proper perspective. He does so in Romans 8:18: 'I consider that the sufferings of this present time are not worth comparing with the glory that is to be revealed to us.' When Paul says 'I consider', he gives not his private opinion but his settled conviction. Verse 18 amplifies the previous one: we are God's children and heirs and Christ's co-heirs if we suffer with

---

[37] Schreiner 1998: 255–256.

him to gain future glory, glory so enormous that in comparison our sufferings are negligible.

Two other texts inform Romans 8:18. In one Paul reinforces his message here: '[T]his light momentary affliction is preparing for us an eternal weight of glory beyond all comparison' (2 Cor. 4:17). In another text informing ours John anticipates a time when suffering will be a thing of the past: God 'will wipe away every tear from their eyes, and death shall be no more, neither shall there be mourning, nor crying, nor pain any more, for the former things have passed away' (Rev. 21:4). Moo makes accurate measurements:

> We must, Paul suggests, weigh suffering in the balance with the glory that is the final state of every believer; and so 'weighty,' so transcendently wonderful, is this glory that suffering flies in the air as if it had no weight at all.[38]

God's glory and heaven

Paul teaches that although God's people often have to endure suffering now, great glory awaits them in Christ's presence and in the resurrection of their bodies. Moreover, the whole creation will share in that glory on the last day.

Hope of glory (Rom. 5:2)

'Through him we have also obtained access by faith into this grace in which we stand, and we rejoice in hope of the glory of God' (Rom. 5:2). In the past God has already saved us by grace through the death and resurrection of the Mediator, Jesus Christ. At present we live by God's grace through faith. In the future we shall see God. In the meantime our lives are characterized by joy and hope as we wait for the final revelation of God's glory. Cranfield exults in this great, future glory:

> By the δόξα τοῦ θεοῦ [glory of God] is meant here (cf. 3:23; 8:17, 18, 21, 30; 9:23) that illumination of man's whole being by the radiance of the divine glory which is man's true destiny but which was lost through sin, as it will be restored (not just as it was, but immeasurably

---

[38] Moo 1996: 511.

enriched through God's own personal participation in man's humanity in Jesus Christ – cf. 8:17), when man's redemption is finally consummated at the parousia of Jesus Christ.[39]

The Christian life is paradoxical. God has given us a free and marvellous salvation in Christ that transforms our lives, and we await even greater glory. But at the same time we still struggle against sin, and we, 'who have the firstfruits of the Spirit, groan inwardly as we wait eagerly for adoption as sons, the redemption of our bodies' (Rom. 8:23).

The creation and glory (Rom. 8:19–22)

The work of Christ is so magnificent and efficacious that it not only defeats our spiritual foes and redeems God's people but also redeems the creation:

> the creation waits with eager longing for the revealing of the sons of God. For the creation was subjected to futility, not willingly, but because of him who subjected it, in hope that the creation itself will be set free from its bondage to corruption and obtain the freedom of the glory of the children of God. For we know that the whole creation has been groaning together in the pains of childbirth until now. (Rom. 8:19–22)

Thanks be to God that because the Lord Jesus died and arose, the creation will be redeemed. As a woman delivering a baby groans, so the personified created order is eager to experience deliverance. Cranfield points out how Paul eloquently ties together the redemption of God's people and the creation:

> With poetic boldness and with a penetrating prophetic insight Paul sees the whole splendid theatre of the universe together with all sub-human life within it as eagerly awaiting the time when the sons of God will be made manifest in their true glory.[40]

Sometimes, therefore, Paul uses 'glory' to speak of heaven; that is, the final salvation of believers and even of the whole creation.

---

[39] Cranfield 2004: 260.
[40] Ibid. 412.

God's glory and Israel

Paul's complex message (Rom. 2:23–24; 11:26–29)

Paul sounds a complex message concerning Israel. He condemns the Israelites for their unfaithfulness to God: 'You who boast in the law dishonour God by breaking the law. For, as it is written, "The name of God is blasphemed among the Gentiles because of you"' (Rom. 2:23–24).

Paul laments, 'I bear them witness that they have a zeal for God, but not according to knowledge. For, being ignorant of the righteousness of God, and seeking to establish their own, they did not submit to God's righteousness' (10:2–3). Concerning Jews he declares, 'As regards the gospel, they are enemies' (11:28). Nevertheless, he pours out his heart in anguished prayer to God for their salvation (10:2–3). He lists eight blessings given to no other people but Israel (9:4–5). Finally, he says that God is not finished with ethnic Israel: '[A]s regards election, they are beloved for the sake of their forefathers. For the gifts and the calling of God are irrevocable' (11:28–29). So he promises that 'all Israel will be saved' (v. 26).

Israelites and glory (Rom. 9:4)

Paul begins chapters 9–11, on God's dealing with Israel, by emphatically expressing his burden for the salvation of his fellow Israelites. He could wish for what is impossible – his own damnation – if that would save them (v. 2). He then cites eight blessings God bestowed on Israel, culminating in the Christ:

> They are Israelites, and to them belong the adoption, the glory, the covenants, the giving of the law, the worship, and the promises. To them belong the patriarchs, and from their race, according to the flesh, is the Christ who is God over all, blessed for ever. Amen. (Rom. 9:4–5)

Among these blessings is 'the glory' (v. 4).

> The use of the simple term, without the addition of a divine name, is unusual (there is no clear OT example, and Str-B [Strack and

Billerbeck] find no parallel in the rabbis [3.262]), but it may be the product of Paul's desire for stylistic parallelism (ἡ υἱοθεσία/ἡ δόξα [adoption/glory]; cf. Dunn).[41]

A number of scholars have noted that the first six blessings (all in v. 4) occur in three couplets of two:

1 'The adoption to sonship' / 'The receiving of the law'
2 'The divine glory' / 'The temple worship'
3 'The covenants' / 'The promises'

The combination of 'glory' and 'worship' in the second couplet above suggests that the glory Paul mentions here is that which is associated with the worship of God in tabernacle and temple, as Schreiner summarizes:

> The coupling of δόξα with λατρεία suggests that the reference is to the cult in which the glory of God was manifested in the tent and the temple (Exod. 29:42–43; 40:34–35; Lev. 9:23; Num. 14:10; 16:19; 20:6; 1 Kings 8:11; 2 Chron. 5:13–14; 7:1, 2, 3; Ezek. 10:4, 18–19; 11:22–23) . . . Israel has been blessed with the glorious presence of God and access to him through the cult.[42]

God's glory and election

God's name proclaimed (Rom. 9:18)

God also displays his glory in election. After quoting Exodus 33:19 to show that God has freedom in showing mercy and compassion (Rom. 9:17), Paul turns to God's dealings with Pharaoh: 'For this very purpose I have raised you up, that I might show my power in you, and that my name might be proclaimed in all the earth' (Rom. 9:17, citing Exod. 9:16). God's 'name' is his character, in this case his great power. God displayed his power in punishing the Egyptians in the plagues and delivering his people from slavery in the exodus. In so doing he got glory for himself, as Exodus records: '[T]he Egyptians shall know that I am the LORD, when I have

---

[41] Moo 1996: 563, n. 43.
[42] Schreiner 1998: 484.

gained glory over Pharaoh, his chariots, and his horsemen' (Exod. 14:18; cf. 14:4, 17).

Vessels of mercy, prepared for glory (Rom. 9:23)

Later in Romans 9 God tells why he patiently endured 'vessels of wrath prepared for destruction' (v. 22) instead of condemning them immediately. He did so 'in order to make known the riches of his glory for vessels of mercy, which he has prepared beforehand for glory' (v. 23).

Further, Paul teaches that God will be glorified in the fate of every human being. Schreiner unpacks this difficult theme:

> The mercy of God would not be impressed on the consciousness of human beings apart from the exercise of God's wrath, just as one delights more richly in the warmth, beauty, and tenderness of spring after one has experienced the cold blast of winter.[43]

Universalism is false (Rom. 9:14–24)

Although many modern theologians and even a few evangelicals teach universalism, the view that all human beings will be saved in the end, Scripture does not teach it. It is true that even in hardening, God's ultimate purpose is to show mercy. This mercy, however, is not universal. Only 'the vessels of mercy' receive it (v. 23). By contrast, 'the vessels of [his] wrath' are hardened (v. 22). Moo is correct:

> Therefore we must not allow the preeminence of God's purpose in bestowing mercy *on some* to cancel out the reality and finality of his wrath *on others.* Paul is clear here, as he is elsewhere: some people receive God's mercy and are saved, while others do not receive that mercy and so are eternally condemned.[44]

Ultimately, God's glory is beyond our ability to understand fully, and his sovereignty is one of the areas in which this truth manifests itself.

---

[43] Ibid. 523.
[44] Moo 1996: 608; emphases original. For more on the doctrine of hell see Morgan and Peterson 2004.

God's glory and church unity

The 'strong' and the 'weak' (Rom. 14:1 – 15:13)

From 14:1 to 15:13 Paul is concerned with matters pertaining to the 'strong' and the 'weak' in the Roman church. These correspond to ethnic divisions in the church. The 'strong' are Gentile Christians who have no scruples about Jewish dietary laws or holy days. The 'weak' are Jewish believers who observe Jewish dietary laws and holy days and are suspicious of meat or wine dedicated to idols. Moo's summary of these passages captures Paul's message:

> 14:1–12 – Both 'strong' and 'weak' Christians need to stop condemning each other because it is the Lord, and he alone, who has the right to access the believer's status and conduct.
>
> 14:13–23 – The 'strong' Christians must be careful not to cause the 'weak' Christians to suffer spiritual harm by their insistence on exercising their liberty on disputed matters . . .
>
> 15:1–6 – The 'strong' Christians should willingly tolerate the tender consciences of the 'weak' Christians, seeking thereby to foster unified praise of God in the community . . .
>
> 15:7–13 – Both 'strong' and 'weak' Christians should receive each other as full and respected members of the Christian community, for God himself has shown, in fulfillment of Scripture, that he accepts both Jews and Gentiles as his people.[45]

Jesus' example (Rom. 15:2–3)

Paul begins chapter 15 with an exhortation for Christians to please their neighbours, not themselves, and then writes, 'For Christ did not please himself, but as it is written, "The reproaches of those who reproached you fell on me"' (15:2–3). Christ did not please himself but took the reproaches of God (Ps. 69:9) when he suffered and died on the cross for sinners. Believers are to follow their Lord's example. Paul's counsel, in a nutshell, is 'Therefore welcome one another as Christ has welcomed you, for the glory of God' (Rom. 15:7). Morris is correct:

---

[45] Moo: 1996: 833.

God's glory was promoted when Christ received us sinners, and it is further advanced when we who are by nature sinners and wrapped up in our own concerns instead receive our brothers and sisters in Christ with warmth and love.[46]

Paul saw a need to address these issues because there was strife in the Roman church between 'the strong' and 'the weak'. Both groups needed to remember their status before God when he redeemed them, as Schreiner notes:

Paul returns to the fundamental baseline of the gospel. Believers should accept one another because Christ accepted us, despite our hostility to him, in order to bring glory to God. Since Christ accepted us, despite our weakness and sin (5:6–10), then we too should accept one another.[47]

Applied theology (Rom. 15:5–7)

Christopher Morgan summarizes for us: Gentile and Jewish Christians can live in unity while not agreeing on every issue because they agree on many basic truths:

It is precisely *because of these truths* that the church does tolerate certain differences of opinion on culture and tradition . . . He appeals to them to promote church unity . . . He offers many reasons . . . but the glory of God stands behind them. That is why he concludes his argument with the purpose of his prayer-wish: 'so that with one mind and one voice you may glorify the God and Father of our Lord Jesus Christ' (15:6). He then summarizes his argument, 'Therefore, welcome one another as Christ has welcomed you, for the glory of God' (15:7).[48]

---

[46] Morris 1988: 503.
[47] Schreiner 1998: 754.
[48] Morgan 2009: 8–9; emphasis original.

God's glory and worship

It is commonly recognized that Romans is replete with doctrinal teaching. It is not as well known that the letter has much to say about the worship of God. Worship appears in various places in the letter.

Bursts of praise (Rom. 1:25; 9:5)

Twice Paul bursts out in praise to God:

> they exchanged the truth about God for a lie and worshipped and served the creature rather than the Creator, who is blessed for ever! Amen.
> (Rom. 1:25)

> To them belong the patriarchs, and from their race, according to the flesh, is the Christ who is God over all, blessed for ever. Amen.
> (Rom. 9:5)

In the first text Paul expresses disgust at the folly of Gentiles in forsaking the worship of the living and true God for idols. In this context he extols the Creator, who alone is worthy of praise for ever. In the second text, though there is some debate, it seems clear that Paul, as he frequently does, refers to Christ as God. The greatest benefit God bestowed on the Israelites was sending one of their own – Jesus Christ, who is also God and as such deserves everlasting praise.

Boasting in God (Rom. 5:11)

Paul concludes his treatment of reconciliation in Romans 5 with these words: 'More than that, we also rejoice in God through our Lord Jesus Christ, through whom we have now received reconciliation' (Rom. 5:11). The word translated 'rejoice' is often rendered 'boast'. This 'boasting' is the climax of the passage.

Worship in unity (Rom. 14)

Paul returns to the theme of the worship of God as he deals with the controversy between Jews and Gentiles in the Roman church. Paul leaves open the matters of Christians' following the Old Testament dietary code and celebrating Jewish festivals and holy days, as long as persons make their decisions 'in honour of the Lord' and give 'thanks to God' (Rom. 14:6). What is important in indifferent matters is to remember Christ's lordship and to live for him:

> For if we live, we live to the Lord, and if we die, we die to the Lord. So then, whether we live or whether we die, we are the Lord's. For to this end Christ died and lived again, that he might be Lord both of the dead and of the living.
> (vv. 8–9)

As we saw, Paul's aim is that believing Jews and Gentiles in the church in Rome will 'with one voice glorify the God and Father of our Lord Jesus Christ' (15:6). If this comes to pass, they will promote 'the glory of God' (v. 7). Paul reinforces this notion with Old Testament quotations which show that God intended for Gentiles as well as Jews to worship him, using a variation in verbs of worship: 'praise', 'sing', 'rejoice', 'praise' and 'extol'.

> Therefore I will praise you among the Gentiles,
>   and sing to your name.
> (Rom. 15:9, citing Ps. 18:49)

And again it is said,

> 'Rejoice, O Gentiles, with his people.'
> (Rom. 15:10, citing Deut. 32:43)

And again,

> 'Praise the Lord, all you Gentiles,
>   and let all the peoples extol him.'
> (Rom. 15:11, citing Ps. 117:1)

Schreiner writes concerning Romans 15:7–13 that this passage 'not only functions as the conclusion to 14:1–15:6 but also draws attention to the major theme (the glory and praise of God) of the entire letter'.[49]

---

[49] Schreiner 1998: 704.

Doxologies (Rom. 11:36; 16:27)

As he frequently does in his epistles, Paul includes two outstanding doxologies in Romans:

> from him and through him and to him are all things. To him be glory for ever. Amen.
> (Rom. 11:36)

> to the only wise God be glory for evermore through Jesus Christ! Amen.
> (Rom. 16:27)

The first doxology occurs at the end of Paul's lengthy treatment of the place of Jews in God's plan. Paul has just told how in God's merciful plan he sidelined the Jews because of unbelief and opened the door for the Gentiles to be saved. Paul's summary? 'God has consigned all to disobedience, that he may have mercy on all' (v. 32). Next Paul extols God's wisdom, knowledge, judgments, inscrutable ways and grace (vv. 33–35):

> Oh, the depth of the riches and wisdom and knowledge of God! How unsearchable are his judgements and how inscrutable his ways!
>
> 'For who has known the mind of the Lord,
>   or who has been his counsellor?'
> 'Or who has given a gift to him
>   that he might be repaid?'

Paul adds, 'For from him and through him and to him are all things. To him be glory for ever. Amen' (v. 36). Jonathan Edwards captured it well: 'The whole is *of* God, and *in* God, and *to* God; and he is the beginning, middle, and end.'[50] Because God is the Creator, sustainer and end of all things, no one is qualified to know his mind or to counsel him. And for the same reasons no one is God's debtor. It is fitting for Paul to end this passage with an acclamation of God's glory.[51]

---

[50] Edwards 1998: 247; emphases original.
[51] Schreiner 1998: 638.

We should not be surprised to find that Paul ends his marvellous epistle thus: '[T]o the only wise God be glory for evermore through Jesus Christ! Amen' (Rom. 16:27). Over and over again Paul has related his theological themes to God's glory. He wrote of God's glory and the gospel, the image of God, sin, the work of Christ, faith and justification, sanctification, suffering, heaven, Israel, election, church unity and finally worship.

4

The glory of God and the resurrection: 1 Corinthians 15

No study of the glory of God in Paul would be complete without a look at 1 Corinthians 15, the 'resurrection chapter'. This is a good label, for in this chapter Paul authors Scripture's major treatment of Christ's and believers' resurrection in glory. As 1 Corinthians 15:3–4 summarizes, Paul begins this letter with Christ's crucifixion (1:17–25) and ends the body of the letter here with Christ's resurrection. Casting a larger vision, we see that Scripture begins in Genesis with Adam, who brought death and shame to humans, and here contrasts him with 'the last Adam . . . the second man', who brings life and glory to believers (15:45, 47).

Background

Four background sources shed light on glory in 1 Corinthians 15, the first two from the Old Testament, the third from the epistle itself and the fourth from Paul's experience. We will examine these in turn. First, the underpinnings for Paul's teaching concerning glorious bodily resurrection, according to Richard Bauckham, 'are firmly laid in the Old Testament portrayal of God as Sovereign Creator, Righteous Judge, and Divine Warrior'.[1] We cite one text for each portrait of God:

> *Sovereign Creator*: 'Have you not known? Have you not heard? / The LORD is the everlasting God, / the Creator of the ends of the earth.'
> (Isa. 40:28)

---

[1] As cited by Ciampa and Rosner (2010: 740).

Righteous Judge: '[H]e comes to judge the earth. / He will judge the world in righteousness, / and the peoples in his faithfulness.' (Ps. 96:13)

Divine Warrior: 'The LORD goes out like a mighty man, / like a man of war he stirs up his zeal; / he cries out, he shouts aloud, / he shows himself mighty against his foes.' (Isa. 42:13)

The One whom the Old Testament portrays as sovereign Creator here in 1 Corinthians 15 authors the new creation by raising Christ from the dead and thereby pledging to raise believers to eternal glory.

The Old Testament's righteous Judge does right in the death and resurrection of Christ, which are the foundation for his setting all things right when he subjects all things to the Son, who in turn submits to the Father, 'that God may be all in all' (v. 28).

The One depicted by the Old Testament as divine Warrior defeats 'the last enemy', death, in Christ's resurrection (v. 26) and mocks death in anticipation of glorious victory in the resurrection of the righteous (vv. 54–55).

Second, three Old Testament texts lay a foundation for bodily resurrection in 1 Corinthians 15. They display resurrection as the hope of believers for life after death:

He will swallow up death for ever; / and the Lord GOD will wipe away tears from all faces, / and the reproach of his people he will take away from all the earth, / for the LORD has spoken. (Isa. 25:8)

Your dead shall live; their bodies shall rise. / You who dwell in the dust, awake and sing for joy! / For your dew is a dew of light, / and the earth will give birth to the dead. (Isa. 26:19)

many of those who sleep in the dust of the earth shall awake, some to everlasting life, and some to shame and everlasting contempt. (Dan. 12:2)

Ultimately, these three texts point to what Paul describes elsewhere: '[W]e await a Saviour, the Lord Jesus Christ, who will transform our lowly body to be like his glorious body' (Phil. 3:20–21).

Third, 1 Corinthians 5 – 15 deals with the idea of the body, and chapter 15 caps this off by highlighting how God will transform believers' bodies from dishonour in death to glory in resurrection. Chapters 5–7 treat the body's sexual purity, chapters 8–11 treat eating and drinking and chapters 12–14 treat the body as a metaphor for the church's worship. Sanctification, of both individuals and the community, is a central theme of chapters 5–14. In the light of this, chapter 15, as Ciampa and Rosner teach, relates

> what it means to be God's holy people in this present age to God's ultimate plans for the complete transformation of our bodies (= ourselves) and of our world and the final glorification of God in and through his creation.[2]

Fourth, we must not miss the autobiographical aspect to Paul's message on resurrection and glory in 1 Corinthians 15. Before he began to think about how Jesus Christ's resurrection relates to ours, he met the glorious Christ on the Damascus road:

> suddenly a light from heaven flashed around him. And falling to the ground, he heard a voice saying to him, 'Saul, Saul, why are you persecuting me?' And he said, 'Who are you, Lord?' And he said, 'I am Jesus, whom you are persecuting'.
> (Acts 9:3–5)

Paul is never the same again. He knows that Jesus, who is alive, gives life to others, both now in regeneration and on the last day in resurrection. Ciampa and Rosner point out that, though Paul knows this from the Old Testament, he also knows it through encounter with 'Christ as the powerful, glorious, wholly spiritual, life-giving spirit'.[3]

Themes

Four theological themes underscore the role of the glory of God in 1 Corinthians 15:

---

[2] Ibid. 737.
[3] Ibid. 820.

1 Christ appears in resurrection glory (1 Cor. 15:5–8).
2 Christ's resurrection and God's grace (1 Cor. 15:8–11).
3 Christ is 'the last Adam', 'the second man' (1 Cor. 15:20–26, 45–49).
4 God will raise believers in glory (1 Cor. 15:35–58).

The chapter's first eleven verses play a foundational role that is not always recognized. Both Christ's post-resurrection appearances and God's sovereign grace shown to Paul set the stage for the tremendous revelation of God's glory in resurrection in the rest of the chapter.

Christ appears in resurrection glory (1 Cor. 15:5–8)

Viewed from an Old Testament perspective, Paul's citation of Christ's appearances after his resurrection (in 1 Cor. 15:5–8) introduces the theme of eschatological glory. The risen Christ

> appeared to Cephas, then to the twelve. Then he appeared to more than five hundred brothers at one time, most of whom are still alive, though some have fallen asleep. Then he appeared to James, then to all the apostles. Last of all, as to one untimely born, he appeared also to me.

Paul's words introduce eschatological glory, as the Psalms and Prophets anticipate a future *appearance* of God associated with glory:

> Nations will fear the name of the Lord,
>   and all the kings of the earth will fear your glory.
> For the Lord builds up Zion;
>   he appears in his glory.
> (Ps. 102:15–16)

> the glory of the Lord shall be revealed,
>   and all flesh shall see it together,
>   for the mouth of the Lord has spoken.
> (Isa. 40:5)

> Arise, shine, for your light has come,
>   and the glory of the Lord has risen upon you.

For behold, darkness shall cover the earth,
 and thick darkness the peoples;
but the LORD will arise upon you,
 and his glory will be seen upon you.
(Isa. 60:1–2)

Then the LORD will appear over them,
 and his arrow will go forth like lightning;
the Lord GOD will sound the trumpet
 and will march forth in the whirlwinds of the south.
(Zech. 9:14)

Thiselton argues cogently that 'in the light of this background *appearing* marks . . . the end of the time of waiting for eschatological and transcendent glory. Christ's risen presence serves as God's eschatological manifestation.'[4] His glorious resurrection fulfils Old Testament expectation and points to the resurrection of his people to life and glory when he returns.

Christ's resurrection and God's grace (1 Cor. 15:8–11)

When verses 8–11 put side by side Christ's resurrection and God's grace shown to Paul, they prepare readers for Scripture's grandest revelation of God's grace and glory in verses 12–58. Thiselton is correct: 'Divine grace and the person and work of Christ provide the foundation for the rest of the chapter,'[5] which like no other focuses on believers' resurrection life in final glory.

As with most New Testament themes, the roots of this one sink deep in Old Testament soil. There only God kills and makes alive:

See now that I, even I, am he,
 and there is no god beside me;
I kill and I make alive;
 I wound and I heal;
 and there is none that can deliver out of my hand.
(Deut. 32:39)

---

[4] Thiselton 2000: 1199; emphasis original.
[5] Ibid. 1177.

when the king of Israel read the letter, he tore his clothes and said, 'Am I God, to kill and to make alive, that this man sends word to me to cure a man of his leprosy?'
(2 Kgs 5:7)

It is the same in the New Testament, for God alone destroys 'both soul and body in hell' (Matt. 10:28) and 'gives life to all things' (1 Tim. 6:13). Moreover, only God 'gives life to the dead and calls into existence the things that do not exist' (Rom. 4:17). God's raising the righteous dead is the epitome of grace. This is why Paul writes of spiritual resurrection (regeneration), 'God . . . even when we were dead in our trespasses, made us alive together with Christ – by grace you have been saved' (Eph. 2:4–5). Nothing displays God's grace like raising to life the spiritual dead in regeneration or the physical dead in resurrection, for the dead are powerless to make themselves alive. This is why Paul follows his list of Christ's post-resurrection appearances by describing God's powerful grace at work in his life and ministry. Paul prepares his readers for God's sovereign grace in the resurrection of his people from the grave to life and eternal glory.

Paul stresses how unlikely it was for the risen Christ to appear to him, a persecutor of Christians: 'Last of all, as to one untimely born, he appeared also to me. For I am the least of the apostles, unworthy to be called an apostle, because I persecuted the church of God' (1 Cor. 15:8–9). His unworthiness puts the spotlight on God's grace and propels Paul forward in the service of Christ. Paul revels that Christ would save him, 'the foremost' of sinners (1 Tim. 1:15–16), and that his grace would drive him to work 'harder than any of' the other apostles (1 Cor. 15:10).

Thiselton, pointing to verse 10, deserves quotation:

We come to the heart of Paul's point. Undeserved, unmerited grace (χάρις) which springs from the free, sovereign love of God alone and becomes operative in human life not only determines Paul's life and apostolic vocation but also characterizes all Christian experience, not least the promise of resurrection and the reality of the activity of Christ as Lord.[6]

---

[6] Ibid. 1211.

God's grace shines in his turning the chief opponent of the church into its chief proponent. Paul thus introduces the main subject of the 'resurrection chapter' – the ultimate triumph of God's sovereign grace for his glory. Fee underscores the crucial significance of Christ's resurrection:

> Thus the concern is ultimately theological; not just the death of individuals concerns Paul here, but death itself as the final enemy of God and God's sovereign purposes in the universe. The work of Christ is therefore the key to everything, both the resurrection of believers, set in motion by his own resurrection, and at the same time through that resurrection the consummation of the 'saving acts of God,' including the utter defeat of all of God's enemies.[7]

Christ is 'the last Adam', 'the second man' (1 Cor. 15:20–26, 45–49)

In verses 12–19, after confronting Corinthian objections to the resurrection of the dead that, if cogent, would also deny Christ's resurrection, Paul affirms, 'But in fact Christ has been raised from the dead, the firstfruits of those who have fallen asleep' (v. 20). This last phrase reverses the meaning of verses 17–18: '[I]f Christ has not been raised, . . . [t]hen those also who have fallen asleep in Christ have perished.' Paul thus dramatically affirms Christ's resurrection and its effects: those who died in Christ have not perished but will triumph when he returns and the righteous dead are 'raised in glory' (v. 43). Fee is insightful: 'This is the final mention of Christ's resurrection in the argument, but everything that follows is predicated on it.'[8] His mighty resurrection causes his people's resurrection to glorification and their giving eternal glory to the Trinity.

Christ the firstfruits (1 Cor. 15:20, 23)

Paul uses an Old Testament image, 'firstfruits' (Deut. 26:1–11), that refers to the practice, ordained by God, of offering to him the first portion of crop or flock. The firstfruits served two purposes, one human and one divine. First, worshippers brought firstfruits in gratitude for God's bounty, trusting that he would provide the rest of the harvest. They thereby

---

[7] Fee 1987: 827–828.
[8] Ibid. 829.

acknowledged that the whole harvest came from and belonged to God. Second, God's causing the firstfruits to grow was his pledge that he would bless the remainder of the harvest.

When applied to resurrection, the risen Christ is 'firstfruits' (1 Cor. 15:20), guaranteeing our resurrection to life and glory at his return. The link between Christ's resurrection and ours is very close, as Beale explains:

> Christ's resurrection is referred to as 'first fruits' to show not only that his resurrection is the first of more to come, but also that the additional future resurrections must necessarily come because they actually belong to Christ's resurrection itself; this is the meaning of the phrase 'Christ the first fruits, after that those who are Christ's [those resurrected ones who are part of the remainder of Christ's firstfruits resurrection] at his coming' (v. 23).[9]

Just as the firstfruits sacrifice was the same in kind as the final harvest, so the resurrection of Jesus, our representative, is the same in kind as ours. We will have glorious resurrection bodies, like Christ's. Paul says that from heaven 'we await a Saviour, the Lord Jesus Christ, who will transform our lowly body to be like his glorious body, by the power that enables him even to subject all things to himself' (Phil. 3:20–21).

Moreover:

> By calling Christ the 'firstfruits,' Paul is asserting by way of metaphor that the resurrection of the believing dead is absolutely inevitable; it has been guaranteed by the eternal God, the *living* God, who in Christ's life, death, and resurrection has set that future in motion.[10]

Christ the second Adam (Rom. 5)

Christ as firstfruits points to his role as second Adam, a theme Paul unpacks in verses 21–22 and 45–49. Paul depicts the history of the world in terms of two people: Adam and Christ, the second Adam. In Romans 5:12–21 Paul primarily treats Christ's atonement as the basis of justification. But in so doing he offers Scripture's fullest treatment of original

---

[9] Beale 2011: 261.
[10] Fee 1987: 830; emphasis original.

sin. Adam's sin opened the door for the usurpers sin and death to invade humanity (v. 12) and tarnish the 'glory and honour' God had given our first parents (Ps. 8:5). In Romans 5:12–21 Paul assumes a commonality between how Adam and Christ related to the human race. But before Paul shows how the two Adams were alike, he shows how they differ. Adam's one trespass brought death, condemnation and the reign of death (vv. 15–17). Christ brought life and justification and made believers 'reign in life' (v. 17). Paul then shows how the two Adams are alike. They both exerted tremendous influence on their respective people. Adam's sin brought death and condemnation to humanity. Christ's 'one righteous act', his 'obedience' to death on the cross, brought justification and eternal life to all believers (vv. 18–19).

Christ the second Adam (1 Cor. 15)

Paul also treats Christ as second Adam in 1 Corinthians 15:21–22, 45–49, calling him 'the last Adam' (v. 45) and 'the second man' (v. 47), from which comes the theological shorthand 'the second Adam'. Christ is the second man because he is only the second human being made without sin (Eve is not in the two-Adams theology). Their origins differ, for Adam was a special creation of God, whereas Christ was born via the virginal conception. Nevertheless, unlike all other humans (Eve excepted), both came into the world without sin. Christ is also 'the last Adam' because he is the saving representative of humanity, whose work of death and resurrection eliminates the need for any other deliverer. '[T]here is one God, and there is one mediator between God and men, the *man* Christ Jesus' (1 Tim. 2:5). Jesus is the Mediator who leads humanity to life and glory.

Two strands of Old Testament revelation undergird Christ as the second Adam in 1 Corinthians 15: God's creation of Adam and Eve and Isaiah's promise of a new creation. Adam is the first human being, created by God 'of dust from the ground' and animated by God, who 'breathed into his nostrils the breath of life' so that 'the man became a living creature' (Gen. 2:7). God's making Adam and Eve was the highlight of God's original creation. It points to the second strand of OT background – the new creation.

Although the major prophets dwell on Israel's rebellion and idolatry and warn of captivity, they also pray for God's mercy and deliverance from exile. Isaiah speaks of this deliverance as a new creation, a theme captured by Beale:

Both Isa. 40–66 and Ezek. 36–48 predict Israel's deliverance from exile and restoration into a new creation, though these themes also occur earlier in these books. The most explicit hopes for new creation are expressed in these major prophets, especially the book of Isaiah. The return from exile is prophesied as an eschatological period when new-creational conditions will exist on the earth. The idea of end-time new creation … is a natural part of a broader theme of new creation woven throughout chapters 40–66, the most explicit texts being 43:18–19; 65:17; 66:22.[11]

In chapters 65–66 Isaiah tells of God's making this new creation, recalling the language of Genesis 1:1:

> Behold, I create new heavens
>   and a new earth,
> and the former things shall not be remembered
>   or come into mind.
> (Isa. 65:17)

God promises immense joy, for the new creation shall be characterized by long life, no more sorrow, 'smiles of fulfillment and satisfaction',[12] answered prayer and peace on earth (Isa. 65:18–25; cf. 66:22–24).

Paul asserts that the risen Christ has brought this new creation: '[I]f anyone is in Christ, he is a new creation. The old has passed away; behold, the new has come' (2 Cor. 5:17). Christ inaugurated the new creation in his resurrection and in pouring out the Holy Spirit at Pentecost. The new creation has 'already' come in Christ, but its full and glorious manifestation is 'not yet': it awaits his return, the resurrection of his people and God's glory filling the new earth.

Commonalities between the two Adams

Before contrasting the two Adams we study their commonalities. First, both Adam and Christ are genuine humans: '[A]s by a man came death, by a man has come also the resurrection of the dead' (1 Cor. 15:21). God

---

[11] Beale 2011: 81.
[12] Oswalt 1998: 659.

made Adam in his image as the first human. Christ's miraculous conception produced the God-man, as Scripture abundantly testifies:

> the Word became flesh.
> (John 1:14)

> [He who existed] in the form of God . . . [took] the form of a servant, being born in the likeness of men.
> (Phil. 2:6, 7)

> Since therefore the children share in flesh and blood, he himself likewise partook of the same things, that through death he might destroy the one who has the power of death, that is, the devil, and deliver all those who through fear of death were subject to lifelong slavery.
> (Heb. 2:14)

The last quotation above not only demonstrates our Lord's true humanity but also presents it as a prerequisite for his work of salvation. Although it is not always recognized, Christ's genuine humanity is as essential for our salvation as is his deity. He has to be God, for only God can *save* us. He also has to become a human being, for only a man could save *us*, his fellow humans, by dying in our place and rising to newness of life and glory.

Gerald Bray underlines the necessity of our Lord's humanity for his saving work:

> What God did was to bring a second Adam into being, a man who was not encumbered by the legacy of the fall, but who was nevertheless a real human being who shared our nature. In order to bridge the gap between man and God, this second Adam also had to be divine, since no creature has the right to stand in the presence of the Creator and be heard. In order to save us from our sins, God opened himself up by sending his Son into the world. He shared with us the deepest love that one person can have for another – he gave his life on earth for us in order that we might live forever in heaven with him.[13]

---

[13] Bray 2012: 516.

Second, both Adams are similar in that they did not act as isolated individuals but were representatives of their respective people. Adam's primal transgression condemned and polluted humanity, and Christ's obedience to death results in the justification of all who trust him as substitute (Rom. 5:19). Paul also presents the two Adams' representative functions in 1 Corinthians 15. Adam's sin brings death to all humans; Christ's death and resurrection bring resurrection glory to all his people (vv. 21–22).

Contrasts between the two Adams

Although Paul teaches what Adam and Christ have in common – both are authentic humans and representatives – he chiefly contrasts them. '[A]s by a man came death, by a man has come also the resurrection of the dead' (1 Cor. 15:21). Although God created Adam without sin, Adam succumbed to the evil one's temptation and committed the primal transgression of humanity. By contrast, though Christ was tempted by the evil one at the beginning of and throughout his public ministry, he did not succumb. Where Adam failed, Christ succeeded.

In their representative roles the two Adams brought different results for their people: Adam's sin brought death; Christ's saving accomplishment brought life. Paul draws attention to this contrast by omitting names in verse 21: '[A]s by a man came death, by a man has come also the resurrection of the dead.' He thereby puts 'death' and 'life' in bold relief. Even before naming them he focuses on what the two Adams bring to their people.

Paul then names them: 'For as in Adam all die, so also in Christ shall all be made alive' (v. 22). The fact that Paul here mentions Adam for the first time in the epistle and offers no comment shows that he assumes his readers are familiar with Genesis 1 – 3. What does Paul mean when he speaks of people as 'in Adam' and 'in Christ'? Ciampa and Rosner elucidate:

> To be *in Adam* is to be part of the group which finds in Adam its representative and leader, which finds its identity and destiny in Adam and what he has brought about for his people. To be *in Christ* is to be part of the group which finds in Christ its representative and leader, which finds its identity and destiny in Christ and what he has brought about for his people.[14]

---

[14] Ciampa and Rosner 2010: 763; emphases original.

All those who have not come to know Christ as Redeemer are still 'in Adam'. All those who have trusted Christ as Saviour are 'in Christ'. They already have eternal life in union with him and eagerly await the day when they will experience eternal life on the new earth. Paul's emphasis is on the latter because he uses the future tense, 'shall all be made alive', which points to the resurrection of the body, anticipating his argument in verses 23–28. Thiselton makes an important point:

> 'Shall all be made alive,' has an eschatological meaning here . . . The resurrection of Jesus was not to restore life in the conditions of continuing earthly existence (and eventual death) but to initiate a transformed mode of existence as the *firstfruits* (v. 20) of the eschato-logical new creation with all its attendant glory.[15]

All humans are implicated in Adam's original sin. Only Christ is excluded. Is it the same for Christ's resurrection? Will all humans be raised to eternal life on the last day? The answer is no, because Paul qualifies 'all' in the clause 'in Christ shall all be made alive' in the very next verse. 'All' in verse 22 refers to 'those who belong to Christ' in verse 23.[16]

In verses 45–49 Paul resumes his contrasts between the two Adams, speaking of life: 'The first man Adam became a living being; the last Adam became a life-giving spirit' (v. 45). Paul refers to Genesis 2:7: '[T]he LORD God formed the man of dust from the ground and breathed into his nostrils the breath of life, and the man became a living creature.' At the apex of God's good creation, he made Adam (and Eve, vv. 21–23). God's inbreathing animated Adam, who became 'a living creature' or 'being'. By contrast, in his resurrection Christ 'the last Adam became a life-giving spirit'. God gave Adam physical life, but the risen Christ gives spiritual life to others.

Ferguson skilfully juxtaposes Adam and Christ:

> Paul says that 'The first man Adam became a living being' (1 Cor. 15:45). But while the first Adam received the breath of God, the last Adam is the One with the very Breath which gives life to his people:

---

[15] Thiselton 2000: 1229; emphasis original.
[16] Paul teaches eternal punishment in 2 Thess. 1:5–10. For refutations of universalism see Packer 2004 and R. A. Peterson 1995: 139–159.

'the last Adam [became] a life-giving spirit' (1 Cor. 15:45). By this statement, Paul indicates the way in which Christ as last Adam was fully possessed by and came into the full possession of the Spirit in his glorification. Its implication is that the resurrected and glorified Christ, the Adam of the Spirit, now creates life of a new order, life like his own through the power of the Spirit: *eschatological* life whose dominant feature is [S]pirituality.[17]

The bodies of the two Adams also stand in contrast (1 Cor. 15:44–46), in terms of both fragility and peccability. First, Adam is the model for 'the natural', humanity from the earth, a 'man of dust' (Gen. 2:7). As such he has fragile humanity (vv. 46–47), which after the fall is consigned to death, to return to dust (Gen. 3:19). Sadly, for humanity, whom Adam represented, 'As was the man of dust, so also are those who are of the dust' (1 Cor. 15:48). We too have fragile bodies that grow old, become weak and die.

By contrast, the living Christ is the model for another order of existence, for 'the second man is from heaven' (v. 47). His body, raised by God, is powerful and no longer subject to death. By God's sovereign grace, 'as is the man of heaven, so also are those who are of heaven' (v. 48). They too, like Christ, will be raised with bodies that are 'of heaven' – powerful and immortal. In a word, God will raise them 'in glory' (v. 43), with bodies ruled by the Holy Spirit.[18] 'Just as we have borne the image of the man of dust, we shall also bear the image of the man of heaven' (v. 49).

Second, we compare Adam and Christ in terms of their bodies' peccability. God created Adam 'after the likeness of God in true righteousness and holiness' (Eph. 4:24).[19] His whole person, including his body, was without sin. But he was capable of sinning and in his body did so. The risen Christ also has a genuine human body (and soul), but, unlike Adam, he cannot sin. This points to the work of the Holy Spirit in Christ and in his people, as Thiselton affirms:

For Paul *new creation* and *transformation came from beyond and were constituted by the agency of the Holy Spirit* ... Paul does not

---

[17] Ferguson 1996: 251–252; emphasis original.

[18] Thiselton 2000: 1287.

[19] Since the renewal of the image of God in humans is described in this way, it must also describe the original image.

devalue the physical, which is God's gift, but the natural is bound up with human sin and bondage, and there is no hope of full salvation without *transformation* by an act of the sovereign God which entails the mediate agency also of Christ and the Spirit . . . It means not only transformation from weakness to power but also from sin to holiness.[20]

Another contrast between the two Adams is frequently overlooked: Adam's glory as created compared to Christ's glory as risen. Although Adam forfeited glory in the fall, Christ recovers and surpasses it, as Horton explains:

It is this lost glory that is recovered – and because it is no less than the glory of the God-Man, it is greater than the original glory of 'the first man . . . from the earth, a man of dust' (1 Cor. 15:47).[21]

God will raise believers in glory (1 Cor. 15:35–58)

Background

To appreciate Paul's presentation of the glory of Christ's resurrection and ours we must become acquainted with background, including Greek philosophical ideas about resurrection, contemporary Jewish ideas of the same and the biblical doctrines of creation and new creation. Inevitably, all humans are influenced by their culture. The first-century Corinthians were no exception, as they were swayed by leading values and ideas of Roman culture.[22]

The Corinthians' understanding of life after death was influenced by Greek philosophical ideas. We catch a glimpse of these in the response of Epicurean and Stoic philosophers to Paul's preaching in Athens:

Some of the Epicurean and Stoic philosophers also conversed with him. And some said, 'What does this babbler wish to say?' Others

---

[20] Thiselton 2000: 1283–1284, 1291; emphases original.
[21] Horton 2007: 244–245.
[22] Ciampa and Rosner 2010: 794. Some were not heeding Rom. 12:1–2.

said, 'He seems to be a preacher of foreign divinities' – because he
was preaching Jesus and the resurrection.
(Acts 17:18)

N. T. Wright is on point:

> Christianity was born into a world where its central claim was
> known to be false. Many believed the dead were non-existent; out-
> side Judaism, nobody believed in resurrection . . . Everybody knew
> dead people didn't and couldn't come back to bodily life.[23]

Jewish ideas outside the Old Testament were also confused. 'Evidence
from Jewish apocalyptic . . . presupposes a view that the resurrection body
is an organism composed of particles reassembled from those of the
rotting or rotted corpse.'[24]

What specific doctrinal problem did Paul address in 1 Corinthians?
Fee answers:

> Behind that denial [of the resurrection] is a view of the material
> order that found the resurrection of material bodies (or dead
> corpses) to be a doctrine most foul . . . The real concern behind their
> denial of the resurrection of the dead was an implicit understanding
> that this meant the reanimation of dead bodies, the resuscitation of
> corpses.[25]

Paul's teaching on the resurrection of the body affirms the doctrines
of creation and new creation. The Corinthians' rejection of bodily resurrection was an affront to God as Creator. Fee sums up Paul's response to
them.

> At stake is the biblical doctrine of creation. According to Scrip-
> ture, God created the material order and pronounced it good. But in
> the fall it also came under the curse. In Paul's view, therefore, the
> material order must also experience the effects of redemption in
> Christ, and that involves the physical body as well. Since in its

---

[23] Wright 2003: 35, 316, as quoted in Ciampa and Rosner 2010: 754.
[24] Thiselton 2000: 1262, citing *2 Baruch* 49.2; 50.1–2.
[25] Fee 1987: 858–859.

present expression it is under a curse, it must be transformed; and that happens at the Eschaton.[26]

Paul reflects on Genesis 1 – 2 when he depicts the resurrection of believers' bodies in glory. In fact, the resurrection of believers' bodies *is* the new creation, as Beale explains: 'Resurrection is conceptually equivalent to new creation because the way redeemed humans participate in the new creation is through having transformed, newly created bodies.'[27]

Nature of the resurrection body (1 Cor. 15:35–44)

After affirming the resurrection of Christ and his people Paul treats the nature of the resurrection body: 'But someone will ask, "How are the dead raised? With what kind of body do they come?"' (1 Cor. 15:35). As we have seen, for some of the Corinthian congregation bodily resurrection conjured up images of resuscitated corpses. Paul rebukes anyone who questions the Creator's power and wisdom in raising the dead to glory: 'You foolish person!' (v. 36). Jesus had made the same criticism of the Sadducees' denial of the resurrection: 'You are wrong, because you know neither the Scriptures nor the power of God' (Matt. 22:29).

First, Paul helps readers understand the nature of believers' resurrected bodies by speaking of the 'bodies', the corporeal substances, God gives to other parts of his creation, such as plants. 'What you sow does not come to life unless it dies' (v. 36). Someone plants ('buries') a seed in the earth, and it therefore 'dies', disappears. We put seeds, not the full-grown plants, in the ground. But what comes up is not the seed but the plant that springs from it, and each plant comes up according to its type of seed. Paul's point? 'God gives it a body as he has chosen, and to each kind of seed its own body' (v. 38). David Garland encapsulates Paul's idea:

> A bare seed is sown, dies, is made alive, and is given a new body as it is transformed through God's creative power into 'a plant luxuriantly clad in leaves' (Edwards 1885: 434). The same is true of humans. The eye sees nothing in a mortal, perishing body that promises any hope of a resurrection to come, but God will transform

---

[26] Ibid. 861.
[27] Beale 2011: 227.

it into a body clothed with glory through the same creative power that gives life to seeds.[28]

Paul teaches that seed/plant is somewhat analogous to natural body / resurrection body in God's raising the dead. There is continuity between the person who dies and the body that is raised. But God gives to believers the resurrected bodies he desires, and these do not resemble the decaying bodies put into graves but are incredibly new, powerful and glorious.

Second, Paul appeals to the 'bodies' God gives to living beings: humans, animals, birds and fish. In doing so he reverses the order of God's creation on the fifth and sixth days in Genesis 1 (1 Cor. 15:39). Once more the point is that God gives his various creatures different 'bodies' as he deems appropriate. Ciampa and Rosner are succinct: 'The opening clause, *All flesh is not the same*, is the key to everything else in vv. 39–41.' In the light of the great variety of 'bodies' in the world, the Corinthians should not assume that our present bodies provide the blueprints for our resurrection bodies.[29]

Third, the apostle recalls the fourth day of creation and looks to the heavenly bodies, contrasting them with the earthly ones he has just discussed:

> There are heavenly bodies and earthly bodies, but the glory of the heavenly is of one kind, and the glory of the earthly is of another. There is one glory of the sun, and another glory of the moon, and another glory of the stars; for star differs from star in glory.
> (1 Cor. 15:40–41)

Garland captures Paul's argument:

> The items in 15:41 are listed in descending order of their radiance: the blazing of the sun, the soft glow of the moon, the twinkling of the stars . . . Since the stars have a resplendence unlike anything on earth, one can expect the resurrected body, fit for a heavenly existence, to be unlike anything known on earth . . . Paul wants to disabuse the Corinthians of the mistaken impression that all bodies

---

[28] Garland 2003: 729. He cites Edwards 1979: 434.
[29] Ciampa and Rosner 2010: 804.

are the same so that they can begin to appreciate that the resurrection body is not identical with the familiar, earthly body . . . Even heavenly bodies emit different levels of brightness. The body that is raised will be transformed into something entirely different from what is known on earth and something appropriate for heavenly existence.[30]

Paul resumes his plant analogy to discuss resurrection bodies. After the bridge statement 'So is it with the resurrection of the dead' (v. 42), four times he says, 'It is sown . . . it is raised' (vv. 42–44). That is, four times he contrasts believers' earthly bodies with their resurrection bodies. Paul describes earthly bodies as 'perishable', 'sown in dishonour', 'sown in weakness' and 'natural'. But he describes resurrection bodies as 'imperishable', 'raised in glory', 'raised in power' and 'spiritual'.

We will investigate these contrasts in turn. First, earthly bodies are 'perishable'. Since the fall they have been subject to decomposition in burial. By contrast, resurrection bodies are imperishable, not subject to decay or death. They are immortal. Fee concludes, 'So important is this basic set of contrasts to Paul's argument that this is the only language picked up in the description of the final transformation (vv. 50–54), where it is repeated three times (vv. 50/52, 53, 54).'[31]

Second, earthly bodies are 'sown in dishonour', and resurrection bodies are 'raised in glory' (1 Cor. 15:43). Our current bodies are subject to dishonour, as the mistreatment of both Paul and Jesus demonstrates. Earlier in 1 Corinthians Paul, with sarcasm directed toward opponents in Corinth, spoke of the dishonour apostles experience:

God has exhibited us apostles as last of all, like men sentenced to death, because we have become a spectacle to the world, to angels, and to men . . . To the present hour we hunger and thirst, we are poorly dressed and buffeted and homeless, and we labour, working with our own hands. When reviled, we bless; when persecuted, we endure; when slandered, we entreat. We have become, and are still, like the scum of the world, the refuse of all things.
(1 Cor. 4:9–13)

---

[30] Garland 2003: 730–732.
[31] Fee 1987: 868.

Of course, the greatest example of someone (and his body) being dishonoured is that of 'the Lord of glory', who was crucified (1 Cor. 2:8). Jesus was rejected by his creatures, specifically his covenant people (John 1:10–11). They disbelieved his word, rejected his messianic claims, condemned him and delivered him to Gentiles, who mocked, flogged and crucified him.

When Paul says our physical bodies are sown in dishonour, he speaks of the dishonour all humans experience in life and especially in death. God did not create Adam and Eve to die! On the contrary, he made Adam 'a little lower than the heavenly beings / and crowned him with glory and honour' (Ps. 8:5). But humanity fell into sin, with the result that 'all have sinned and fall short of the glory of God' (Rom. 3:23). What is more, 'Claiming to be wise, they became fools, and exchanged the glory of the immortal God for images resembling mortal man and birds and animals and creeping things' (Rom. 1:22–23). Humanity was made for God's glory but exchanged it for idols.

God did not abandon his rebellious image-bearers, however, but granted glory to sinners who had forfeited it. God's plan of rescue centres on Jesus Christ, the glorious Lord (1 Cor. 2:8), who died for our sins, 'was raised from the dead by the glory of the Father' (Rom. 6:4) and was 'taken up in glory' (1 Tim. 3:16). 'Our blessed hope' is 'the appearing of the glory of our great God and Saviour Jesus Christ' (Titus 2:13). Ciampa and Rosner state that although 'glory' (in 1 Cor. 15:43) is the same word rendered 'glory' in verses 40–41, 'The word's antithetical relationship with "dishonor" in this verse clearly indicates that glory in the sense of (majestic) honor is in mind, not luminescence, although it will certainly involve magnificent splendor as well.'[32]

Like many New Testament themes, God's saving glory is both 'already' and 'not yet'. In conversion God reveals 'the riches of the glory of this mystery, which is Christ in you, the hope of glory' (Col. 1:27). Astonishingly, in this life believers, 'beholding the glory of the Lord, are being transformed into the same image from one degree of glory to another' (2 Cor. 3:18). However, the best is yet to come, for 'we rejoice in hope of the glory of God' (Rom. 5:2).

How do our present sufferings stack up against our future resurrection glory? They 'are not worth comparing with the glory that is to be revealed

---

[32] Ciampa and Rosner 2010: 814.

to us' (Rom. 8:18). Why does God call us to salvation through the gospel? He did this 'so that [we] may obtain the glory of our Lord Jesus Christ' (2 Thess. 2:14). When will we share Christ's resurrection glory? 'When Christ who is your life appears, then you also will appear with him in glory' (Col. 3:4). To whose praise does all this redound? To God alone 'be glory in the church and in Christ Jesus throughout all generations, for ever and ever. Amen' (Eph. 3:21).

Leon Morris contrasts the faulty ideas held by some Corinthians with the glory of our resurrection bodies:

> Look at it how you will, there is nothing honourable about a decaying body as it is put into a grave. But that has no relevance to the way the body is when it is raised. The resurrection body is a glorious body, just as far surpassing the present body as the beautiful plant surpasses the seed from which it sprang. The Greek's doubts arising from the dishonourable nature of the body that now is are groundless. The body that is to be raised will be a body in glory.[33]

Ciampa and Rosner remind us of Paul's experience with the glorious resurrected Christ on the road to Damascus (1 Cor. 15:8): 'The themes of Christ's glory and the glory that awaits believers were important ones for Paul, and they grew out of his personal experience of Christ.'[34]

Third, earthly bodies are 'sown in weakness', whereas resurrection bodies are 'raised in power'. 'Some Corinthians had a mistaken understanding of strength and weakness, and in doubting the resurrection they showed a particularly grave underestimation of God's power.'[35]

Even those few in the Corinthian congregation who considered themselves powerful in the world's eyes (1 Cor. 1:26), the rich and socially influential, would grow weak and die. Thiselton is frank when he remarks concerning pre-resurrection bodies 'sown in weakness'. This language, he writes, shows

> Paul's realism about the frailty, fragility, vulnerability, and constraints of human existence (including that of Christians) without

---

[33] Morris 1985: 222.
[34] Ciampa and Rosner 2010: 814.
[35] Ibid. 816.

diminishing the power of the cross, which is the presupposition for the triumph of the resurrection mode of existence.[36]

However, weakness will not have the last word for believers, for God will raise us 'in power' (1 Cor. 15:43). God's sovereign grace will reverse the effects of weakness and decay and raise bodies full of power and glory.

Fourth, earthly bodies are 'natural', while resurrection bodies are 'spiritual': 'It is sown a natural body; it is raised a spiritual body. If there is a natural body, there is also a spiritual body' (v. 44). So far we have seen that earthly bodies are perishable, dishonoured and weak and that resurrection bodies are imperishable, glorious and powerful.

But what is the meaning of the contrast between 'natural' and 'spiritual' bodies? The view that the distinction is between 'physical' and 'immaterial' bodies is wrong, for 'The material/immaterial dichotomy is a modern one and . . . in Paul's world soul and spirit were not considered to be immaterial but of a lighter, thinner material than visible stuff.'[37] Most importantly, 'spiritual' bodies are not immaterial, for 1 Corinthians 15 is all about the bodily resurrection of Christ and believers.

Rather, the distinction between 'natural' and 'spiritual' bodies is between bodies fitted for ordinary human life on earth and those fitted for eternal life on the new earth. It is a distinction between bodies animated by the soul in this age and those animated by the Spirit in the age to come. It is a distinction between natural, earthly bodily life and supernatural, heavenly bodily life. It is a distinction between believers' present common bodies and their future transformed bodies. Fee is correct:

> The transformed body, therefore, is not composed of 'spirit'; it is a *body* adapted to the eschatological existence that is under the ultimate domination of, and animated by, the Spirit. Thus for Paul, to be truly *pneumatikos* [spiritual] is to bear the likeness of Christ (v. 49) in a transformed body, fitted for the new age.[38]

---

[36] Thiselton 2000: 1274.
[37] Ciampa and Rosner 2010: 816.
[38] Fee 1987: 869; emphasis original.

The certainty of resurrection (1 Cor. 15:45–49)

We previously studied the two Adams, and we now treat briefly Paul's return to that theme (in vv. 45–49). He contrasts Adam and Christ, the two heads of humanity. God imparted life to Adam by inbreathing, and Adam 'became a living being' (v. 45). By contrast Christ the risen 'last Adam became a life-giving spirit' (v. 45). As Jesus said, 'Because I live, you also will live' (John 14:19). Paul speaks here not of eternity but of the history of salvation: Adam and his normal body came first in time, and Christ and his resurrected body came later (v. 46). The story follows the principle of 'As with the two Adams, so with God's people.' Believers too now have normal bodies like Adam's postfall, and when Christ returns they will have resurrection bodies like Christ's.

Paul next points to the origins of the two Adams – earthly and heavenly, respectively – to differentiate the two orders of existence they introduce. God created Adam 'of dust from the ground' (Gen. 2:7), and God said concerning his death, 'you are dust, / and to dust you shall return' (3:19). Adam epitomizes the normal order of human existence since the fall, marked by weakness and death. In contrast, the raised Christ is 'from heaven', a different order of existence, marked by a resurrection body filled with power and glory and fitted for eternity on the new earth.

The two Adams are representatives of their respective people. Adam represents people in the first fallen creation, and Christ represents redeemed people in the new creation (v. 48). Adam's descendants are like him – characterized by normal bodies, perishable and full of weakness, sin, death and dishonour in this age. Christ's descendants will be like him – characterized by resurrection bodies, imperishable and full of power, righteousness, life and glory in the age to come (v. 49).

Paul's use of the word 'image' twice in verse 49 echoes God's creation of Adam and Eve in his image and likeness (Gen. 1:26–27). Paul mentions 'image' and 'glory' in several passages (Rom. 1:23; 1 Cor. 11:7; 15:43, 48; 2 Cor. 3:18; 4:4), sometimes tying them together. Ciampa and Rosner helpfully bring these data to bear on 1 Corinthians 15:49:

> We are to understand that the image of the earthly man lacks the glory with which it was previously created and is now an image of impermanence, weakness, ignobility, and of earthly humanness

while the image of the heavenly man reflects God's glory in its incorruptible, powerful, honorable, and spiritual nature (cf. vv. 42–44).[39]

Resurrection means transformation (1 Cor. 15:50–58)

Paul concludes his masterful treatment of resurrection by answering the earlier question 'How are the dead raised?' (v. 35). The answer is by transformation. Paul shows that for the redeemed to enjoy eternal life on the new earth the transformation of their bodies is necessary. This transformation affects the living and the deceased and marks the ultimate defeat of death.[40]

The transformation of believers' bodies is necessary. Paul explains that 'flesh and blood cannot inherit the kingdom of God, nor does the perishable inherit the imperishable' (v. 50). Our present mortal bodies are fitted for this age, not the one to come. He describes our present bodies as 'flesh and blood' and 'perishable'. Our current bodies are dishonoured, weak and natural bodies we inherited from Adam (vv. 43–44). Ironically, in this Paul agrees with those among the Corinthians who then wrongly conclude that there is no resurrection. Ciampa and Rosner insist that our current bodies need transformation and that will be accomplished only by God's 'inconceivable power that makes the inconceivable conceivable'.[41] What we need for the coming age are 'imperishable' bodies, as Paul taught in verse 42. He underscores the need for this transformation: 'For this perishable body must put on the imperishable, and this mortal body must put on immortality' (v. 53). Garland is succinct: 'What is raised is not flesh and blood. The earthly frame will be utterly changed into a heavenly body of glory.'[42]

This transformation of believers' bodies affects the living and the dead. Paul declares, 'Behold! I tell you a mystery. We shall not all sleep, but we shall all be changed' (v. 51). A mystery is something previously unknown now revealed through divine revelation.[43] Paul uses 'sleep' as a euphemism for death (cf. vv. 6, 18, 20). God will transform the deceased, those who 'sleep', and those alive when Jesus returns.

---

[39] Ciampa and Rosner 2010: 824.
[40] Fee 1987: 882.
[41] Ciampa and Rosner 2010: 828.
[42] Garland 2003: 742.
[43] Ciampa and Rosner 2010: 829.

God has now revealed this mystery of his grace in raising dead believers and in transforming them along with living ones to share Christ's glory.

The resurrection and transformation will occur suddenly, 'in a moment, in the twinkling of an eye, at the last trumpet. For the trumpet will sound, and the dead will be raised imperishable, and we shall be changed' (v. 52). Fee notes that the imagery of the trumpet 'had been taken up into Jewish prophetic-apocalyptic in a variety of senses to herald the Eschaton'.[44] The exact meaning of the blowing of the trumpet as a signal here is uncertain. Paul repeats the main idea of transformation of the resurrected dead and living believers: '[W]e shall be changed' (v. 52).

Paul's theme in the remaining verses of 1 Corinthians 15 is that transformation signals the ultimate defeat of death:[45]

When the perishable puts on the imperishable, and the mortal puts on immortality, then shall come to pass the saying that is written:

'Death is swallowed up in victory.'
'O death, where is your victory?
　O death, where is your sting?'

The sting of death is sin, and the power of sin is the law. But thanks be to God, who gives us the victory through our Lord Jesus Christ. Therefore, my beloved brothers, be steadfast, immovable, always abounding in the work of the Lord, knowing that in the Lord your labour is not in vain.
(1 Cor. 15:54–58)

God's mighty work of changing his people's bodies from perishability to imperishability crushes the 'last enemy . . . death' (v. 26). Paul creatively alludes to Isaiah 25:8 and Hosea 13:14 to mock death. He likens death to a venomous creature swallowed by a predator and rendered harmless. Thiselton is correct: Paul

projects an eschatological vision of a stingless death precisely because Jesus Christ has himself absorbed the sting on the basis of

---

[44] Fee 1987: 887.
[45] Ibid. 882.

how his death and resurrection addresses the problem of human sin and the law ([1 Cor. 15] vv. 55–57).[46]

Paul exults in the great victory God gives his people through Christ. As a result of this victory, believers find stability in the risen Christ and can work diligently for him, knowing that he will raise us and reward our labours (vv. 57–58).

Christ was raised in glory, and by God's grace we shall be also. Because Christ is the firstfruits of the resurrection, God assures us that we will share his glory in resurrection. Even as Adam brought death and shame to humanity, Christ, the second and last Adam, will bring life and glory to all believers. Although we do not at present fully understand the nature of our resurrection bodies, our resurrection is as certain as Christ's, and it will mean transformation from perishability to imperishability and from dishonour to glory.

Paul elsewhere sums up the message of 1 Corinthians 15: from 'heaven . . . we await a Saviour, the Lord Jesus Christ, who will transform our lowly body to be like his glorious body, by the power that enables him even to subject all things to himself' (Phil. 3:20–21). Horton deserves the last word:

> On the last day, however, the whole person – and the whole church – will be radiant with the light that fills the whole earth with the glory of God, and this new humanity will be joined by the whole creation as it is led by the Servant-Lord of the covenant into the day whose sun never sets.[47]

---

46 Thiselton 2000: 1300.
47 Horton 2007: 292–293.

5
The glory of God and the new covenant: 2 Corinthians 3 – 4

Philip Hughes is eloquent:

> [The new covenant] so far surpasses in glory [the old covenant] that in comparison with it the latter may be said to be no longer glorious . . . just as the brightness of the sun altogether transcends and supersedes the brightness of the moon . . . The impermanence of the earlier dispensation is confirmed by the fact that . . . it was accompanied with the manifestation of divine glory at mount (*sic*) Sinai when it was mediated to the people through Moses, whose face also shone with glory. The permanence of the gospel dispensation, on the other hand, is confirmed by the fact that . . . it is established in the sphere of glory. Its glory is the glory that surpasses; and it is *all* glory, glory leading to glory.[1]

This chapter will focus on the glory of God and Christ in the new covenant:

- God's glory is abundantly revealed in the new covenant (2 Cor. 3:7–18)
- The gospel of the glory of Christ (2 Cor. 4:1–6)
- Suffering, thanksgiving and the glory of God (2 Cor. 4:7–18)

---

[1] Hughes 1962: 105–106; emphasis original.

God's glory is abundantly revealed in the new covenant (2 Cor. 3:7–18)

God's glory in the old covenant (Exod. 19 – 24)

The 'old covenant' (also called the Mosaic covenant or simply 'the law') is found in Exodus 19 – 24, although that expression commonly refers to the epitome of the covenant – the Ten Commandments (Exod. 20:1–21; Deut. 5). Gentry and Wellum are correct: 'The Ten Words form the heart of the covenant between God and Israel at Sinai.'[2] Paul in 2 Corinthians 3 contrasts the new covenant in Christ and its glory with the old covenant and its glory. If we read Paul's words only there concerning the old covenant, we gain a very bad impression of that covenant. Paul calls it the following:

- The ministry of death, carved in letters on stone (3:7)
- The ministry of condemnation (3:9)
- What was being brought to an end (3:11, 13)

Paul finds it and its glory deficient compared to the new covenant:

> the letter [of the old covenant] kills, but the Spirit [of the new covenant] gives life.
> (3:6)

> what once had glory [the old covenant] has come to have no glory at all, because of the glory [of the new covenant] that surpasses it.
> (3:10)

Therefore, in order to obtain a fuller picture of the old covenant, we must consider it on its own terms. When we do, we see that it was God's blessing to his people in at least five ways.

The old covenant was God's gracious gift (Exod. 20:2)

This is true in two respects. First, the covenant with Moses was founded on redemptive grace, as God declares in its preamble: 'I am the LORD your

---

[2] Gentry and Wellum 2012: 327.

God, who brought you out of the land of Egypt, out of the house of slavery' (Exod. 20:2).[3] This is Paul's point in Galatians 3:17–18:

> This is what I mean: the law, which came 430 years afterwards, does not annul a covenant previously ratified by God, so as to make the promise void. For if the inheritance comes by the law, it no longer comes by promise; but God gave it to Abraham by a promise.

Second, Psalm 119 and other psalms view God's commandments not as a burden but as his gracious gift. The law *is* a burden to law-breakers, but God's people, saved by his grace, love God and his law (Ps. 119:48, 167) and find it to be a 'delight' (vv. 16, 174), life-giving (vv. 50, 156), a comfort (vv. 50, 52), better than 'thousands of gold and silver pieces' (v. 72; cf. v. 127), 'sweeter than honey' (v. 103), a 'joy' (v. 111) and 'wonderful' (v. 129).

The old covenant was exclusive (Deut. 7:6–8)

Out of all the nations in the ANE, God chose Israel alone to be his people:

> The LORD your God has chosen you to be a people for his treasured possession, out of all the peoples who are on the face of the earth. It was not because you were more in number than any other people that the LORD set his love on you and chose you, for you were the fewest of all peoples, but it is because the LORD loves you and is keeping the oath that he swore to your fathers, that the LORD has brought you out with a mighty hand and redeemed you from the house of slavery, from the hand of Pharaoh king of Egypt.
> (Deut. 7:6–8)

God made a covenant only with Israel, as Waltke asserts: 'At Mount Sinai Moses initiates God's word that seals God's covenant relationship with Israel and defines Israel as a nation set apart from other nations . . . No other nation is defined by its holiness.'[4] No other ancient people held the belief that their god entered into a covenant with them, as Israel did with regard to God's covenants with Abraham and Moses.

---

[3] 'The very genesis of the law is grace, for it is instituted by Yahweh, who led Israel out of Egypt based not on intrinsic merit but based rather on Yahweh's promises to Abraham' (House 1998: 118).

[4] Waltke 2007: 405.

The old covenant had gracious purposes (Exod. 19:5–6)

The old covenant contains God's gracious purposes expressed in amazing words. As the people of Israel camped in front of Mount Sinai prior to God's giving them the law, he called them his 'treasured possession', his 'kingdom of priests' and 'a holy nation' (Exod. 19:5–6). Christopher Wright writes of how these words describe both Israel's identity and its mission. Israel is its great King's 'treasured possession', much as an earthly king owns all in his realm but

> also had his own personal treasure, in which he took particular delight . . . The *status* is to be a special treasured possession. The *role* is to be a priestly and holy community in the midst of the nations.[5]

In spite of God's gracious purposes, Israel presumed upon its elevated status, went after idols, and largely failed at being a light to the nations.

The old covenant was a clear revelation of God's character (Exod. 20:5–6)

The God of glory revealed himself to Moses and the people. Even before giving the law he manifested his holiness and justice in prohibiting humans and animals from touching Mount Sinai, on penalty of death. The thunder and lightning so frightened the people that they thought they might die (Exod. 20:18–19).

After the commandment prohibiting idolatry, God proclaimed himself to be 'a jealous God', who punishes the descendants of those who hate him but shows 'steadfast love to thousands' who love and obey him (vv. 5–6).

God not only revealed his attributes to his old covenant people but did so clearly. We see this in the vehicle of revelation he used. God used a then-current suzerain–vassal Hittite treaty form to set forth the old covenant. 'Clearly, then, God's revelation comes in an understandable, recognizable form. It can be written down, read, grasped and obeyed.'[6]

The old covenant is the core of biblical ethics (Deut. 5:6–21)

The old covenant was a blessing to Israel in another way. Waltke explains, 'The center of biblical theology is the message that God's will [should] be

---

[5] Wright 2006: 256; emphases original.
[6] House 1998: 117.

done on earth to his glory and . . . the most important expression of God's will is the Ten Commandments.'[7] Those commandments constitute the very core of the Scripture's ethics. As a result, the canonical implications of Exodus 19 – 24 are immense, as House shows:

> Everyone from Moses (Deut 5:6–21), to Jeremiah (Jer 7:1–15), to Jesus (Mt 5–7), to Peter (1 Pet 2:9), and every other biblical writer who has anything to say about covenant, morality and relationship to God reflects directly or indirectly on this passage [Exod. 19 – 24].[8]

If the old covenant was such a blessing to Israel, as demonstrated in these five ways, why does Paul stress its inferiority in 2 Corinthians 3? The answer lies in the superiority of the new covenant to the old.

God's glory in the new covenant (2 Cor. 3)

Paul defends himself (2 Cor. 3:1–3)

Before Paul argues for the superiority of the new covenant and its glory in 3:7–18 he defends himself against his critics. When he speaks of 'some' who need letters of recommendation in 3:1, he refers to the 'peddlers of God's word' from 2:17: 'We are not, like so many, peddlers of God's word, but as men of sincerity, as commissioned by God, in the sight of God we speak in Christ.' Unlike the 'peddlers', Paul is sincere, appointed by God to the apostolic office and accountable to him.

Paul begins 3:1 with two questions: 'Are we beginning to commend ourselves again? Or do we need, as some do, letters of recommendation to you, or from you?' It was not unusual in the first century for churches to write 'letters of recommendation' for those who ministered.[9] Recent studies have shown the accepted practice of individuals writing their own letters of recommendation as well. Such letters were not regarded as signifying self-approval but rather served as introductions.[10] Paul implies negative answers to his two questions because, as God's apostle, he does not need

---

[7] Waltke 2007: 414.

[8] House 1998: 117.

[9] Seifrid (2014: 110–111) is helpful: 'We know, in fact, that the church in Corinth received such a letter of commendation for Apollos (Acts 18:27). Paul himself commends Phoebe, a prominent member of the church in Cenchreae, to the church at Rome (Rom 16:1–2).'

[10] Garland 1999: 154–155.

letters of recommendation, '[f]or it is not the one who commends himself who is approved, but the one whom the Lord commends' (2 Cor. 10:18).

Paul is discouraged to think the Corinthians would seek a letter of recommendation for him. The Corinthian believers are Paul's metaphorical letter of recommendation: 'You yourselves are our letter of recommendation, written on our[11] hearts, to be known and read by all' (v. 2). The Corinthians are a living testimony to Paul's apostleship. Moreover, Paul says, the Corinthians are 'written on our hearts', beloved by Paul and his associates. Since it was common for the person recommended to bear the letter of recommendation, 'Paul carries around in his heart the memory' of how they responded to his ministry.[12] And, unlike the 'peddlers', Paul's ministry and motives are public, so that his living 'letter' is 'known and read by all'.

Paul expands his metaphor: 'And you show that you are a letter from Christ delivered by us' (v. 3). Christ 'wrote' the letter that is the Corinthian congregation. Paul and his fellow workers 'delivered' it. The Corinthian believers are a letter 'written not with ink but with the Spirit of the living God'. Paul contrasts the impermanence of ink and its results with the permanent work of the Holy Spirit.[13] Only here does Scripture call him 'the Spirit of the living God'. This is appropriate for at least two reasons. First, the Corinthians are a living letter written by the Spirit; second, Paul here hints at the contrast between the death-dealing old covenant and the life-giving new covenant.

The Corinthians are Christ's letter inscribed by the Spirit 'not on tablets of stone but on tablets of human hearts'. The latter expression is unusual and even awkward. Paul uses it, of course, as parallel to 'on tablets of stone', a reference to the Ten Commandments. He thereby contrasts the old and new covenants. God engraved the old covenant on 'tablets of stone' (Exod. 24:12; 31:18). The Spirit writes the new covenant 'on tablets of human hearts' in fulfilment of Jeremiah's and Ezekiel's predictions of the new covenant:

> this is the covenant that I will make with the house of Israel after those days, declares the Lord: I will put my law within them, and

---

[11] Some manuscripts have 'your', and both 'our' and 'your' make sense in the context. 'Our' is better attested, which is why the esv and niv adopt it.

[12] Garland 1999: 157.

[13] Harris 2005: 264.

I will write it on their hearts. And I will be their God, and they shall
be my people.
(Jer. 31:33)

I will give them one heart, and a new spirit I will put within them. I
will remove the heart of stone from their flesh and give them a heart
of flesh, that they may walk in my statutes and keep my rules and
obey them.
(Ezek. 11:19–20)

I will give you a new heart, and a new spirit I will put within you.
And I will remove the heart of stone from your flesh and give you a
heart of flesh. And I will put my Spirit within you, and cause you to
walk in my statutes and be careful to obey my rules.
(Ezek. 36:26–27)

The work of the Holy Spirit in the Corinthians both demonstrates the
fulfilment of these Old Testament predictions of a new covenant and
accredits Paul as a minister of that covenant.[14]

Paul's sufficiency is from God (2 Cor. 3:4–6)

Next Paul writes, 'Such is the confidence that we have through Christ
towards God. Not that we are sufficient in ourselves to claim anything as
coming from us, but our sufficiency is from God' (vv. 4–5). The former
Pharisee previously had confidence in his 'flesh', his pedigree and achieve-
ments, but now has confidence in Christ, crucified and risen (Phil. 3:4–11).
Because of the Holy Spirit's work through Paul's preaching the gospel to
others, including the Corinthians, he has confidence through Christ.
However, he is quick to acknowledge that his competence and confidence
are from God. Paul answers his own question from 2 Corinthians 2:16:
'Who is sufficient for these things?' Paul's sufficiency comes from the
grace of God and results in his glory.

God graciously qualifies the unqualified for his service, even
persecutors of the church, as he did Paul. Paul specifies, God 'has made
us sufficient to be ministers of a new covenant'. Paul introduces the theme
he will treat to the end of the chapter: the glorious new covenant. God has

---

[14] Barnett 1997: 161.

appointed the apostles to be 'ministers', or agents, of the new covenant (v. 6). Paul's role as agent of the new covenant assumes Christ's role as its Mediator (Heb. 9:15).

Paul's reference to the 'new covenant' comes from Jeremiah 38:31 (LXX), apparently mediated through the tradition of the Last Supper (Luke 22:20; 1 Cor. 11:25).[15] Paul no sooner introduces the concept of the new covenant than he speaks of its superiority to the old covenant. God made Paul a minister of a new covenant 'not of the letter but of the Spirit. For the letter kills, but the Spirit gives life' (2 Cor. 3:6).

'Letter' stands for the demands of OT law, whose every 'commandment is holy and righteous and good' (Rom. 7:12) but when disobeyed by humans brings bondage and death. 'Spirit' stands for the Holy Spirit and his power to transform human lives from within, resulting in freedom and life.

The 'letter' and the 'Spirit', then, stand for two different covenants with different descriptions, demands and results. The law's letter 'kills';[16] it 'slays' the disobedient, as Paul has painfully learned (Rom. 7:10–11). The Spirit 'gives life' in regeneration in this age and in resurrection to life in the age to come. This is characteristic of the Spirit, for

> when Paul observes here that the Spirit 'imparts life' or when he describes the Spirit as 'life-giving' (τῆς ζωῆς, Rom. 8:2; cf. Gal. 5:25), he is affirming that one characteristic – perhaps the principal characteristic – of the Spirit is that he perpetually grants the physical and spiritual life of which he is the source.[17]

New covenant ministry is more glorious than Moses' ministry (2 Cor. 3:7–18)

Garland fittingly introduces 2 Corinthians 3:7–18: 'Glory, not the contrast between law and grace, is the key theme of this unit.'[18] Indeed, this passage exalts the glory of new covenant ministry like no other, showing its superiority even to that of Moses, the mediator of the old covenant. Paul bases his comparison on Exodus 34:29–33:

---

[15] Harris 2005: 270–271.
[16] The words 'kills' and 'gives life' are gnomic presents 'depicting what is always and everywhere the case' (ibid. 273).
[17] Ibid. 273–274.
[18] Garland 1999: 167–168.

When Moses came down from Mount Sinai, with the two tablets of the testimony in his hand as he came down from the mountain, Moses did not know that the skin of his face shone because he had been talking with God. Aaron and all the people of Israel saw Moses, and behold, the skin of his face shone, and they were afraid to come near him. But Moses called to them, and Aaron and all the leaders of the congregation returned to him, and Moses talked with them. Afterwards all the people of Israel came near, and he commanded them all that the LORD had spoken with him in Mount Sinai. And when Moses had finished speaking with them, he put a veil over his face.

Paul is not claiming that the old covenant lacked glory. On the contrary, the second time Moses carried the two tablets of the law down the mountain from God's presence, although he did not realize it, 'the skin of his face shone' with God's glory (Exod. 34:29). It shone so much that the people were afraid to approach him (v. 30).

The scene shifts from the historical occasion at Sinai (in vv. 29–33) to a more general setting in verses 34–35:

Whenever Moses went in before the LORD to speak with him, he would remove the veil, until he came out. And when he came out and told the people of Israel what he was commanded, the people of Israel would see the face of Moses, that the skin of Moses' face was shining. And Moses would put the veil over his face again, until he went in to speak with him.

The setting here is not Mount Sinai but the later meetings of Moses with God that resulted in his delivering God's message to the people at the tent of meeting. Moses is the mediator of the old covenant, the one who went into God's presence to talk with him. During these times he would remove the veil. He did the same when he addressed the people, after which he would reapply the veil until he visited God again.

Even before we get to 2 Corinthians 3, Exodus 34:29–35 provides much insight into the divine glory. Eager for God to accompany his people to the Promised Land, Moses had made the bold request of God 'Please show me your glory' (Exod. 33:18). In reply God said:

'I will make all my goodness pass before you and will proclaim before you my name "The Lord". And I will be gracious to whom I will be gracious, and will show mercy on whom I will show mercy. But,' he said, 'you cannot see my face, for man shall not see me and live.' And the Lord said, 'Behold, there is a place by me where you shall stand on the rock, and while my glory passes by I will put you in a cleft of the rock, and I will cover you with my hand until I have passed by. Then I will take away my hand, and you shall see my back, but my face shall not be seen.'
(Exod. 33:19–23)

Then the living and true God, who had covenanted himself to his people Israel, revealed his glory to Moses by his presence, passing before him and in words proclaiming his name:

The Lord descended in the cloud and stood with him there, and proclaimed the name of the Lord. The Lord passed before him and proclaimed, 'The Lord, the Lord, a God merciful and gracious, slow to anger, and abounding in steadfast love and faithfulness, keeping steadfast love for thousands, forgiving iniquity and transgression and sin, but who will by no means clear the guilty, visiting the iniquity of the fathers on the children and the children's children, to the third and the fourth generation.'
(Exod. 34:5–7)

Of what does God's revelation of his glory in words consist? Stuart answers well:

God manifested himself specially and personally in Moses' presence. Thereby Moses could perceive that a real personal being had come to him and not a concept, or a feeling, or a numinous impression . . . He then 'proclaimed his name, the LORD [Yahweh].' . . . [He revealed] the (divine) person behind the name . . . God cited five attributes that characterize him – all of which would be welcome to Moses and the Israelites, who needed very much to count on his compassion toward them in light of their having previously angered him by their behavior.[19]

---

[19] Stuart 2006: 714–715.

Moses responded appropriately: he 'quickly bowed his head towards the earth and worshipped' (v. 8). Moses, a mere sinful mortal, had the audacity to ask God to reveal his glory to him! And astoundingly, God acceded to his request!

So what did the Israelites see when Moses' face glowed with the glory of God? Moses himself was not allowed to see God's face, lest he die. God showed Moses, the man to whom 'the LORD used to speak . . . face to face, as a man speaks to his friend' (Exod. 33:11), his 'back', a partial glimpse of his glory. And even this greatly reduced sense of God's glory made Moses' face so radiant that the people could not bear to look upon it.

In 2 Corinthians 3:7–18 Paul does not offer a straightforward exegesis of this Exodus passage, and scholars debate reasons for the differences between the two texts. Harris helpfully summarizes: cognizant of the differences, some label 2 Corinthians 3:7–18 a 'midrash' on Exodus 34, some call it 'pesher' or 'midrash pesher' and still others label it an allegory.

> Given the fact that specific reference to the Exodus story is found only in vv. 7, 13, and 16 of 2 Corinthians 3, it may be wiser to follow Hays's lead and describe 3:7–18 as 'an allusive homily based on biblical incidents'.[20]

We agree and will follow Hays's lead, beginning with verses 7–11. We are immediately struck by two things. First, the word 'glory' appears ten times, and second, a stark contrast is drawn between the covenants (see Table 1).

Table 1 The contrast between the old and new covenants

The old covenant	*The new covenant*
the ministry of death: glory	the ministry of the Spirit: more glory
the ministry of condemnation: glory	the ministry of righteousness: exceeding glory
what once had glory: no glory now	what has surpassing glory
what was ending: glory	what is permanent: more glory

Before examining these vibrant contrasts between the old and new covenants we note that Paul begins verse 7 with a contrast to verse 6. Verse 6 had said 'the letter kills', and now the apostle speaks of the great

---

[20] Harris 2005: 277, citing Hays 1989: 132.

glory of the 'letter' and its ministry: it 'came with such glory that the Israelites could not gaze at Moses' face because of its glory' (v. 7).

In addition, Paul extends the contrast of verse 6, 'For the letter kills, but the Spirit gives life.' Instead of 'letter' Paul now writes 'ministry'; instead of 'kills' he writes 'of death'; and he expands 'the Spirit' to 'the ministry of the Spirit'. His contrast is sharp: 'Now if the ministry of death, carved in letters on stone, came with such glory . . . will not the ministry of the Spirit have even more glory?' (vv. 7–8). Paul, of course, refers to the Ten Commandments, written by God's finger on the stone tablets. Paul calls it 'the ministry of death' not because of deficiencies in that covenant or a lack of glory but because of the sinful people's inability to keep the covenant.[21] Paul contrasts this with the life-giving Spirit in the new covenant.

In verses 7–11 Paul employs a rabbinical Jewish argument of *qal wāḥômer* (the light and the heavy), 'from the lesser to the greater', as Harris explains:

> The movement of thought is from 'what is true' to 'what is even more certainly true.' This seems to be the case in vv. 7–8: 'If the dispensation that brought death . . . was attended by glory . . . , even more certainly will the dispensation of the Spirit be accompanied by glory.'[22]

The new covenant abounds in glory (2 Cor. 3:7–11)

Paul amplifies the protasis ('if' clause) of the comparison over against the apodosis ('then' clause):

> Now if the ministry of death, carved in letters on stone, came with such glory that the Israelites could not gaze at Moses' face because of its glory, which was being brought to an end, will not the ministry of the Spirit have even more glory?
> (vv. 7–8)

This imbalance makes readers linger on the protasis and its final words, 'which was being brought to an end'. Paul envisions the temporary nature

---

[21] Barnett 1997: 180.
[22] Harris 2005: 279.

of the old covenant as being on display from its inception. The longer protasis also lays stress on the shorter apodosis, which glorifies 'the ministry of the Spirit'. In so doing Paul continues his argument from verses 1–6 to justify his role in new covenant ministry.

It is sometimes overlooked that in Paul's argument the glory of the new covenant depends on the glory of the old covenant. Garland explains: Paul does not 'denigrate Moses and his glory but wants to stress it so he can show how much greater is the glory attached to his ministry'.[23]

But how exactly is the ministry of the Spirit more glorious than that of the law? Taking our cue from verse 6, we conclude that it is because the Spirit, fulfilling the promise of the new covenant, regenerates sinners and inclines their hearts to obey God's law.[24]

In 3:9 Paul makes his second contrast: 'For if there was glory in the ministry of condemnation, the ministry of righteousness must far exceed it in glory.' Here he again sets the old covenant against the new, this time in terms of ministries of condemnation and of righteousness and their respective glories. Because of its contrast with its opposite, condemnation, righteousness here is not ethical but legal and therefore means acquittal or forgiveness.[25]

Paul increases the degrees of difference with each of his three contrasts between the covenants. In verses 7–8 the Spirit's ministry has 'even more glory' than the law's 'ministry of death'. Now in verse 9 the 'ministry of righteousness' of the new covenant 'far 'exceed[s]' the 'ministry of condemnation' of the old one. In verses 10–11 the new covenant's glory is so great that it eclipses that of the former covenant, rendering it 'no glory at all'.

As we found concerning God's glory and the resurrection of Christ and believers in 1 Corinthians 15, so here there is an autobiographical element to Paul's words. Saul of Tarsus was never the same after the risen Christ appeared to him in glory on the road to Damascus. Garland speaks to Paul's changed views of Christ and righteousness:

Paul's self-centered devotion to the law had blinded him to the glory of God in the person of Christ. Only when the Lord encountered him on the Damascus road was he constrained to recognize the

---

[23] Garland 1999: 171.
[24] Barnett 1997: 184.
[25] Ibid. 185.

truth ... Jesus' crucifixion was not God's retribution against some imagined blasphemy committed by a counterfeit prophet but a vicarious sacrifice for the sins of humanity ... making him the beneficiary of staggering sacrificial love. He also learned that his righteousness according to the law (Phil 3:6) was nothing more than filthy rags.[26]

Paul knew the truth of verse 9 personally; he rejoiced to have Christ's righteousness credited to him and to be accepted by God. The glory of this ministry of free justification and life far exceeds the glory of the law's death-dealing character. Here he again demonstrates the superiority of the new covenant, which in turn demonstrates to the Corinthians that he is Christ's apostle and minister of that covenant. Barnett comments wisely:

> The 'glory' that Paul saw on that one life-changing occasion serves to describe – metaphorically – the experience of those who, through the 'light of the gospel' (4:4), have come under the righteousness of the new covenant (cf. 5:21). What Paul saw with his eyes also tells the story of the people in whose hearts the 'light of the knowledge of the glory of God' has shone (4:6). It is this 'glory,' shining in their hearts, arising from the preaching of the gospel, which is greater, infinitely surpassing, and indeed 'out-paling' the glory associated with 'Moses.'[27]

In verses 10–11 Paul sets forth his third antithetical parallel to demonstrate even more emphatically the new covenant's supremacy over the old:

> Indeed, in this case, what once had glory has come to have no glory at all, because of the glory that surpasses it. For if what was being brought to an end came with glory, much more will what is permanent have glory.

Although Paul has repeatedly affirmed the glory of the old covenant to highlight the greater glory of the new covenant, now in his final

---

[26] Garland 1999: 285.
[27] Barnett 1997: 184.

comparison of the two he says that, compared to the glory of the new covenant, the old covenant's glory is 'no glory at all' (v. 10).

Once more Paul views the glory of Moses' face coming down from Mount Sinai as representative of the glory of the old covenant generally. But this time the key to his comparison is the matter of permanence. The old covenant is 'what was being brought to an end', whereas the new covenant is 'what is permanent'. Garland is terse: 'The breathtaking glory of the new so outshines the old that it makes its glory seem nonexistent.'[28]

The surpassing glory of the new covenant and its ministry is the focus of 2 Corinthians 3:7–11, and this text is its apex. New covenant glory is the glory that arrested Saul of Tarsus and is 'the light of the gospel of the glory of Christ, who is the image of God' (2 Cor. 4:4), that Paul the apostle now proclaims. Paul thus reinforces the claim of his apostolic ministry to the Corinthians.

The glorious new covenant brings hope and openness (2 Cor. 3:12–18)

In verses 12–18 Paul draws conclusions from verses 7–11. He does so based on the new covenant's superior glory: 'Since we have such a hope, we are very bold' (v. 12). What 'hope' creates this boldness? Paul answers later: it is 'an eternal weight of glory beyond all comparison' (2 Cor. 4:17). The apostles, including Paul, are new covenant ministers and are confident that this covenant as the fulfilment of God's plan is permanent and will never be outshone in glory.[29]

Paul alternates quotations from Exodus 34 with his own comments on them. His expositional strategy for the passage may be outlined as follows:

In 2 Cor. 3:13a Paul quotes Exod. 34:33 and comments on it in 2 Cor. 3:13b–15.

In 2 Cor. 3:16 Paul quotes Exod. 34:34 and comments on it in 2 Cor. 3:17.

In 2 Cor. 3:18 Paul quotes and comments on Exod. 34:35.[30]

It is understandable that Paul, as a minister of the new covenant, would speak of Moses, the mediator of the old covenant, as he does in verse 7.

---

28 Garland 1999: 177–178.
29 Harris 2005: 295.
30 Garland 1999: 179.

But now Paul has the audacity to assert that a new state in redemptive history eclipses that of Moses. Paul speaks of Moses' veiling himself: 'Since, then, we have such a hope, we act with great boldness, not like Moses, who put a veil over his face to keep the people of Israel from gazing at the end of the glory that was being set aside' (2 Cor. 3:12–13, NRSVA).

Paul contrasts Moses with himself and other new covenant believers. He juxtaposes the boldness or, perhaps better, openness[31] of ministers of the new covenant with Moses' wearing a veil under the old covenant. Moses would uncover his face when he was in the Lord's presence and when he brought the Lord's word to the Israelites. Then he would veil his face until the next time he went into God's presence.

That much is clear, but there is much disagreement over why Moses veiled his face. Garland, who credits Hafemann, makes a good case. He claims that Paul interpreted Exodus 34:29–35 with regard to its context in Exodus. Moses' veiling was for the safety of the Israelites, who feared God because he had punished their sin.

> No hint appears in the text in Exodus or in contemporary Jewish tradition that the glory on Moses' face was fading. The glory of God was mediated on Moses' face, and the repeated veiling rendered inoperative (stopped, cut off) the effects of the glory on his face . . . Moses was protecting the people from a dire consequence if they gazed continually at the reflected glory of God radiating from his face.[32]

Thus Moses, by concealing his face, bright with glory, was protecting the Israelites from looking at God's glory for long periods of time and reaping his judgment. Though the emphasis falls on judgment, we should not miss God's mercy and blessing to his people in allowing them glimpses of his glory.

Paul next extends the 'veiling' metaphor to apply it to the Jews of his day. He likens the unbelieving Jews of the first century to the Israelites of Moses' time:

> But their minds were hardened. For to this day, when they read the old covenant, that same veil remains unlifted, because only through

---

[31] So Harris (2005: 295) and Barnett (1997: 188).
[32] Garland 1999: 187. He relies on Hafemann 1995.

Christ is it taken away. Yes, to this day whenever Moses is read a veil
lies over their hearts.
(2 Cor. 3:14–15)

As their worship of the golden calf at the foot of Mount Sinai while Moses
received the law atop the mountain showed, the Israelites were an idolatrous and 'stiff-necked people' (Exod. 34:9).

Moreover, 'Paul implies that any who fail to see God's glory manifest
in his own ministry of the Spirit are in the same hardened condition as
Israel of old', as Garland says.[33] By 'reading the old covenant' and 'Moses
being read' Paul refers to the reading of the Law and the Prophets in the
synagogue. Paul as an unbelieving Jew and later as a Christian preacher
had first-hand knowledge of people's being 'hardened by the deceitfulness
of sin' (Heb. 3:13).

The veil lies not over the Old Testament but over unbelievers' hearts,
including those of unbelieving Jews. Paul tells of the veil being lifted:
'[O]nly through Christ is it taken away' (2 Cor. 3:14). He knows this first-
hand too, for the glorified Christ appeared to him with a light from heaven
on the Damascus road and answered his question 'Who are you, Lord?'
with these words: 'I am Jesus, whom you are persecuting' (Acts 9:5). It seems
likely, based on 2 Corinthians 4:1–6, that Paul addresses Jewish criticism
of his ministry to the effect that if Paul's preaching was the fulfilment of
Old Testament new covenant prophecies, why did more Jews not believe?[34]
Those who failed to respond demonstrate the truth of Paul's words:

> even if our gospel is veiled, it is veiled only to those who are perish-
> ing. In their case the god of this world has blinded the minds of the
> unbelievers, to keep them from seeing the light of the gospel of
> the glory of Christ, who is the image of God.
> (2 Cor. 4:3–4)

In 2 Corinthians 3:16 Paul speaks of salvation: 'But when one turns to
the Lord, the veil is removed.' The apostle has stated frankly the condition
of his fellow Jews without Christ: they are heading for 'death' (v. 7) and
'condemnation' (v. 9), which he describes elsewhere as 'wrath and fury'

---

[33] Garland 1999: 191.
[34] Harris 2005: 301.

(Rom. 2:8) and 'the punishment of eternal destruction' (2 Thess. 1:9). But Paul is not disheartened and will not give up on his 'own people', his 'kinsmen according to the flesh' (Rom. 9:3), for his 'heart's desire and prayer to God for them is that they may be saved' (10:1).

For that to happen they must turn to the Lord (2 Cor. 3:16). Garland is instructive: 'In the Old and New Testaments the verb "turn" can refer to conversion (see Deut 4:30; 30:2, 9–10; 2 Chr 30:9; Isa 6:9; Hos 6:1; see also *Tob* 13:6; Acts 9:35; 11:2; 15:19; 26:20).'[35] Israelites must turn from their sins 'to the *Lord*' to see God's glory and be saved. Scholars disagree as to the meaning of 'Lord'; some think it refers to the Father and others to the Son.[36] We agree with those who conclude that in context 'Lord' refers to Jesus.[37] Paul understands turning to Christ as believing the gospel, which 'is the power of God for salvation to everyone who believes, to the Jew first and also to the Greek' (Rom. 1:16).

Verse 16 serves as a bridge between the previous verses in chapter 3 and verse 17: 'Now the Lord is the Spirit, and where the Spirit of the Lord is, there is freedom.'[38] Scholars likewise debate the identity of the 'Lord' of verse 17, some favouring Yahweh from Exodus 34 and others Christ from the context of 2 Corinthians 3.[39] It seems clear that Paul is not making an absolute identity between 'the Spirit' and 'the Lord', for he distinguishes the two in verse 17 when he speaks of 'the Spirit of the Lord'.

What does Paul mean by 'Now the Lord is the Spirit'? Correlating a parallel text in 1 Corinthians 15:45, 'the last Adam became a life-giving spirit', Gaffin answers this question persuasively:

> The equation or unity expressed in both [texts] is not ontological but economic or functional. By his exaltation the incarnate Christ and the Spirit are one; in 2 Corinthians 3:17 they are one in granting eschatological freedom, and the Lord-Christ is now the eschatological glory-image (v. 18, cf. 'the image of the man of heaven,'

---

[35] Garland 1999: 194.

[36] Garland (1999: 195) is an example of the former and Barnett (1997: 198) the latter.

[37] E.g. Barnett 1997: 196. Another way that Scripture speaks of this 'unveiling' is 'in Luke 24:45, 46, where the disciples' "minds" are opened (and no longer obtuse) and they can then see the OT as full of messianic prefigurations' (Martin 2014: 69).

[38] As Garland (1999: 196) shows, crediting Belleville (1991: 257–262), v. 17 specifically clarifies v. 16: 'Belleville cogently makes the case that 3:17a, "Now the Lord is the Spirit," explains 3:16a, "But whenever anyone turns to the Lord"; and 3:17b, "and where the Spirit of the Lord is, there is freedom," explains 3:16b, "The veil is taken away."'

[39] For discussion see Harris 2005: 309–312.

invested by the Spirit with resurrection and ascension glory, 1 Cor. 15:49).[40]

Paul now parallels 'freedom' here with 'boldness' from verse 12, for they are closely related. We previously defined 'boldness' as 'openness', and we likewise define 'freedom' from the context. Unlike Moses, new covenant believers are free from the veil and are free to speak openly as they proclaim the gospel. Garland is convincing: 'The greater glory of Paul's ministry does not require an even thicker veil to protect the people but no veil at all because the Spirit radically changes the disposition of the people's heart.'[41]

Because the new covenant is the covenant of 'the Spirit of the living God' (v. 3), 'the Spirit' who 'gives life' (v. 7), and because new covenant ministry is the glorious 'ministry of the Spirit' (v. 8), its ministers are characterized by the Spirit's openness (v. 12). Because 'the last Adam', the risen, glorious Christ, 'became a life-giving spirit' (1 Cor. 15:45) and he, 'the Lord' who 'is the Spirit' (2 Cor. 3:17), is alive with heavenly glory, he gives freedom to his people (v. 17), enables them to behold his gospel glory and will transform them fully when he comes again (v. 18).

Paul draws a powerful conclusion in verse 18 as he comments on Exodus 34:35. Although vocabulary counts are not always a reliable guide to exegesis, they sometimes point in a promising direction. This is the case for 2 Corinthians 3:7–18, which, with thirteen instances, has the highest concentration of 'glory' words of any passage in Paul's letters. Garland is accurate: 'Glory . . . is the key theme of this unit' (2 Cor. 3:7–18).[42] Verse 18 has three uses of 'glory' ('from one degree of glory to another' [ESV] is literally 'from glory to glory'), and it also recapitulates some of the themes of the preceding verses: 'unveiled', 'face', 'the Lord' and 'the Spirit', as it rounds out the passage.

Paul begins with 'we all', in contrast to Old Testament saints and Moses. Only Moses 'went in before the LORD' (Exod. 34:34), but all believers in Christ have access to God's presence. The ancient Israelites gazed at Moses' radiant faith only at intervals; we always see God's glory in Christ as presented in the gospel. Believers in Christ have greater

---

[40] Gaffin 2010: 145.
[41] Garland 1999: 198.
[42] Ibid. 167–168.

privileges than Moses, the mediator of the old covenant, for he wore a veil, but we do not.

'[W]e all, with unveiled face, beholding the glory of the Lord'. Scholars have debated the meaning of the verb rendered 'beholding' in the ESV. Harris summarizes the debate and concludes, 'The real options are: "reflect like a mirror/as in a mirror" or "behold/see as in a mirror." This latter alternative is to be preferred.'[43] The ESV, NIV, NASB, NRSVA and we agree. Where do new covenant believers see God's glory? Paul directs us: 'the light of the knowledge of the glory of God' is to be found 'in the face of Jesus Christ' (2 Cor. 4:6).

Specifically, believers see God's glory in 'the gospel of the glory of Christ, who is the image of God' (2 Cor. 4:4). God made Adam and Eve in his image, and in the fall the image was defaced but not obliterated. The image is progressively restored for all who believe in Christ, the true image of God. The image of God in us will be perfected on the last day, when Christ returns to raise the righteous dead, and only then, '[j]ust as we have borne the image of the man of dust [Adam], we shall also bear the image of the man of heaven [Christ]' (1 Cor. 15:49). Harris connects God's glory, the image, the gospel and Christ:

'The glory of the Lord' is God's glory as it is revealed in his image . . . The vision of God's glory accorded Christians is indirect, for it is mediated through the gospel, but it is clear, for the Christ who is proclaimed through the gospel is the exact representation (εἰκών) of God (2 Cor. 4:4).[44]

Paul says that believers in Christ 'are being transformed into the same image from one degree of glory to another', or, more literally, 'from glory to glory'. But either translation seems problematic, for whose Christian life can be described in this manner? Scholars have offered various solutions to the problem. Seifrid, writing from a Lutheran perspective, insists that Paul's words

are not to be understood as signifying linear progress of some sort, as if Paul spoke of movement from one degree of glory to another . . .

---

[43] Harris 2005: 314.
[44] Ibid. 315.

It is not a moral quality within them but God's favor and comfort given to those in need and distress, including the distress of their sin and rebellion.[45]

In other words, 'from glory to glory' speaks of justification, not progressive sanctification. Barnett, Garland, Harris and Martin all reach the opposite conclusion.[46]

We agree with them and the ESV, NIV, NASB and NRSVA. This admittedly is a challenging description of the Christian life, and the key to at least a partial understanding lies in grasping who produces such glory. Plainly, from both the context and verse 18, the Spirit is the change agent working in believers. The Spirit is prominent in the context, appearing six times in verses 3, 6, 8 and 17. And verse 18 plainly states who effects the transformation of believers in glory: 'For this comes from the Lord who is the Spirit.' This refers to Christ, functionally identified with the Holy Spirit, as we said above. Harris captures verse 18 in its context: the Spirit brings the new era and along with it liberation, spiritual knowledge and openness and transformation. Consequently,

> Christians, with unveiled faces, see in the mirror of the gospel the glory of Yahweh, which is Christ. Again, the glory is displayed not outwardly on the face but inwardly in the character . . . the glory experienced under the new covenant progressively increases until the Christian finally acquires a 'glorious body' like that of the risen Christ.[47]

The gospel of the glory of Christ (2 Cor. 4:1–6)

Paul links this passage with the preceding: 'Therefore, having this ministry by the mercy of God, we do not lose heart' (v. 1). 'This ministry' recalls 'the ministry of the Spirit' (3:8), 'the ministry of righteousness' (3:9), that is, the ministry of the new covenant. Paul gladly acknowledges that he is an apostle of the new covenant by God's mercy. Paul did not earn this

---

[45] Seifrid 2014: 183.
[46] Barnett 1997: 207–208; Garland 1999: 200–201; Harris 2005: 316; and Martin 2014: 72.
[47] Harris 2005: 318–319.

privilege: God gave it to him, a former persecutor, as a gift (1 Tim. 1:12–13). Moreover, because of God's gifts of mercy and ministry, Paul does not 'lose heart': he does not allow discouragement to overwhelm him. Instead, he is 'very bold' (2 Cor. 3:12) and determined to press on in gospel ministry despite opposition or disappointment.

Paul disallows behaviour incompatible with new covenant ministry. 'But we have renounced disgraceful, underhanded ways. We refuse to practise cunning or to tamper with God's word, but by the open statement of the truth we would commend ourselves to everyone's conscience in the sight of God' (4:2). Paul repudiates shameful and devious ways, craftiness and corrupting of the gospel. He presents Scripture openly to appeal to his hearers' consciences. Furthermore, Paul ministers 'in the sight of God' (4:2), that is, before God, in God's presence.

Satan blinds people to gospel glory (2 Cor. 4:3–4)

Next Paul faces the fact that some, especially Jews, refuse his message. We can imagine the criticism: Paul, if your gospel is so clear and powerful, why do more people not believe it? Paul responds with boldness (3:12) and freedom (3:17): '[E]ven if our gospel is veiled, it is veiled only to those who are perishing' (4:3). This is not a matter of communication strategies, but concerns the nature of the gospel: 'The Messiah whom God sent to save Israel was not a figure of glory who deposed Israel's pagan oppressors.'[48] Instead, he was crucified.

Are those who reject the gospel accountable to God? Of course they are (Rom. 3:19). Is that the whole story? No, as Paul explains: 'In their case the god of this world has blinded the minds of the unbelievers, to keep them from seeing the light of the gospel of the glory of Christ, who is the image of God' (2 Cor. 4:4). 'The god of this world' is Satan, who prevents the unsaved from believing in Christ. Satan does this specifically by blinding unbelievers' minds to 'the truth and the attractiveness of the gospel'.[49] This blinding pertains to unbelieving Jews, whose 'minds' are 'hardened' (2 Cor. 3:14) and veiled (v. 15). But Barnett is correct: 'Such blindness is not merely the historic incapacity of the people of Israel under the old covenant (3:13–15). The darkness is universal, demonic and cosmic.'[50]

---

[48] Garland 1999: 208–209.
[49] Harris 2005: 328.
[50] Barnett 1997: 220.

Satan is more powerful and intelligent than human beings. But the devil, a creature, is a fallen angel and acts only with the permission of the all-powerful, all-knowing God. Although Satan keeps unbelievers from trusting Christ, the Creator effectually illumines them, defeating Satan (v. 6).

Christ as the glory and image of God (2 Cor. 4:4–6)

In 2 Corinthians 4:1–6 Paul continues the use of images from the previous chapter, which included 'gaze' (3:13), 'veil' (3:14, 15, 16), 'unveiled' (3:18), 'beholding' (3:18) and predominately 'glory' (thirteen times). He adds to them 'veiled' (2× in 4:3), 'blinded', 'seeing', 'image' (4:4), 'light' (4:4, and 2× in v. 6), 'shine' and 'shone' (4:6), while repeating 'glory' two more times (4:4, 6). This time, however, Paul connects 'glory' with Jesus. The gospel concerns 'the glory of Christ, who is the image of God' (v. 4), and salvation brings 'the knowledge of the glory of God in the face of Jesus Christ' (v. 6).

Second Corinthians 4:4, 6 aid our study of the glory of God in Paul, for in these verses he joins the gospel, Christ's glory and Christ as the image of God. The devil works to keep out 'the light', the revelation of the gospel. But God is more powerful than he, and God makes the gospel effective to salvation. Paul heralds 'the gospel of the glory of Christ'.

The exalted Christ radiates his glory when the gospel is preached. His glory is revealed in the history of salvation. The eternal Son shared heavenly glory with the Father and the Holy Spirit before creation (John 17:5). In the incarnation the outward manifestation of his divine glory was veiled. Nevertheless, his disciples beheld 'his glory, glory as of the only Son from the Father, full of grace and truth' (1:14), especially in his miracles (2:11; 11:40–44). His glory was briefly unveiled in his transfiguration when 'his face shone like the sun, and his clothes became white as light' (Matt. 17:2). Ironically, though evil rulers 'crucified the Lord of glory' (1 Cor. 2:8), his glory was revealed in the despised cross (John 12:23–24; 13:31–32). The splendour of the 'Lord Jesus Christ, the Lord of glory' (Jas 2:1), was broadcast in his triumphant resurrection (Acts 3:13; Phil. 2:9; Heb. 2:9; 1 Peter 1:21), ascension (1 Tim. 3:16) and session at God's right hand (John 17:5; Heb. 8:1–2). Christ's glory will be fully revealed only at 'the appearing of the glory of our great God and Saviour Jesus Christ' (Titus 2:13; Matt. 25:46; 1 Peter 4:13).

When Paul speaks of 'seeing the light of the gospel of the glory of Christ', he means that the gospel's content is the glorious Christ himself. After 'the glory of Christ' Paul adds 'who is the image of God' (2 Cor. 4:4). Having briefly traced the image of God in the Bible's storyline previously, here we interpret Christ as the image in the context of gospel preaching. Christ reveals the merciful and loving God, who sends his Son to rescue sinners.[51]

'For what we proclaim is not ourselves, but Jesus Christ as Lord, with ourselves as your servants for Jesus' sake' (2 Cor. 4:5). We noted the prevalence of visual imagery in 2 Corinthians 4:2–6. Here Paul shifts to aural imagery because he speaks of preaching. This is necessary, for 'faith comes from hearing, and hearing through the word of Christ' (Rom. 10:17). The content of Paul's message is not himself but Christ's lordship, which implies that the crucified Jesus (1 Cor. 2:21) is identical to the risen Lord (15:3–4). In fact, 'Jesus is Lord' is the primitive confession of faith (Rom. 10:9; 1 Cor. 12:3). 'This is the only place where [Paul] speaks of himself and his fellow workers as the "slaves" of other believers.'[52] His qualification 'for Jesus' sake' shows that his loyalty lies first with Christ, his Lord and Saviour, and because of that with those he serves. At the same time, Christ is Paul's great example of humble service (Mark 10:45; John 13:14–15).

If Satan, who is stronger than humans, blinds their minds so they do not believe the gospel, how can anyone be saved? Paul replies, 'For God, who said, "Let light shine out of darkness", has shone in our hearts to give the light of the knowledge of the glory of God in the face of Jesus Christ' (2 Cor. 4:6). Jesus, answering the charge that he cast out demons by the power of Satan, their prince, taught, 'How can someone enter a strong man's house and plunder his goods, unless he first binds the strong man? Then indeed he may plunder his house' (Matt. 12:29). God is stronger than Satan, and God frees sinners from Satan's power and saves them.

Paul returns to his light metaphor and teaches that the Creator of light (Gen. 1:3) shines in hearts to free them from satanic blindness to the gospel. Specifically, he shines in hearts with the light of salvation. Once more we are reminded of Christ's saving illumination of Paul on the Damascus road. Outwardly, Christ shone blinding light on Paul to halt

---

[51] Garland 1999: 212–213.
[52] Harris 2005: 333.

his persecution of Christians. Inwardly, God flooded Paul's heart with divine light to dispel his darkness (2 Cor. 4:6). Barnett, quoting Margaret Thrall, connects God's illumination of Paul and God's illumination of lost persons through Paul's preaching the gospel:

> Whereas God's outward revelation of his glory to Paul was unique, his inner enlightenment of the heart also describes the illumination of all who receive the gospel message (cf. 'see the light of the gospel' – v. 4). The gospel is now 'the fundamental re-presentative agency for the splendor of God'; God's glory is present in the proclamation.[53]

Suffering, thanksgiving and the glory of God (2 Cor. 4:7–18)

Suffering and God's glory (2 Cor. 4:7–12)

Paul has defended his new covenant ministry from 2:14 to 4:6. He told of the superiority of its glory compared to that of the old covenant (3:7–18). He declared that the gospel that new covenant ministers preach gleams with Christ's glory (4:1–6). Now, diverging from the previous emphasis on glory, Paul dwells on trials, suffering and death. Barnett notes that Paul addresses a problem: 'How could such glory be mediated by so inglorious an instrument, the suffering Paul?'[54] Anticipating such a question, Paul confesses the frailty and weakness of his body to glorify God's power (v. 7). Paul's hardships do not discredit his apostleship but highlight God's power working through him.[55]

The key to verses 8–11 is union with Christ. In four statements in verses 8–9 Paul shows how Christ's servants 'die and rise' with him daily. The first half of each statement tells of identification with Christ in his humiliation; the second half of each tells of identification with Christ in his exaltation: 'We are afflicted in every way, but not crushed; perplexed, but not driven to despair; persecuted, but not forsaken; struck down, but not destroyed.' Paul's life and ministry reflect union with Christ in his humiliating death and powerful resurrection:

---

[53] Barnett 1997: 224; quoting Thrall 1994: 319.
[54] Barnett 1997: 227.
[55] So Garland (1999: 219).

always carrying in the body the death of Jesus, so that the life of Jesus may also be manifested in our bodies. For we who live are always being given over to death for Jesus' sake, so that the life of Jesus also may be manifested in our mortal flesh.
(vv. 10–11)

All this is the work of God, whose 'power is made perfect in weakness' (2 Cor. 12:9), and is for the sake of those to whom Paul ministers, including the Corinthians: 'So death is at work in us, but life in you' (4:12).

Barnett captures Paul's point:

> Unpalatable as it may have been in Corinth, the truth was that God was leading his minister from place to place in humiliating suffering, replicating Golgotha wherever he went (2:14–15a). The message of Christ crucified, which brought them life, was, and must be (cf. 4:5), borne by one whose own existence was cruciform. Because the glory is God's glory, the bearer must be dependent on God, which, indeed, Paul's missionary sufferings caused him to be.[56]

Evangelism and God's glory (2 Cor. 4:13–18)

In 4:13–18 Paul tells why he keeps preaching despite much suffering: to reach others with the gospel so they will give thanks to God and thereby promote his glory. Paul connects his actions with those of the psalmist. When Paul says, 'I believed, and so I spoke', quoting Psalm 115:1 in the LXX (cf. NIV; Ps. 116:10, MT), he identifies with the psalmist's overcoming faith. The psalmist did not shrink back when suffering 'distress and anguish' (Ps. 116:3) but trusted the Lord, who heard his cry and delivered him (vv. 6–9). Similarly, Paul writes, '[W]e also believe, and so we also speak' (2 Cor. 4:13).

What undergirds Paul's ministry and hope? The answer, as we saw in 1 Corinthians 15, is his belief in Christ's resurrection as the basis for the resurrection of believers, including himself. Paul believes that the Father raised his Son from the dead and therefore Paul speaks the gospel. For he knows that 'he who raised the Lord Jesus will raise us also with Jesus and bring us with you into his presence' (2 Cor. 4:14). The end for which Paul

---

[56] Barnett 1997: 227.

strives is enjoyment of God's presence for ever with all the resurrected saints on the new earth.

The end just mentioned has an even greater end. Paul anticipates resurrection and God's eternal presence as the means to the supreme end – the glory of God. In verse 12 Paul said, 'So death is at work in us, but life in you.' Now he adds, 'For it is all for your sake' (v. 15). In union with Christ Paul travels, serves, preaches and suffers for the sake of his hearers, including the church at Corinth. As he previously said, he preaches Christ, not himself, and ministers as the Corinthians' servant 'for Jesus' sake' (v. 5).

Paul has many goals: personal holiness, faithfulness in ministry, successful church planting and more. But his utmost goal is to bring glory to God. God uses the fact that 'we have this treasure in jars of clay', perishable bodies (v. 7), in two ways: to accentuate the gospel's power and to ensure that God, not humans, receives the glory.[57] Paul envisions grace cascading and producing gratitude for God's glory: Paul endures and preaches 'so that as grace extends to more and more people it may increase thanksgiving, to the glory of God' (v. 15).

Barnett's analysis of the complex relationship between Paul's purpose, means and goal in ministry is accurate:

> He sets out the complex relationship between (1) his *purpose* in giving himself for them ('in order that increasing grace may overflow [to you]'), (2) the *means* by which that grace becomes a reality ('through the thanksgiving of more people'), and (3) the *goal* of that overflowing grace ('to the glory of God') . . . Paul longed that men and women who 'neither glorified [God] as God nor gave thanks to him' (Rom 1:21) would, in ever-growing numbers, 'turn to the Lord [Jesus Christ]' (3:16) and express thankfulness to God, and so glorify him. The glorification of God is the apostolic aim, but it is also the privilege and duty of every believer.[58]

Paul desires the multiplication of God's saving grace to turn up the volume of gratitude to God, which in turn increases his glory.

Paul, as an apostle, speaking for all new covenant believers, draws a conclusion and repeats the thought of 4:1: 'So we do not lose heart' (v. 16).

---

[57] Harris 2005: 338.
[58] Barnett 1997: 244–245; emphases original.

Because Jesus lives and God keeps bringing more people into his kingdom with gratitude that redounds to his glory, Paul is strengthened. He continues, 'Though our outer self is wasting away, our inner self is being renewed day by day' (v. 16). By 'outer' and 'inner self' (lit. 'man') Paul is not distinguishing material and immaterial parts of the human (body and soul). Rather, as Thrall explains, Paul describes the outer as the whole person 'as seen by others from without' and the inner person as 'one's unseen personality, visible only to God and (in part) to oneself'.[59] The 'inner self' is part of God's new creation, for believers now have eternal life in mortal bodies and long for the day when they will have eternal life in immortal bodies.

Outwardly believers are declining due to adversities, but inwardly God's Spirit progressively renews them. Paul contrasts this life's passing hardships with the next life's eternal splendour: 'For this light momentary affliction is preparing for us an eternal weight of glory beyond all comparison' (v. 17). Paul provides an eternal perspective on painful and at times unbearable sufferings that believers endure at present. When viewed against the backdrop of eternity, present sufferings are short in duration and, ultimately, insignificant. Moreover, as we endure, we must keep in mind that God uses our present troubles to produce future unimaginable glory for us.

Paul's readers reveal their lack of eternal perspective when they criticize his sufferings. They are blind to the glory in his ministry because they have been seduced by their culture's concept of glory. People who had honour were the elite who callously squashed those who challenged them. The Corinthian believers must not follow this warped system of values. If they succumb, as Garland asserts, 'they will miss the authentic glory and honor that reside less conspicuously in the hearts of those who have been beaten down by a malevolent world but who will be raised up by God'.[60]

Paul not only contrasts 'light momentary affliction' and a future 'eternal weight of glory' but teaches that God uses the former to prepare the latter for his people. God is not defeated by the suffering of his saints. Rather, he uses it for his own glory, as shown above all in the cross of his Son.

---

[59] Thrall 1994: 349–350, cited by Garland (1999: 240).
[60] Garland 1999: 244.

It is difficult to translate the words indicating the greatness of the glory that awaits God's children, as Harris explains:

> The repetition of ὑπερβολή in the remarkable expression καθ' ὑπερβολὴν εἰς ὑπερβολήν could merely point to intensification, 'beyond all measure' (NRSV), 'out of all proportion' (Martin 82), but it is preferable to represent clearly both emphatic elements, καθ' ὑπερβολήν, 'beyond measure,' 'utterly,' and εἰς ὑπερβολήν, 'to excess,' by renderings such as 'beyond all measure and proportion' (BAGD 840c), 'beyond all comparison and estimate' (Isaacs), 'to a degree immeasurable, to a degree exceeding all bounds' (Cassirer), 'to an utterly extraordinary degree' (Thrall 347).[61]

Truly God has promised to bless his people with incalculable glory! But we benefit now from his promise only 'as we look not to the things that are seen but to the things that are unseen. For the things that are seen are transient, but the things that are unseen are eternal' (v. 18). Faith pertains to the past, present and future. Faith looks to God's past acts, especially the death and resurrection of Christ (1 Cor. 15:1–4). Faith looks to the present, 'for we walk by faith, not by sight' (2 Cor. 5:7). And here faith looks to future invisible realities, even unseen eternal ones (2 Cor. 4:18).

---

61 Harris 2005: 338.

6
The glory of God and the church: Ephesians

Harold Hoehner has called the teaching of Ephesians 'the crown or quintessence of Paulinism because in large measure it summarizes the leading themes of the Pauline letters'.[1] Hoehner's good summary of that teaching includes the Trinity, the fatherhood of God, Christology, pneumatology, soteriology, ecclesiology and reconciliation. An important and often neglected theme that criss-crosses many of these themes is the glory of God, which we will explore under the following heads:

- God's glory and his ultimate goal
- God's glory and his eternal plan
- God's glory and Christ's saving work
- God's glory and union with Christ
- God's glory and the church as his showcase

God's glory and his ultimate goal

Redemption and God's glory (Eph. 1:3–14)

Ephesians encompasses an immense scope, ranging from 'before the foundation of the world' (1:4) to 'for ever and ever' (3:21). This grand perspective is fitting for the eternal God, who makes far-reaching plans. God's plans have many goals or ends, but his supreme goal is the display and recognition of his own glory.

Paul shows this in the epistle's opening long sentence (1:3–14), which begins with praise to God: 'Blessed be the God and Father of our Lord

---

[1] Hoehner 2002: 106.

Jesus Christ, who has blessed us in Christ with every spiritual blessing in the heavenly places' (1:3). God's ultimate and greatest goal is his own glory. Paul continues with praise to God by issuing a similar refrain three times to close three sections:

> In love he predestined us for adoption . . . to the praise of his glorious grace.
> (1:4–6)

> In him we have obtained an inheritance . . . so that we who were the first to hope in Christ might be to the praise of his glory.
> (1:11–12)

> In him you also . . . were sealed with the promised Holy Spirit . . . to the praise of his glory.
> (1:13–14)

These three sections correspond to the three trinitarian persons and their roles. The Father lovingly chooses people for adoption (1:5), the Son redeems them with his blood (v. 7) and the Spirit is God's seal, guaranteeing their salvation (vv. 13–14). Paul's main point is that this trinitarian work of salvation redounds to the glory of God. It is true that one goal of salvation is to make worshippers out of those who previously had 'no hope and [were] without God in the world' (2:12). Nevertheless, as great as God's redemption of his people is in all its complexity and wonder, it is not his greatest goal. That is his own glory, as Stott expresses so well:

> He writes that God destined us to be his children *to the praise of his glorious grace* (5–6); that he made us his heritage and appointed us to live *for the praise of his glory* (verse 12); and that one day he will finally redeem his people who are his possession, *to the praise of his glory* (verse 14) . . . Everything we have and are in Christ both comes from God and returns to God. It begins in his will and ends in his glory. For this is where everything begins and ends.[2]

---

2 Stott 1979: 49–50; emphases original.

Contemplating God's glory raises a question: If God seeks his own glory, does that make him selfish, as it would for humans who sought their own glory? A common answer is that it is not selfish for the supreme being to seek the highest end, which is his glory. This is a good answer, but there is another one, often unnoticed. Linking God's love and glory is instructive:

> God saves us out of his love, displays his kindness toward us for all eternity, and is glorified by putting his greatness, goodness, and fullness on display. God is self-giving and self-exalting, saving us for our good and for his glory. He gives himself to us and acts on our behalf, which simultaneously meets our needs and demonstrates his sufficiency.[3]

Sin, grace and God's glory (Eph. 2:1–10)

Ephesians 2:1–10 is Paul's great text explicating our need for salvation and God's gracious provision of the same. The apostle's portrayal of our plight as sinners is very stark. Before Christ we were spiritually dead (vv. 1, 5), captured by the world system opposed to God (v. 2), unwittingly obeying the evil one (v. 2) and enslaved to 'the passions of our flesh' (v. 3). We were enslaved to the flesh, the world and the devil and 'were by nature children of wrath, like the rest of mankind' (v. 3). When we were trapped in this situation, God showed rich 'mercy' (v. 4), 'great love' (v. 4), 'grace' (vv. 5, 7, 8) and 'kindness towards us in Christ Jesus' (v. 7), who loved us and gave himself for us. Because of his grace God united us to his Son in his death, resurrection, ascension and even his session at God's right hand (vv. 4–6)!

The text illustrates the essence of grace: '[E]ven when we were dead in our trespasses, [God] made us alive together with Christ – by grace you have been saved' (v. 5). Grace is not merely God's undeserved favour; it is his giving eternal life against merit and ability.

Once again, God has multiple goals or ends in mind. He delivers lost persons by making them come alive to him (v. 5) and lead productive lives in 'good works' prepared for them (v. 10). But God has an even loftier goal: he gives saving grace to the lost 'so that in the coming ages he might show the immeasurable riches of his grace in kindness towards us in Christ

---

[3] Morgan 2013: 217.

Jesus' (v. 7). Arnold is succinct: 'God's ultimate purpose in saving a people for himself was to display his grace for all to see forever and ever.'[4]

What will God display for ever in his redeemed people? 'The immeasurable riches of his grace' (v. 7). Paul is the only New Testament author who uses the word 'immeasurable' (the participle *hyperballon*). Hoehner sums up its three uses in Ephesians: the term

> can be translated 'surpassing, extraordinary, exceeding.' In 1:19 it is used of the surpassing greatness of God's power in us, in 3:19 it speaks of the surpassing greatness of Christ's love, and here it speaks of the surpassing greatness of God's grace.[5]

In eternity the church will be a trophy of God's grace. According to Baugh it was common in pagan antiquity to dedicate trophies from victorious battles to the gods. Their temples displayed the spoils of triumphs. In verse 7 Paul says that God's people will be the trophies of battle on exhibition 'in the ages to come'.[6]

The mystery and God's glory (Eph. 3:8–10)

Paul, in prison in Rome, writes of the revelation of the gospel God gave him as the apostle to the Gentiles. Central to this revelation is the concept of mystery. Paul mentions it in Ephesians 3:3, 4, 6 and 9.

Beale and Gladd write, 'We will define mystery generally as *the revelation of God's partially hidden wisdom, particularly as it concerns events occurring in the "latter days."*'[7] Later they expand that definition:

> The majority of occurrences of mystery in the New Testament pertain to Christ in some form or another . . . In addition . . . these salient concepts roughly fall into two categories – the arrival of the end-time kingdom and the unity between Jews and Gentiles.[8]

Ephesians mentions the concept of mystery in four passages. First, Ephesians 1:9–10 speaks of Christ's cosmic rule. Second, Ephesians 3:4

---

[4] Arnold 2010: 137.
[5] Hoehner 2002: 338.
[6] Baugh 2015: 157.
[7] Beale and Gladd 2014: 20; emphasis original.
[8] Ibid. 321–322.

speaks of 'the mystery of Christ' and the incorporation of the Gentiles into the church. Third, Ephesians 5:31–32 speaks of the marriage relationship and the church.[9] Fourth, in Ephesians 6:19–20 Paul asks for prayer that he might boldly proclaim 'the mystery of the gospel'.

We focus on the mystery in Ephesians 3 and God's glory. Paul teaches that this mystery was 'hidden for ages in God' (v. 9), was 'not made known to the sons of men in other generations' but is now revealed by the Holy Spirit to God's 'holy apostles and prophets' (v. 5). This includes Paul, whom God taught this mystery 'by revelation' (v. 3). Its content is 'the mystery of Christ' (v. 4). More specifically, 'This mystery is that the Gentiles are fellow heirs, members of the same body, and partakers of the promise in Christ Jesus through the gospel' (v. 6).

The key to all of this is Christ, as Lincoln indicates: 'Christ himself constitutes the content of the riches of the gospel, and the wealth of the salvation to be found in him is unfathomable.'[10] Isaiah prophesied about the servant of the Lord, who is sometimes Israel and sometimes an individual representing Israel. Isaiah foretold that he would 'bring forth justice to the nations' (Isa. 42:1) and 'sprinkle [sanctify] many nations' (52:15). God said of him:

> It is too light a thing that you should be my servant . . .
>   to bring back the preserved of Israel;
> I will make you as a light for the nations,
>   that my salvation may reach to the end of the earth.
> (49:6)

Thus the Old Testament implied in general terms what Paul explains in detail: Gentiles would gain the inheritance promised to Israel (cf. Eph. 2:11–13) and become members of the church (3:6). Many Gentiles by faith would become 'partakers of the promise in Christ Jesus through the gospel' (v. 6). But when we point to these Old Testament prophecies, this raises a complication, for Paul's mystery was not plainly revealed in the Old Testament but was 'hidden for ages' (v. 9) and 'not made known' as it has 'now been revealed' in the gospel (v. 5).

---

[9] For detailed theological exegesis of Eph. 1:9–10, 3:1–13, 5:31–32 and 6:18–20 see ibid. 148–159, 159–173, 173–183 and 183–186, respectively.
[10] Lincoln 1990: 183.

Scholars hold various views concerning the specific identity of the mystery in Ephesians 3:1–13. Hoehner holds that the mystery was the New Testament reality of believing Jews and Gentiles becoming one as they became members of Christ's church. Beale and Gladd respectfully disagree: 'Christ's identity as true Israel is the key to the mystery: Gentiles identify with him, not Israel's law, to become true Israelites.'[11] We do not have to choose between these two views. Regardless of either view, Paul writes that God gave him grace 'to preach to the Gentiles the unsearchable riches of Christ and to bring to light for everyone what is the plan of the mystery hidden for ages in God', the Creator (Eph. 3:8–9). Paul has multiple purposes in preaching, but chiefly preaches the gospel, including the mystery of God's including the Gentiles among his people, 'so that through the church the manifold wisdom of God might now be made known to the rulers and authorities in the heavenly places' (Eph. 3:10). Bruce is concise: 'This new, comprehensive community is to serve throughout the universe as an object-lesson of the wisdom of God – his "much-variegated" wisdom.'[12]

Although scholars agree that the angel audience includes evil angels, they disagree as to whether good angels are also included.[13] Bruce thinks they are,[14] but Arnold disagrees.[15] Perhaps all angels are included, but, regardless, Paul's main point is clear: the mystery of Christ's church as composed of Jews and Gentiles reveals to the universe the 'beautifully complex'[16] wisdom of God, revealing his glory.

God glorifies himself by creating from Jews and Gentiles 'one new man in place of the two' (Eph. 2:15). Moreover, he continually proclaims his wisdom and glory to the universe by revealing the mystery of his plan to incorporate Gentiles into God's people. Therefore, Paul exclaims, 'to him be glory in the church and in Christ Jesus throughout all generations, for ever and ever. Amen' (3:21).

---

[11] Beale and Gladd 2014: 166.
[12] Bruce 1984: 320.
[13] We reject Walter Wink's view that the church preaches the mystery to the powers (1984: 9–96).
[14] Bruce 1984: 216.
[15] Arnold 2010: 197.
[16] Thielman 2010: 216.

God's glory and his eternal plan

The highest of God's goals is his own glory. It is the same for God's eternal plan. In fact, goals and plans are related. They view the same events from different vantage points. Plans view matters from the beginning, while goals (or ends) view them from the end. Whether we consider God's deeds from the beginning (his plans) or from the end (his goals), we arrive at his eternal glory.

Although God's plans exceed those mentioned in Ephesians, the epistle speaks of three, as Morgan summarizes: 'God's eternal plan encompasses our salvation (1:4–6), the creation of the church as one new people (2:11–22; 3:3–12), and the ultimate reconciliation of the cosmos (1:9–11; 3:9–11).'[17] We will treat the first two of these here and cosmic reconciliation later under 'Cosmic union with Christ (Eph. 1:9–10)' (on pp. 160–163).

God's plan to save and his glory (Eph. 1:4–6, 11)

'Blessed be the God and Father of our Lord Jesus Christ, who has blessed us in Christ with every spiritual blessing in the heavenly places' (Eph. 1:3). This is how Paul begins 'the setting in which God grants his people every spiritual blessing – from eternal election to eternal glory'.[18] The long sentence that begins the epistle (vv. 3–14) is replete with praise. It begins with praise to God the Father, then celebrates the 'praise of his glorious grace' (1:6) and then twice acclaims the 'praise of his glory' (1:12, 14). Arnold depicts the main idea: 'Paul has carefully crafted a heartfelt expression of praise to God for his extraordinary plan of salvation, which he sees as a manifestation of his glory and grace.'[19]

Paul lauds all three trinitarian persons. Christ plays a role in the plan of salvation, for his work rescued sinners 'from the domain of darkness and transferred us to the kingdom of his beloved Son' (Col. 1:13). Indeed, Christ is the 'Beloved' (Eph. 1:6), who 'through his blood' set free prisoners of sin so that they enjoy 'the forgiveness of [their] trespasses' (v. 7). All this is 'according to the riches of his grace . . . which he lavished upon us' (vv. 7–8).

---

[17] Morgan 2013: 219.
[18] Bruce 1984: 254.
[19] Arnold 2010: 73.

Paul also extols the Holy Spirit, who is both seal and guarantee of salvation. The Spirit is seal, for 'in him [Christ]' believers are 'sealed with the promised Holy Spirit' (v. 13), whom God pledged to send in the Old Testament and Christ poured out at Pentecost. The Spirit as seal marks off people as God's own and preserves them for final salvation. Paul underscores preservation when he says that the Spirit is the 'guarantee of our inheritance until we acquire possession of it'. Once again, all this is 'to the praise of his glory' (v. 14).

The passage also lauds the Father, the author of salvation:

he chose us in him [Christ] before the foundation of the world.
(v. 4)

he predestined us.
(v. 5)

[We were] predestined according to the purpose of him who works all things according to the counsel of his will.
(v. 11)

Scripture provides several answers to the question of why people are saved. The most immediate answer is because they believed in Christ for salvation (v. 13). A more ultimate answer is that people are saved because Jesus died and arose to save them (v. 7). The most ultimate answer is that people are saved because God chose them for salvation before creation (v. 4) and predestined them for adoption (v. 5) according to his eternal purpose (v. 11).

Paul expresses God's purpose in salvation as clearly in Ephesians 1:11–12 as in any place in Scripture: 'In him we have obtained an inheritance, having been predestined according to the purpose of him who works all things according to the counsel of his will.' Baugh underscores this point: 'Three terms for God's will – πρόθεσις, βουλή (*prothesis, boulē*), and θέλημα (*thelēma*) – are all used here in v. 11 to show that God's own will and that of no other directs his actions.'[20]

Although good Christians differ over the details of election, God's choosing his people before creation underlines his purpose and grace, as

---

[20] Baugh 2015: 93.

2 Timothy 1:8–9 shows. Paul calls Timothy to suffer for the gospel 'by the power of God, who saved us and called us to a holy calling, not because of our works but because of his own purpose and grace, which he gave us in Christ Jesus before the ages began'. The same principle appears in Romans 9:11–13, where Paul shows that, although Jacob and Esau had the same parents, God chose the former and rejected the latter:

> though they were not yet born and had done nothing either good or bad – in order that God's purpose of election might continue, not because of works but because of him who calls – [their mother] was told, 'The older will serve the younger.' As it is written, 'Jacob I loved, but Esau I hated.'

God's choosing Jacob before birth shows his salvation is all of God's purpose and grace. And God's choosing believers before creation does the same thing. It shows that salvation is due to God's 'love' (Eph. 1:4) and 'glorious grace' (v. 6). God's eternal predestination is 'according to the purpose of him who works all things according to the counsel of his will' (v. 11). Arnold is right: 'God's ultimate purpose in selecting and predestining a people for himself is that it would lead to his own glory.'[21]

God's plan to create the church and his glory (Eph. 2:11–22)

God has many purposes, and the highest and ultimate concerns his own glory. The church too has many purposes, but its highest and ultimate is the glory of God, its Redeemer. Lincoln points this out: 'In the final analysis God's working out of his purpose serves his own glorification and the believing community exists to further that end.'[22]

God gets glory by doing the unexpected – uniting believing Jews and Gentiles in 'one new man' (v. 15). Paul's pattern in 2:11–22 resembles that of 2:1–10. After showing sinners' dire need for salvation (vv. 1–3), he portrayed God's provision in Christ (vv. 4–10). Now he presents Gentiles' hopeless situation (vv. 11–12) and then God's incorporating them into the church for his glory (vv. 13–22). There are, however, differences between the two passages. Chief among them is that Ephesians 2:1–10 is primarily

---

[21] Arnold 2010: 84.
[22] Lincoln 1990: 36.

vertical in orientation, whereas 2:11–22 is primarily horizontal.[23] The former deals with humans' relationship to God; the latter primarily with humans' relationship with one another.

Paul shifts from the third person to the second, addressing 'you Gentiles in the flesh' (2:11). Ephesians 2:11–22 sets forth the spiritual disadvantages of Gentiles compared to Jews. Using familiar biblical language, Paul directs Gentiles to 'remember' (v. 11; cf. Exod. 13:3; Deut. 5:15) their status before salvation. Thielman asserts, 'He begins by describing the tension-filled divide that existed between Gentiles and Jews prior to the coming of the gospel: both groups considered circumcision an insuperable barrier between them.'[24] Jews took pride in their circumcision (cf. Paul's boasting in Phil. 3:4–5), but many Romans and Greeks hated circumcision and often ridiculed it.[25] John Stott shows that the deep animosity cut both ways: 'The Jew had an immense contempt for the Gentile. The Gentiles, said the Jews, were created by God to be fuel for the fires of hell.'[26]

'Therefore remember that at one time you Gentiles in the flesh [were] called "the uncircumcision" by what is called the circumcision, which is made in the flesh by hands' (Eph. 2:11). Later Paul will list Gentiles' sins:

> They are darkened in their understanding, alienated from the life of God because of the ignorance that is in them, due to their hardness of heart. They have become callous and have given themselves up to sensuality, greedy to practise every kind of impurity.
> (Eph. 4:18–19)

But now, in addition to circumcision he adds five other religious obstacles that Gentiles had to hurdle: they were 'separated from Christ, alienated from the commonwealth of Israel and strangers to the covenants of promise, having no hope and without God in the world' (2:12).[27]

First, they were 'separated from Christ'. This item is most important, which is why it is first. Before believing in Christ, 'in general, Gentiles

---

[23] Thielman 2010: 148.
[24] Ibid. 159.
[25] Arnold 2010: 153.
[26] Stott 1979: 91, citing Barclay 2002: 123.
[27] Arnold (2010: 154) perceptively notes that 'this passage is the inverse of Rom 9:3–5, which lists all of the blessings and advantages of the Jews'.

knew nothing of the anticipated Messiah nor did they care to learn'.[28] The result was that they did not know the living God and were headed for hell.

Second, they were 'alienated from the commonwealth [*politeia*] of Israel'. This term has been understood as (1) a way of life, (2) the rights of a social group ('citizenship') or (3) a political body ('commonwealth').[29] Thielman combines these and suggests that Paul had in mind the privileges of citizenship and the way of life of a distinct people.[30] The Gentiles knew nothing of this way of life or these privileges.

Third, they were 'strangers to the covenants of promise'. Scholars debate which Old Testament covenants are in view. However, all agree that Paul speaks of at least two: the Abrahamic and the new covenant. These covenants are found only in Israel's Scriptures. In the Abrahamic covenant God promised to bless all nations through his descendant (Gen. 12:3; 22:18). That descendant is Christ (Gal. 3:16), and through him God brought gospel blessings to Gentiles (3:7–9). Christ is the Mediator of the new covenant, which he ratified in his death (Luke 22:20; Heb. 9:15; 12:24). Gentiles 'had no access to Israel's Scriptures and therefore no clear access to the saving purposes of God'.[31]

Fourth, they had 'no hope', for they lacked the Scriptures and God's promises of a Redeemer. Bruce depicts the Gentiles' hopelessness: 'The absence of hope in the face of death is amply attested in the literature and epigraphy of the Graeco-Roman world of that day.'[32]

Fifth, they were 'without God in the world'. This statement is ironic, for two reasons. The Ephesian Gentiles were not atheists but were polytheists with a special devotion to Artemis (Diana), whose temple in Ephesus was one of the seven wonders of the ancient world. Baugh notes that the Ephesians had 'a full panoply of deities . . . alongside the state goddess, Artemis Ephesia', which Paul had observed.[33]

The term *atheos* (without God) is also ironic, since it 'was used with disdain by Gentiles to describe Jews, who refused to worship their gods (Josephus, *Ag. Ap.* 2.148) and in later times was a favorite slander against Christians (Justin, *1 Apol.* 6.1; 13.1; 46.3; Athenagoras, *Leg.* 6.3;

---

28 Ibid.
29 Thielman 2010: 155.
30 Ibid.
31 Ibid. 157.
32 Bruce 1984: 294.
33 Baugh 2015: 186.

Mart. Pol. 3.2)'.[34] How, then, were the Ephesian Gentiles *atheos*? They were not in covenant relationship with him; they did not 'know' God (cf. Gal. 4:8–9) or glorify him.

Having described the Gentiles' terrible plight, Paul says, remarkably, 'But now in Christ Jesus you who once were far off have been brought near by the blood of Christ' (Eph. 2:13). The words 'but now' play a similar role to 'but God' in verse 4: they announce 'the dramatic change in the Gentiles' situation'.[35]

How did God accomplish this? He did so 'in Christ Jesus' and 'by the blood of Christ'. The expression 'in Christ' has played a key role in Ephesians until now (cf. 1:3, 4, 7, 11; 2:7, 10) and does so here as well. Arnold summarizes:

> Paul uses it to speak of being united with Christ in a profound, dynamic relationship that not only extends to a present experience of the risen Christ, but reaches back to an objective participation with him in his death, resurrection, and exaltation (see 2:6).[36]

When Paul speaks of Christ's 'blood', he taps into a common idea in the first-century Roman world, where sacrifices were routine. The 'blood of Christ' refers to Christ's atoning sacrifice of himself on the cross. Paul thus shows Gentiles' deep need and the way in which God has met that need in Christ to move them to give God glory.

Inhabitants of the Roman world benefited from the Pax Romana achieved by Caesar Augustus (Octavian). Results included an end of hostilities, and unrivalled economic growth and prosperity as Arnold notes.[37] Startlingly, although Paul sometimes says that Christ *brought* peace, here he proclaims, '[H]e himself is our peace' (Eph. 2:14).

He 'has made us both one and has broken down in his flesh the dividing wall of hostility' (v. 14). Christ has unified believing Jews and Gentiles by his death, thereby making peace between them, peoples previously at enmity. His crucified body broke down 'the dividing wall of hostility'. What is that wall? Lincoln surveys the two main views:

---

[34] Thielman 2010: 157.
[35] Lincoln 1990: 138.
[36] Arnold 2010: 157.
[37] Ibid. 158.

Some take it as a reference to the temple balustrade separating the Court of Gentiles from the inner courts and the sanctuary in the Jerusalem temple (cf. Josephus, *Ant.* 15.11.5; *J. W.* 5.5.2). In 1871 one of its pillars was found and on it was the warning inscription: 'No man of another race is to enter within the fence and enclosure around the Temple. Whoever is caught will have only himself to thank for the death which follows.' ... If 'having broken down the dividing wall, the fence' is paralleled by 'having abolished . . . the hostility, the law . . . ,' then it seems more likely that the fence is a reference to the law.[38]

Exegetes defend both views. To cite only two, Stott interprets the dividing wall as the wall in the temple, and Thielman as the law.[39] Arnold prudently suggests that if even 'the dividing wall' does not refer directly to the law, there is a connection between the two.[40] Christ has united Jewish and Gentile believers by dying on the cross to break down the 'wall of hostility' that divided them (v. 14). He did this 'by abolishing the law of commandments expressed in ordinances' (v. 15). All agree that 'the law was like a fence that separated the Jewish people from their Gentile neighbors'[41] and that Christ abolished it in some sense, but there agreement ends. Some hold that Paul refers to the entire Mosaic law.[42] Others maintain that Christ abolished the law only in certain aspects. 'Jesus abolished both the regulations of the ceremonial law and the condemnation of the moral law.'[43]

Nevertheless, everyone agrees that the moral law is still relevant. Although Arnold holds that Christ has abolished the law, he urges that Gentiles should retain 'the moral content of the Mosaic code'. This is because its commands reflected God's holy character that he expected to see reflected in their lives.[44]

---

[38] Lincoln 1990: 141.

[39] See Stott 1979: 91–92 for the view that the dividing wall was in the temple. Paul himself was almost killed when he was falsely accused of bringing Trophimus, an Ephesian Gentile, past the temple court of the Gentiles (Acts 21:28–31). See Thielman 2010: 166–167 for the view that the dividing wall was the law.

[40] Arnold 2010: 161.

[41] Ibid. 159.

[42] Thielman 2010: 169.

[43] Stott 1979: 101.

[44] Arnold 2010: 162.

Of course, those like Bruce, who holds that Christ abolished only some aspects of the law, insist that he did not abolish the law as a disclosure of God's holy character. 'The righteousness required by the law of God is realized more fully by the inward enabling of the Spirit – in Jew and Gentile alike – than was possible under the old covenant.'[45]

Christ did an amazing thing: he created 'in himself one new man in place of the two, so making peace' (Eph. 2:15). Paul had employed the theme of a new creation in 2:10: '[W]e are his workmanship, created in Christ Jesus for good works, which God prepared beforehand, that we should walk in them.' There Paul applied the new creation motif to individual believers. Now he applies it to the church, when Christ makes peace between believing Jews and Gentiles. In uniting the two groups to himself, Christ had created 'one new human being . . . and so, like Christ himself, [they] become a new Adam', as Thielman shows.[46]

Jesus Christ is the second Adam (1 Cor. 15:45–47), who via his death and resurrection brings believers from death to life now and from the grave to resurrection later. When the Holy Spirit spiritually unites believers to Christ, he also unites them to one another in one body, the church. In this way the Mediator overcomes the great antipathy between Jews and Gentiles. He makes the two groups into one and in himself constitutes a new race – and thus brings glory to the triune God.

Jesus, 'the Prince of Peace' (Isa. 9:6), by his divine work of recreation makes a new humanity comprising *all* believers. Consequently, we all must heed Baugh, who warns that excluding certain humans who believe in Jesus from full participation in the church contradicts the church's essence as a new creation and dishonours its Lord.[47]

Paul expands his theme: Christ died to 'reconcile us both to God in one body through the cross, thereby killing the hostility' (Eph. 2:16). Jesus, 'our peace', died and arose to reconcile those estranged to God and to one another. Jesus thereby killed 'the hostility'. Christ, our great high priest and reconciler, is also God's great and final prophet (Heb. 1:2), who proclaims the peace that he accomplished. '[H]e came and preached peace to you [Gentiles] who were far off and peace to those who were near' (Eph. 2:17). Paul uses Old Testament language when he speaks of those 'far off'

---

45 Bruce 1984: 298–299.
46 Thielman 2010: 170–171.
47 Baugh 2015: 193.

and those 'near'. God was near to his people Israel: '[W]hat great nation is there that has a god so near to it as the LORD our God is to us . . . ?' (Deut. 4:7; cf. Ps. 148:14).

Originally, Isaiah 57:19 referred to two groups of Israelites, those in the land (the 'near') and those in exile (the 'far'). Thielman captures Paul's artistry: he alludes to Isaiah 52:7a and 57:19 by restructuring Isaiah's words 'so that one occurrence of the word "peace" goes with "far" and another with "near"'.[48] In this way, Paul shows that both Jews and Gentiles have received the message of peace.

When did Jesus, the Reconciler, preach 'peace'? Stott replies that this occurred in Jesus' post-resurrection messages and in the preaching of the gospel throughout the world by the apostles and their heirs.[49]

Paul relates another benefit of Christ's work of recreation: '[T]hrough him we both have access in one Spirit to the Father' (v. 18). The Gentiles, formerly far off from God, now have equal access with Jews to the living and true God. Paul here refers to the Trinity. Through Jesus, the Mediator, Gentiles and Jews can approach God the Father in worship united in the Holy Spirit. Stott exults, 'Thus the highest and fullest achievement of the peacemaking Christ is this trinitarian access of the people of God, as through him and by one Spirit we come boldly to our Father.'[50]

With 'so then' (*ara oun*) Paul concludes the passage (Eph. 2:11–22): 'So then you are no longer strangers and aliens, but you are fellow citizens with the saints and members of the household of God' (v. 19). This contrasts starkly with Paul's description of the Gentiles in verse 12. Baugh defines the first-century terms 'strangers', 'aliens' and 'citizens' as categories Paul's Ephesian readers would have known.

> Strangers (ξένοι, *xenoi*) were foreigners in the city with no guaranteed civil rights or privileges (see Acts 16:20–23) . . . 'Sojourners,' or better, 'resident free aliens' (πάροικοι, *paroikoi*), may have been born in and lived in the city for generations but were not citizens with full access to legal privileges and protections (cf. Heb 11:13;

---

[48] Thielman 2010: 173–174. He quotes Isa. 52:7a, which 'refers to the beauty of "the messenger who announces peace, who brings good news" (NRSV)' (173).

[49] Stott 1979: 103. Later in the epistle Paul speaks of the 'gospel of peace' (Eph. 6:15).

[50] Ibid. 104.

13:14; 1 Pet 2:11). Most of the residents of Ephesus had this resident alien status.[51]

Therefore, when Paul regards his believing Gentile audience (including slaves in Eph. 6:5–6!) as 'fellow citizens with the saints', this expressed a splendid privilege.

God's glory and Christ's saving work

God reveals his glory magnificently in the salvific work of his Son. Five texts in Ephesians variously portray that work:[52]

- Redemption (Eph. 1:7)
- Victory (Eph. 1:20–22)
- Reconciliation (Eph. 2:13–16)
- Sacrifice (Eph. 5:2)
- Sanctification (Eph. 5:25–27)

Redemption (Eph. 1:7)

'In him we have redemption through his blood'. One biblical picture of Christ's saving accomplishment is redemption. It involves five truths. First, since the fall humans have lived in bondage to sin, self and even Satan (Gal. 4:3; 1 John 3:10), in the 'domain of darkness' (Col. 1:13). We were unable to free ourselves (Ps. 49:7). But thanks be to God for providing a Redeemer, who brings redemption and 'the forgiveness of our trespasses' (Eph. 1:7).

Second, our Redeemer is Christ, who delivered us by paying the redemption price or ransom. Baugh tells how in first-century Ephesus 'redemption' was often used for deliverance of 'kidnapped people or of slaves into the status of freedmen through payment of . . . a ransom'.[53] Mark's famous ransom saying highlights this truth: '[E]ven the Son of Man came not to be served but to serve, and to give his life as a ransom for many' (Mark 10:45). The ransom paid was Christ's 'blood' – his sacrificial death on the cross for us (Eph. 1:7), as Lane affirms:

---

[51] Baugh 2015: 199–200.
[52] For a treatment of Christ's saving events and biblical pictures that interpret them see Peterson 2012. For a systematic treatment see Morgan with Peterson 2020: 267–332.
[53] Baugh 2015: 89.

The ransom metaphor sums up the purpose for which Jesus gave his life . . . The prevailing notion behind the metaphor is that of deliverance by purchase . . . Because the idea of equivalence, or substitution, was proper to the concept of a ransom, it became an integral element in the vocabulary of redemption in the OT. It speaks of a liberation which connotes a servitude or an imprisonment from which man cannot free himself. In the context of verse 45a . . . it is appropriate to find an allusion to the Servant of the Lord in Isa. 53, who vicariously and voluntarily suffered and gave his life for the sins of others . . . Jesus, as the Messianic Servant, offers himself as a guilt-offering (Lev. 5:14–6:7; 7:1–7; Num. 5:5–8) in compensation for the sins of the people.[54]

Third, as a result of Christ's redemption, believers enjoy the freedom of the children of God. Though we

were enslaved to the elementary principles of the world . . . God sent forth his Son . . . to redeem [us] . . . so that we might receive adoption as sons . . . So you are no longer a slave, but a son, and if a son, then an heir through God.
(Gal. 4:3–5, 7)

Paul's words apply to us as well: 'For freedom Christ has set us free; stand firm therefore, and do not submit again to a yoke of slavery' (5:1).

Fourth, at the same time we have been purchased by a new Master: 'You are not your own, for you were bought with a price. So glorify God in your body' (1 Cor. 6:19–20). The redemption price was very costly; it was nothing less than the Son of God's redemptive death! Redeemed believers belong not to themselves but to Christ, their new Lord, and must live accordingly, as John Stott drives home:

Our body has not only been created by God and will one day be resurrected by him, but it has been bought by Christ's blood and is indwelt by his Spirit. Thus it belongs to God three times over, by creation, redemption and indwelling. How then, since it does not belong to us, can we misuse it? Instead, we are to honour God with

---

[54] Lane 1974: 383–384.

it, by obedience and self-control. Bought by Christ, we have no business to become the slaves of anybody or anything else.[55]

Fifth, because Christ is the Lamb who was slain, whose 'blood . . . ransomed people for God / from every tribe and language and people and nation', he deserves praise now and for ever: 'Worthy is the Lamb who was slain, to receive power and wealth and wisdom and might and honour and glory and blessing!' (Rev. 5:9, 12).

Victory (Eph. 1:20–22)

Ironically, Jesus' death is also a mighty victory. Paul asks God, 'the Father of glory', to grant his readers wisdom to know 'the immeasurable greatness of his power towards us who believe, according to the working of his great might' (vv. 16–19). Paul cites two awe-inspiring instances of that power: God's raising Christ and Christ's ruling over all at God's right hand (vv. 20–22).

When we think of what Jesus did to save us, his crucifixion comes to mind, and rightly so. But Scripture presents Jesus' death and resurrection as inseparable (John 10:17–18; 1 Cor. 15:3–4). Together they form the heart of Jesus' saving work. In total, he performs nine saving deeds: his incarnation, sinless life, death, resurrection, ascension, session, pouring out the Spirit at Pentecost, intercession and second coming. The first two events are preconditions of his death and resurrection, which are central, and the last five events are consequences of his death and resurrection. Moreover, Scripture interprets Christ's saving deeds by painting six big pictures. Christ is reconciler, redeemer, legal substitute, victor, second Adam and sacrifice.

Ephesians 1:20–22 focuses on Christ our victor. We have deadly, powerful enemies: humans, sin, the world system against God, demons, Satan, death and hell. We could never prevail over these foes on our own. However, God sent his Son to defeat them for us. The victor's work includes his incarnation (Gal. 4:4–5), temptation (Matt. 4:1–11), exorcisms (12:22–29), especially his death (Col. 2:14–15) and resurrection (1 Cor. 15:4, 54–57), ascension (Eph. 4:8), session (Rom. 8:33–34) and return (2 Thess. 1:6–8).

---

[55] Stott 1986: 181–182.

God raised our mighty champion 'from the dead and seated him at his right hand in the heavenly places, far above all rule and authority and power and dominion' (Eph. 1:20–21). Christ's resurrection and session place him above rule, authority, power and dominion. Arnold notes:

> These believers lived in an environment with many competing claims of spiritual power: the Artemis cult and fifty other gods and goddesses, magical curses and incantations . . . but Paul wants them to have an accurate understanding of the omnipotence of the God they now serve.[56]

Arnold explains that Paul's four terms ('rule', 'authority', 'power' and 'dominion') for supernatural forces are

> used in Jewish texts for evil and for good angels. The fact that Paul is referring to *hostile* powers here is strongly suggested by the fact that these forces were subjected to [Christ] (1:22), will ultimately be brought completely under his headship in the future (1:10), and are the same powers believers struggle with throughout their lifetimes (6:12).[57]

For emphasis Paul adds that God exalted Christ 'above every name that is named, not only in this age but also in the one to come' (Eph. 1:21). Bruce shows that Paul's language is comprehensive: no authority in the universe is superior to Christ:

> Whether the rank or honor be borne by human or superhuman beings, whether it be borne 'in this present age' or 'in the coming one,' it disappears from view in comparison with the glory which Christ has received from the Father.[58]

Paul shows Christ's limitless power from two Old Testament texts. He cites Psalm 110:1, 'The LORD says to my Lord: / "Sit at my right hand, / until I make your enemies your footstool"', to locate the place where God seated the risen Christ – at God's right hand, the place of the greatest

---

[56] Arnold 2010: 121.
[57] Ibid.
[58] Bruce 1984: 273.

honour and power in the universe. He also points to Psalm 8:6, where God says of Adam:

> You have given him dominion over the works of your hands;
>   you have put all things under his feet.[59]

God has 'put all things under' the feet of Christ, the second Adam, who succeeds where Adam failed in defeating our enemies.

Paul completes his thought: 'And he put all things under his feet and gave him as head over all things to the church, which is his body, the fullness of him who fills all in all' (Eph. 1:22–23). The all-powerful Christ has vanquished his enemies and ours (Ps. 110:1). As coregent with the Father he is head over the church, for which he wields his power.

God has highly exalted his Son, and so should we. Christ our champion has defeated our foes and deserves universal honour and glory.

Reconciliation (Eph. 2:13–16)

Scripture also paints a picture of reconciliation to describe Jesus' work. The picture comes from the domain of relationships, and the need for reconciliation is estrangement from God and one another due to sin. We once were God's 'enemies' (Rom. 5:10) and were 'alienated and hostile in mind, doing evil deeds' (Col. 1:21). Christ is our peacemaker, who through his death and resurrection (Rom. 5:10) reconciles God to us and us to God and to one another.

Vertical reconciliation is between God and aliens. God took the initiative, and Christ was the peacemaker, the Mediator of reconciliation:

> we were reconciled to God by the death of his Son.
> (Rom. 5:10)

> God ... through Christ reconciled us to himself ... that is, in Christ God was reconciling the world to himself, not counting their trespasses against them.
> (2 Cor. 5:18–19)

---

[59] 'In the NT the words of the psalm are applied to Christ as the last Adam, notably by Paul in 1 Cor. 15:27 and by the writer to the Hebrews in Heb. 2:6–9' (ibid. 274).

[God reconciled] us both [Jews and Gentiles] to God in one body through the cross.
(Eph. 2:16)

God was pleased . . . through him to reconcile to himself all things, whether on earth or in heaven, making peace by the blood of his cross.
   And you . . . he has now reconciled in his body of flesh by his death.
(Col. 1:19–22)

Horizontal reconciliation is between God and human beings and is based on vertical reconciliation. As we saw on pages 138–140, God reconciled both believing Jews and Gentiles to himself (Eph. 1:16) and thereby to one another:

now in Christ Jesus you who once were far off have been brought near by the blood of Christ. For he himself is our peace, who has made us both one and has broken down in his flesh the dividing wall of hostility . . . that he might create in himself one new man in place of the two, so making peace.
(Eph. 2:13–15)

Cosmic reconciliation is between God and the world he created. God was pleased to have the 'fullness of deity' dwell in Christ bodily (Col. 2:9). God was also pleased 'through him to reconcile to himself all things, whether on earth or in heaven, making peace by the blood of his cross' (Col. 1:20). This means not that every human will be saved in the end but that God will deliver his creation from the curse (Rev. 22:3; 2 Peter 3:13).

The consequences of reconciliation? First, we have a new relationship with God. We will not experience his wrath but now 'have peace with God through our Lord Jesus Christ' (Rom. 5:1). Second, God pledges to preserve his reconciled: '[I]f while we were enemies we were reconciled to God by the death of his Son, much more, now that we are reconciled, shall we be saved by his life' (v. 10). Third, Christ the Reconciler gives the church the 'ministry of reconciliation' (2 Cor. 5:18), which involves taking the 'message of reconciliation' (v. 19) to those estranged from God.

Fourth, there is great joy, for 'we also rejoice in God through our Lord Jesus Christ, through whom we have now received reconciliation' (Rom. 5:11). Christ, the Mediator, accomplishes reconciliation and is the cause of 'ceaseless exultation', as Cranfield notes.[60] And that ceaseless exultation redounds in ceaseless glory to God.

Sacrifice (Eph. 5:2)

Christ's atoning death is also a sacrifice. Paul enjoins his readers, 'Therefore be imitators of God, as beloved children. And walk in love, as Christ loved us and gave himself up for us, a fragrant offering and sacrifice to God' (Eph. 5:1–2). Reminding his readers of their adoption ('beloved children'), Paul sets forth the Father and the Son as examples for Christians to follow. Christ's sacrifice is the greatest example of love. But first it is God's means of atonement. Its background is the Old Testament sacrificial system. We cannot know the number of animals that were sacrificed, but it probably exceeds one million.

God forgave Old Testament saints when in faith they presented animals for sacrifice. But that forgiveness depended ultimately not on the blood of bulls and goats but on the sacrifice of Christ (Heb. 9:13–14). His sacrifice was so effective that it availed for sins committed under the old covenant (Heb. 9:15). At the same time, Jesus' one new covenant sacrifice made the old covenant and all its sacrifices obsolete (Heb. 8:13), because it accomplished what they never could:

> every priest stands daily at his service, offering repeatedly the same sacrifices, which can never take away sins. But when Christ had offered for all time a single sacrifice for sins, he sat down at the right hand of God . . . For by a single offering he has perfected for all time those who are being sanctified.
> (Heb. 10:11–14)

Thielman underlines Christ's readiness to die for us: 'Paul says that Christ stepped forward willingly, out of his love for God's people, to sacrifice himself and atone for their sins.'[61] Moreover, Jesus' willing sacrifice of himself saves!

---

[60] Cranfield 2004: 269.
[61] Thielman 2010: 322.

Ephesians 1:7 and 2:13 speak of Christ's redemptive death as his 'blood'. When Paul speaks of salvation by Christ's 'blood', he taps into a common idea in the first-century Roman world, as Baugh makes plain. 'Blood' for persons in that world signifies blood sacrifices, which were part of everyday life. Almost all meat was offered in sacrifice. Indeed, besides many shrines, Ephesus was home to 'the largest temple in the ancient world, the Artemisium of Artemis Ephesia, with its large, enclosed altar nearby, where regular animal sacrifices took place'.[62]

Christ's blood, his sacrificial death, purifies sinners who put their trust in him and brings them eternal life. This is because 'the blood of Christ, who through the eternal Spirit offered himself without blemish to God', died as 'the mediator of a new covenant, so that those who are called may receive the promised eternal inheritance' (Heb. 9:13–15). Believers can join the chorus in giving glory to the Son of God who loved us and gave himself for us: 'To him who loves us and has freed us from our sins by his blood and made us a kingdom, priests to his God and Father, to him be glory and dominion for ever and ever. Amen' (Rev. 1:5–6).

Sanctification (Eph. 5:25–27)

Paul penned Ephesians 5:25–27 to Christian husbands. Their model for loving their wives is Christ and his love for the church. That love shines supremely in his cross. Scripture says that he 'gave himself up for her' here (v. 25) and in Galatians 1:3–4; 2:20; Ephesians 5:2; 1 Timothy 2:5–6; and Titus 2:13–14. Jesus' self-giving is the epitome of his love for the lost. 'Greater love has no one than this, that someone lay down his life for his friends' (John 15:13). Moreover, '[W]hile we were still sinners, Christ died for us' (Rom. 5:8). At the centre of the Christian faith is Christ, at the centre of his saving work is the cross and at the centre of the cross is Jesus' giving himself to rescue sinners like us.

Christ died to 'sanctify' the church, to make her holy (Eph. 5:26). Sanctification is both individual and corporate in Scripture. It is individual: 'This is the will of God, your sanctification: that you abstain from sexual immorality' (1 Thess. 4:3). Here it is corporate: 'Christ loved the church and gave himself up for her, that he might sanctify her' (Eph. 5:25–26).

Since the Reformation Protestants have rightly distinguished sanctification from justification. In justification God declares righteous all who

---

[62] Baugh 2015: 189.

trust Christ, and they move from condemnation to acceptance by God. In sanctification God works practical holiness in those whom he has justified. Thus sanctification follows justification. To confuse the two leads people to seek to be accepted by God (justified) by being 'good Christians' (sanctified). The Reformation view is correct if we define the sanctification involved as progressive sanctification.

A full-orbed study reveals that sanctification is initial, progressive and final. Initial sanctification is the Spirit's work of setting apart unclean people to God (1 Cor. 6:11). This once-for-all act is also called definitive sanctification because it defines believers as saints (1 Cor. 1:2). Progressive sanctification is the Spirit's continuing work of building holiness into Christians' lives (1 Thess. 4:3–5). The Spirit works progressive holiness into believers, using the Word and prayer (John 17:17). This aspect of sanctification the Reformers rightly distinguished from justification. Final sanctification is the Spirit's work of confirming believers in complete holiness when Jesus comes again (Eph. 5:27; 1 Thess. 5:23–24).

Jesus cleanses the church 'by the washing of water with the word' (Eph. 5:26). This 'washing of water' seems to refer to a bridal bath, common in many cultures, in preparation for a wedding. Although many interpreters understand this as a reference to baptism, we agree with Thielman: 'The minority of interpreters who argue that the phrase "with the water bath" is a metaphorical reference to the cleansing power of the gospel are probably correct.'[63]

Jesus loved the church and died to sanctify it. His goal is to 'present the church to himself in splendour, without spot or wrinkle or any such thing, that she might be holy and without blemish' (Eph. 5:27). Christ's efficacious atonement will result in the perfect sanctification of his bride, the church. For that reason the announcement of the wedding supper of the Lamb, Christ the groom, and his bride, the church, is filled with the glory of God:

> Hallelujah!
> For the Lord our God
>   the Almighty reigns.
> Let us rejoice and exult
>   and give him the glory,

---

[63] Thielman 2010: 384.

for the marriage of the Lamb has come,
    and his Bride has made herself ready.
(Rev. 19:6–7)

Conclusion

We have examined Paul's message to the Ephesians regarding Jesus' saving work viewed in terms of redemption, victory, reconciliation, sacrifice and sanctification. Scriptural songs of praise such as this one form a fitting conclusion:

I heard every creature in heaven and on earth and under the earth and in the sea, and all that is in them, saying, 'To him who sits on the throne and to the Lamb be blessing and honour and glory and might for ever and ever!' And the four living creatures said, 'Amen!' and the elders fell down and worshipped.
(Rev. 5:13–14)

God's glory and union with Christ

God reveals his glory and gets glory for himself in many ways. One way is through union with Christ.[64] Union is best understood in trinitarian terms. Each person of the Trinity plays a role in salvation (Eph. 1:3–14). The Father chooses people for salvation (1:3–4). The Son redeems people with his blood, his sacrificial death (v. 7). The Holy Spirit joins people spiritually to Christ, so that they experience salvation. Here Paul presents union with Christ by depicting the Spirit as God's seal on believers (v. 13).

Paul describes our need for union with Christ: separation from him (Eph. 2:12). The Spirit meets that need by joining people to the Son of God in salvation. 'In Christ' we receive all the benefits of salvation, including regeneration (Eph. 2:4–5), justification (2 Cor. 5:21), adoption (Gal. 3:26–27), sanctification (Eph. 2:10), perseverance (Rom. 8:1), resurrection (1 Cor. 15:21–22) and glorification (Col. 3:4). Union is thus the most comprehensive category for the application of salvation.

---

[64] For a book-length treatment of union see Peterson 2014b. For a concise systematic treatment see Morgan with Peterson 2020: 334–339.

Paul communicates union with Christ in various ways. He says Christians are 'in Christ' or 'in him'. He also says that believers participate in Christ's saving deeds. By grace through faith we take part in Jesus' death (Col. 2:20), resurrection and session (Eph. 2:6) and even his return (Col. 3:4), in the sense that our full identity in Christ will only then be made known.

We live and die in union with Christ. We live in him: 'Christ . . . lives in me. And the life I now live in the flesh I live by faith in the Son of God, who loved me and gave himself for me' (Gal. 2:20). We also die in union with Christ: 'Blessed are the dead who die in the Lord from now on' (Rev. 14:13).

Ephesians glorifies God by presenting union with Christ in three spheres:

1 Personal union (Eph. 1:3–14; 2:1–10)
2 Communal union (Eph. 2:11–22)
3 Cosmic union (Eph. 1:9–10)

Personal union with Christ (Eph. 1:3–14; 2:1–10)

Ephesians 1:3–14

Paul's long paragraph blessing God is saturated with references to union with Christ. Of nine occurrences of 'in Christ' or 'in him', at least six pertain to union. These deal with aspects of the great salvation God has graciously given believers for his glory: spiritual blessings (v. 3), election (v. 4), grace (v. 6), redemption (v. 7), our inheritance (v. 11) and sealing (v. 13).

First, 'Blessed be the God and Father of our Lord Jesus Christ, who has blessed us in Christ with every spiritual blessing in the heavenly places' (v. 3). Thielman notes, 'The opening line of Paul's benediction follows a pattern [of a prayer of blessing God, a *berakhah*] familiar from Israel's Scriptures and Jewish literature of the Second Temple period.'[65] Paul fills this pattern full of Christian meaning. He begins his blessing with God the Father. He is Jesus' God and Father. He is Jesus' God because the eternal Son became a man in Jesus of Nazareth. He is Jesus' Father, whom the incarnate Son obeyed and to whom he prayed.

---

[65] Thielman 2010: 45.

Paul blesses the Father, who bestows 'every spiritual blessing' on his people. Further, God gave these blessings 'in the heavenly places'. This is where God dwells as the Father of lights and source of '[e]very good gift and every perfect gift' (Jas 1:17). Most important, God bestows these abundant blessings 'in Christ'. All of God's spiritual blessings are 'in Christ', to the glory of God.

Second, 'he chose us in him before the foundation of the world that we should be holy and blameless before him' (Eph. 1:4). God chooses people for himself before creation. This is similar to Paul's words elsewhere: 'God . . . saved us . . . not because of our works but because of his own purpose and grace, which he gave us in Christ Jesus before the ages began' (2 Tim. 1:8–9). In both passages God chooses people before creation for salvation. In addition, in both texts election is in union with Christ:

he chose us in him before the foundation of the world.
(Eph. 1:4)

God . . . saved us . . . because of his own purpose and grace, which he gave us in Christ Jesus before the ages began.
(2 Tim. 1:8–9)

How can union with Christ occur before creation? Union with Christ happens in time and space when people believe in Jesus as Lord and Saviour: '[I]n Christ Jesus you are all children of God through faith' (Gal. 3:26, niv). The two passages above speak of God's planning to unite people to his Son for salvation. 'In Christ' 'describes the means by which God's choice became effective for believers'.[66] The Father selects his own and plans how to bring salvation to them – by uniting them to Christ.

Third, 'he predestined us for adoption as sons through Jesus Christ, according to the purpose of his will, to the praise of his glorious grace, with which he has blessed us in the Beloved' (Eph. 1:5–6). Here Paul switches from '[God] chose us' to 'he predestined us', but the meaning is much the same. After considering different possible nuances between the words, Thielman concludes that Paul's emphasis is on election's occurrence and the resultant need of God's people to praise him for such grace. When Paul mentions predestination he describes 'God's primordial action

---

on behalf of his people not as his choice but as his predetermination of them'.[67]

In verse 3 Paul taught that God's election results in sanctification. Here he demonstrates how God's predestination results in adoption. The Father places us as adult sons and daughters in his family 'through Jesus Christ', the Mediator (John 14:6; Acts 4:12). This is a sovereign act of God, who works 'according to the purpose of his will' (Eph. 1:5; cf. v. 11). Moreover, God's adoption of believers leads 'to the praise of his glorious grace' (v. 6). Bruce explains, 'In this saving work, and its becoming effective in the lives of believers, God is glorified: his grace is manifested as worthy of "glorious praise."'[68]

Paul expands on this grace by continuing, 'with which he has blessed us in the Beloved' (v. 6). The substantive 'beloved' is used in both Testaments to describe people.[69] Although the very word is used only here in the New Testament of Christ, it resembles the adjective 'beloved' used by the Father of the Son at his baptism and transfiguration (Matt. 3:17; 17:5). It is also akin to 'his beloved Son', used of Christ in Colossians 1:13. Once more union with Christ is connected to salvation, here expressed as 'his glorious grace', as Hoehner asserts: 'In the NT God the Father calls his Son the beloved One, which is evidence of his love for him. Since believers are in Christ, they are also the object of God's love.'[70]

Fourth, 'In him we have redemption through his blood' (v. 7). Because we treated the concept of redemption under 'God's glory and Christ's saving work' on pages 142–144, here we summarize. Redemption is God's act in Christ of purchasing slaves of sin and making them the free sons of God. Redemption as an atonement theme thus has adoption as its counterpart in the application of salvation. Redemption involves the payment of a ransom, 'the blood of Christ', his violent death.[71] '*In him* we have redemption through his blood' (v. 7). We are redeemed through Christ's work, which is 'in him', in union with Christ, the Father's Beloved One.

Fifth, 'In him we have obtained an inheritance, having been predestined according to the purpose of him who works all things according to the counsel of his will' (v. 11). This blessing is closely connected to the

---

[67] Ibid. 51.
[68] Bruce 1984: 258.
[69] E.g. Deut. 33:12; 2 Sam. 1:23; Isa. 5:1; Rom. 9:25; 1 Thess. 1:4; 2 Thess. 2:13.
[70] Hoehner 2002: 204.
[71] So Morris (1965a: 358–359).

preceding, because 'an inheritance' belongs to a son, and one way to attain the status of sonship is through adoption. Baugh helps us understand the momentous meaning of verse 5 in the ancient world. In the Roman world slaves were possessions and not persons. For slaves in Ephesus to hear that God chose them in Christ to become not just 'God's freedmen (1 Cor 7:22) or free children (1 John 1:12) but through *huiothesia* to become ruling sons (whether male or female) was an astounding magnificent statement of God's lavish grace'.[72]

The omnipotent God planned adoption for believers, for this inheritance had 'been predestined according to the purpose of him who works all things according to the counsel of his will' (Eph. 1:11). Indeed, God the Father has blessed every believer in his Son with sonship, regardless of gender, race, social status or locale. The Spirit incorporates believers into God's family 'in him', that is, in union with the divine Son of God, 'the firstborn among many brothers' (Rom. 8:29). Our inheritance includes resurrection in immortal bodies for eternal life on the new earth (cf. 1 Cor. 3:21–22). The purpose of adoption? '[S]o that we . . . might be to the praise of his glory' (Eph. 1:12).

Sixth, 'In him you also . . . were sealed with the promised Holy Spirit' (Eph. 1:13). Paul has not mentioned the Holy Spirit until now. He presents the Spirit as God's seal on believers. The Father is the sealer: he 'has also put his seal on us and given us his Spirit in our hearts as a guarantee' (2 Cor. 1:22). The Spirit is God's seal given to believers: '[Y]ou also, when you heard the word of truth, the gospel of your salvation, and believed in him, were sealed with the promised Holy Spirit' (Eph. 1:13). The Spirit as seal is permanent: '[D]o not grieve the Holy Spirit of God, by whom you were sealed for the day of redemption' (4:30). As with all the blessings of salvation, sealing is 'in him' (1:13). Hoehner accurately describes the response God desires: 'God sealed the believers with the Holy Spirit of promise until the day he redeems them, his possession, and for this he is to be praised.'[73]

Ephesians 2:1–10

Personal union with Christ is evident also in Ephesians 2:1–10. Having studied this passage under the heading 'Sin, grace and God's glory (Eph.

---

72 Baugh 2015: 85, 88.
73 Hoehner 2002: 245.

2:1–10)' on pages 129–130, now we only underline personal union with Christ. The first three verses depict the woeful condition of people outside Christ; Paul summarizes, 'when we were dead in our trespasses' (v. 5). Surrounding this statement are expressions of God's favour toward those who deserved his disfavour. Paul speaks of God's rich 'mercy' (v. 4), his 'great love' (v. 4), his 'grace' (vv. 5, 8) and 'the immeasurable riches of his grace in kindness towards us in Christ Jesus' (v. 7). The last three words are suggestive because they point once more to union with Christ.

Union appears three times in verses 5–7. First, Paul says that God 'made us alive together with Christ' (v. 5). In mercy God regenerated those spiritually dead, and Paul regards this as cutting 'to the heart of the gospel and of grace'[74] (v. 5). Of course, God 'made us alive together with Christ' (v. 5). Salvation never comes to us apart from Christ but always in union with him.

Second, Paul writes that God 'raised us up with him and seated us with him in the heavenly places in Christ Jesus' (v. 6). Believers participated in Jesus' story: we died with him, were raised with him to newness of life and anticipate our future bodily resurrection. Only here Paul teaches that God 'seated us with him in the heavenly places in Christ Jesus' (v. 6). The fact that Paul puts the three verbs ('made us alive', 'raised' and 'seated') in the past tense is significant. Bruce accurately interprets why Paul does so: God's purpose 'is so sure of fulfillment that it can be spoken of as having already taken place: "whom he justified, them he also glorified"'.[75]

At the same time Paul wrote to affect Christians' lives now, as Hoehner notes: 'Hence, the position of being seated with Christ in the heavenlies gives the believer a heavenly status with heavenly power to overcome the power of sin and death.'[76] Salvation is the work of God alone, beyond our ability to understand, and by union with Christ in his death and resurrection believers are overcomers in this life and are raised immortal in the next.

Third, Paul announces that 'in the coming ages' God will 'show the immeasurable riches of his grace in kindness towards us in Christ Jesus' (v. 7). This is the goal of God's great grace. Paul struggles to express the richness of God's grace: it is the 'immeasurable riches of his grace in

---

[74] Baugh 2015: 155.
[75] Bruce 1984: 287.
[76] Hoehner 2002: 334.

kindness towards us'. Though we do not follow Lincoln in rejecting Pauline authorship of Ephesians, we appreciate his comments at this point:

> As the writer's thought and style attempt to capture something of the extravagance of God's display of grace, it becomes not just grace but 'the richness of his grace' (cf. also 1:7), and not just the richness of his grace but 'the surpassing richness of his grace.'[77]

Needless to say, the exceeding richness of God's saving grace poured out upon the church in ages to come is 'in Christ Jesus' (v. 7). Bruce unpacks the significance of these three words:

> Because they are 'in Christ Jesus,' he deals with them as he has dealt with him. The vindication and exaltation that Christ has received is his by right; the share in that bestowed on believers in Christ is theirs by divine mercy, grace, and kindness.[78]

Communal union with Christ (Eph. 2:11–22)

When people trust Christ, the Holy Spirit unites them to Christ spiritually so that all of his saving benefits become theirs. Simultaneously, the Spirit unites them to all other believers. In other words, union is both an individual soteriological truth and a corporate soteriological truth. We previously treated this passage, so here we summarize with reference to the church's union with Christ.

After detailing the awful predicament of the unsaved Gentiles (Eph. 2:11–12), Paul declares, 'But now in Christ Jesus you who once were far off have been brought near by the blood of Christ' (Eph. 2:13). Formerly they were 'separated from Christ . . . having no hope and without God' (v. 12), but now 'in Christ Jesus' God has given them access to himself in salvation. Though some have rendered the words 'by Christ Jesus' (an instrumental use), Arnold correctly says it has 'incorporational significance'.[79] In grace God has replaced separation from Christ with union with Christ.

---

[77] Lincoln 1990: 109.
[78] Bruce 1984: 288.
[79] Arnold 2010: 157.

It is important to highlight the fact that the rescue of the Gentiles is accomplished 'by the blood of Christ' (v. 13). 'Blood' in Scripture often refers to the death of Old Testament animal sacrifices and to the death of 'the Lamb of God, who takes away the sin of the world' (John 1:29). Believers thus receive 'redemption through his blood' (Eph. 1:7).

Paul powerfully portrays corporate union with Christ in Ephesians 2. He teaches that through his crucifixion Christ created 'in himself one new man in place of the two, so making peace, and [so reconciled] us both to God in one body through the cross, thereby killing the hostility' (2:15–16). God overcame the deep-seated animosity between Jews and Gentiles through Jesus' atonement. Through the work of the Mediator, God reconciled believing Jews and Gentiles to himself and one another. Having used the imagery of the new creation in 2:10 to speak of the salvation of individual Christians, Paul now applies it corporately to the church. Christ 'create[d] in himself one new man in place of the two' (2:15). He did so 'in himself', in union with himself. Thielman encapsulates Paul's message: 'By their union with Christ, believers become united with one another across the social barriers that formerly divided them, and so, like Christ himself, become a new Adam.'[80]

Paul says that through the Mediator Jewish and Gentile believers 'both have access in one Spirit to the Father' (Eph. 2:18). He then contrasts the Gentiles' former state of alienation from God, his people, his Messiah and salvation with their new identity: 'So then you are no longer strangers and aliens, but you are fellow citizens with the saints and members of the household of God' (v. 19). The former aliens are at home with God and his people.

Paul paints the image of a building, whose foundation is 'the apostles and [New Testament] prophets, Christ Jesus himself being the cornerstone' (Eph. 2:20). It turns out that the building is a temple, and in Christ 'the whole structure, being joined together, grows into a holy temple in the Lord' (v. 21). The omnipresent God dwells in his people, individually and corporately as the church. In fact, this living temple is home for the special presence of the Trinity (v. 22).

In the space of fourteen Greek words Paul uses 'in Christ' language three times: 'the cornerstone, in whom the whole structure, being joined together, grows into a holy temple in the Lord. In him you also are being

80 Thielman 2010: 171.

built together into a dwelling place for God by the Spirit' (Eph. 2:20, 21, 22). Paul tells of the importance of Christ, the primary stone, to the whole temple (v. 21), describes the temple as 'in the Lord' and says that 'in him' his Gentile readers are living stones that the Holy Spirit puts into that temple (v. 22).

The use of these three prepositional phrases is debated, with some capable scholars opting for a local sense each time, denoting the locale or sphere of action.[81] However, we agree with Arnold: 'This spiritual temple is "in the Lord"; that is, it exists only in the corporate unity that Christ has created by bringing individuals into a dynamic union with himself.'[82] Eternal praise will redound to the Trinity for individual and communal union with Christ.

This temple differs from two other first-century temples of note, as Stott explains:

> there stood in Ephesus the magnificent marble temple of Artemis . . . one of the seven wonders of the ancient world, and in whose inner shrine there was a statue of the goddess. At the same time in Jerusalem there stood the Jewish temple built by Herod the Great, barricading itself against the Gentiles, and now also against God . . . Two temples, one pagan and the other Jewish, each designed by its devotees as a divine residence, but both empty of the living God. For now there is a new temple, *a dwelling place of God in the Spirit*. It is his new society, his redeemed people scattered throughout the inhabited world.[83]

Two applications flow from this great passage (Eph. 2:11–22). First, because 'no privilege is bestowed on the people of God in which Gentiles do not enjoy an equal share',[84] Christian churches today must live out Paul's teaching that the church transcends cultural, racial and ethnic boundaries.

Second, Arnold singles out the Son, 'who created the new humanity, who reconciled us to God (and to one another), and who serves as the foundation stone of the new temple . . . Because of his great work, Jesus deserves our praise and devotion.'[85] As do God the Father and the Holy Spirit!

---

[81] Hoehner 2002: 407, 411, 412.
[82] Arnold 2010: 172.
[83] Stott 1979: 109–110; emphasis original.
[84] Bruce 1984: 307.
[85] Arnold 2010: 177.

Cosmic union with Christ (Eph. 1:9–10)

God also manifests his glory in his eternal plan to reconcile the cosmos in union with Christ (Eph. 1:9–10). Paul has spoken of Christ our Redeemer, who died to free us from bondage and bring us 'forgiveness of our trespasses' (v. 7). This expressed the 'riches of [God's] grace' and adds to God's glory.

'[I]n all wisdom and insight' God made 'known to us the mystery of his will' (vv. 8–9). Paul's conception of 'mystery' is far different from that of many Ephesians, as Arnold reveals: 'Many of the readers of this letter had perhaps once been initiated into the mystery rites of Artemis, Isis, Cybele, Dionysus, or any of a number of pagan gods.'[86]

As we have seen, Beale and Gladd define a biblical mystery as 'the revelation of God's partially hidden wisdom, particularly' related to the 'latter days' and pertaining 'to Christ'.[87] This definition holds true for Ephesians 1:8–10. God's great plan to unite all things in Christ was revealed only in 'the last days'. It was only after Christ died, rose, ascended and sent the Spirit that God disclosed this mystery. And at its centre is Jesus himself.

God revealed his great 'wisdom and insight' (v. 8) when he made known the mystery of Christ's cosmic rule over all. God got glory in doing this, for he included it in his Word, that the church might praise him for his redemptive wisdom. Further, this mystery fulfilled God's 'purpose, which he set forth in Christ' (v. 9). God planned before creation to send his Son to die, rise and eventually reign over all things.

Paul speaks of God's 'purpose, which he set forth in Christ as a plan for the fullness of time' (Eph. 1:9–10). Arnold elucidates the concept of 'plan' (*oikonomia*) in Greco-Roman culture: 'Every household [*oikos*] . . . was overseen by a household manager (*oikonomos*) . . . In this passage, Paul portrays God as the household manager.'[88] Paul focuses on God's plan, which is comprehensive and centres on Christ.

Before creation (v. 3) God planned to glorify himself by uniting the universe in Christ. This plan involved many steps, including bringing a great nation from Abraham, the history of Old Testament Israel, bringing the Messiah into the world and the events in Christ's life from incarnation

---

86 Ibid. 86.
87 Beale and Gladd 2014: 20, 321–322.
88 Arnold 2010: 87–88.

to future return. God's sovereign plan in Christ clashes with the pagan view dominant in Ephesus, as Baugh shows. In Ephesus both gods and humans bowed to fate:

> Even Zeus, 'the father of the gods and of men,' bowed to the inevitable will of the inscrutable fates . . . The Ephesians themselves bowed to 'Lady Luck' (or Fate) in their affairs by prefacing their many public actions with a dedication to the goddess Τυχή (*Tychē*) ('Luck'), or more commonly Ἀγαθὴ Τυχή (*Agathē Tychē*) ('Good Luck').[89]

Paul refuses to bow to Lady Luck, but serves an all-powerful God who has in grace disclosed 'the mystery of his will' in the person and work of his Son (v. 9).

Furthermore, God is a person who delights in summing up all things in Christ, even as he delighted to choose persons to be part of his family (Eph. 1:4–5, NIV): '[H]e made known to us the mystery of his will according to his good pleasure, which he purposed in Christ . . . to bring unity to all things in heaven and on earth under Christ' (vv. 9–10, NIV).

The key word in Ephesians 1:9–10 occurs in verse 10: 'as a plan for the fullness of time, to unite [*anakephalaioō*] all things in him, things in heaven and things on earth'. Paul uses an unusual word composed of two words (*ana* ['again', as a prefix] and *kephalaioō* [to sum up]). Thielman sorts out the options. Two approaches err by focusing on either element of the word, rather than taking it as a whole. The first emphasizes the prefix to focus on Christ's repetition and culmination of redemptive history in himself. The second approach interprets *kephalaioō*, linked with *kephalē*, to mean 'to head up' all things in Christ. Thielman rejects these approaches for a third:

> The noun ἀνακεφαλαίωσις (*anakephalaiōsis*) and its corresponding verb ἀνακεφαλαιόω were commonly used in rhetorical contexts of an orator's or author's 'recapitulation' or 'summary' of the various elements of a speech or composition . . . If Paul used the term in Eph. 1:10 with this . . . meaning, then he is metaphorically describing God's plan to sum up his disparate creation in Christ. Just as an orator or writer draws together the elements of an argument and

---

[89] Baugh 2015: 95–96.

shows how they demonstrate the chief point of the speech or composition, so Christ will bring order to the universe.[90]

Questions remain. Why must all things be summed up in Christ? Two
other Pauline passages answer this question. Due to the fall, the creation
longs to 'be set free from its bondage to corruption' (Rom. 8:20–21). In
addition:

> 'God was pleased ... through [Christ] to reconcile to himself all
> things, whether on earth or in heaven, making peace by the blood of
> his cross' (Col. 1:19–20). Now peace does not reign in the universe,
> but when Christ returns he will bring unity, and under his headship
> discord will be no more.[91]

Who or what will be involved in the summing up? Redeemed humanity
will be a part (Eph. 2:13–19), as will angels, both elect (1 Tim. 5:21) and
vanquished, fallen (Eph. 1:20–22) ones. The summing up of all things in
Christ will not entail salvation for all humans, the devil or demons but an
acknowledgment of Christ's lordship and their just condemnation.
Moreover, the summing up will be cosmic, involving the entire creation.
Lincoln is succinct:

> The elaboration τὰ ἐπὶ τοῖς οὐρανοῖς καὶ τὰ ἐπὶ τῆς γῆς [things in
> heaven and things on earth] indicates that we are right to take τὰ
> πάντα [all things] in its widest sense of all things and all beings, that
> is, the cosmos as a whole and not just humanity.[92]

Thielman tells how Paul expands 1:10 later in Ephesians. God will sum
up the created universe in Christ. Through Christ's resurrection and ascension, God has vanquished all hostile powers and put them at Christ's feet
(1:20–22). God has given this triumphant Christ to his body, the church
(1:22–23), which is made up of believers taken from Jews and Gentiles, both
once estranged from God (2:1–10) and one another (2:11–22). As a result,
Christ will be Lord over all (1:22), especially over the church (4:15; 5:23).[93]

---

[90] Thielman 2010: 65–67. Some church fathers adopted the first approach (see ibid. 65–66).
For a defence of the second approach see Arnold 2010: 87–88.

[91] Stott 1979: 42; see also Lincoln 1990: 33.

[92] Ibid. 34.

[93] Thielman 2010: 67; see also Stott 1979: 44.

When will the summing up occur? Although some understand it to have 'already taken place',[94] it is better to regard it as still future. Bruce compares the expression 'the fullness of time' (Eph. 1:10) to its occurrence in Galatians 4:4:

> As, according to Gal. 4:4, God sent his Son into the world 'when the fullness of the time had come,' that is, when the time was ripe for his coming, so, when the time is ripe for the consummation of his purpose, in his providential overruling of the course of the world, that consummation will be realized.[95]

Baugh fittingly brings to a close our treatment of God's glory and his eternal plan in Christ by returning to Paul's beginning to recount God's gracious redemption. Paul begins, 'Blessed be the God and Father of our Lord Jesus Christ, who has blessed us in Christ with every spiritual blessing in the heavenly places' (v. 3). Baugh writes, 'Here doctrine and practice meet in sweet fellowship of grateful praise . . . All focus in this passage of praise is on God in Christ through the Spirit.'[96]

God's glory and the church as his showcase[97]

God creates one church to showcase cosmic reconciliation

As we have seen, God's plan addresses the personal, communal and cosmic consequences of the fall to bring all things together in Christ (1:9–10). He reconciles people to himself and to one another, even uniting the cosmos in Christ.

Does the church fit into this? Absolutely! God's new creation – the church – relates to all three spheres of God's plan for cosmic unity. The church is linked to the personal dimension, for it comprises individuals who were alienated from God but through Christ's saving work have been united to him (2:1–10). Second, the church is also linked to the

---

[94] Lincoln 1990: 34–35.
[95] Bruce 1984: 262.
[96] Baugh 2015: 101–102.
[97] This section is dependent on Morgan 2013: 225–233.

communal dimension, as the people of God reconciled to one another (2:11–22). Third – and this is often overlooked – the church plays a key role in the cosmic dimension. As the people reconciled to God and to one another, the church showcases God's plan of cosmic reconciliation:

> To me, though I am the very least of all the saints, this grace was given, to preach to the Gentiles the unsearchable riches of Christ, and to bring to light for everyone what is the plan of the mystery hidden for ages in God who created all things, so that through the church the manifold wisdom of God might now be made known to the rulers and authorities in the heavenly places. This was according to the eternal purpose that he has realized in Christ Jesus our Lord. (Eph. 3:8–11)

Therefore the current existence of one new people, the church, testifies that God is on a project to create unity. The reality of the unity of Jews and Gentiles together as one new humanity is an incredible testimony to God's broader purposes. The intended audience of this showcase is here described as the rulers and authorities in the heavenly realms, likely referring to both angels and demons. The point seems to be that the beings in the heavenly realms are put on notice: God is going to do cosmically what he has already done for individuals in Christ and corporately for Jews and Gentiles. He will bring together in Christ all things in heaven and on earth (Eph. 1:10); all things will highlight Christ as the focal point of the cosmos. So, not only is Christ the Saviour of sinners and the head of the church, but he is also the goal of the entire cosmos! Paul's idea here is similar to that of Colossians 1:16, where he teaches that 'all things were created through [Christ] and for him'.

The church as God's visible exhibition proclaims these cosmic purposes. The church preaches Christ not only to humanity in the verbal proclamation of the gospel but also to the entire cosmos through the visible display of unity. As believers preach the gospel, God enacts a drama for the audience. But who are the members of this audience? Stott answers:

> They are the cosmic intelligences, *the principalities and powers in the heavenly places.* We are to think of them as spectators of the drama of salvation . . . It is through the old creation (the universe)

that God reveals his glory to humans; it is through the new creation (the church) that he reveals his wisdom to angels.[98]

Thus as the church we showcase God's purposes not just to one another and to the world but, according to Ephesians 3:9–12, even to the heavenly realms! And as we display God's eternal purpose of cosmic unity to the world, we are demonstrating that the kingdom of God has already broken into history. Certainly, there is still a 'not yet' aspect of the kingdom. God's eternal purpose of cosmic reconciliation is not yet perfectly realized, for sin and injustice still occur. Yet sin will not have the last word; disorder and division will not last for ever. Though the present age can still to some extent be characterized as being 'not the way it is supposed to be',[99] God will bring about a new creation, as he has promised:

> according to his promise we are waiting for new heavens and a new earth in which righteousness dwells.
> (2 Peter 3:13)

> No longer will there be anything accursed, but the throne of God and of the Lamb will be in it, and his servants will worship him. They will see his face, and his name will be on their foreheads. And night will be no more. They will need no light of lamp or sun, for the Lord God will be their light, and they will reign for ever and ever.
> (Rev. 22:3–5)

Strikingly, God's new creation is already underway – in the church! God brings peace out of disorder by forming a 'new creation' (Eph. 2:10). He reconciles Jews and Gentiles to create one new humanity, the church (2:13–16). Fulfilling Old Testament hopes, Christ has brought the kingdom and the new age. He, the second Adam, the firstborn, the Son of God and God's perfect image, inaugurates the new creation. Christ, 'who as the Son of God bears the divine image is also the one who by virtue of his death and resurrection is now re-creating a people into that same image'.[100] The unity of Jews and Gentiles is the creation of one new humanity! God's new creation is already underway – in the church!

---

[98] Stott 1979: 123–124; emphasis original.
[99] Plantinga 1995: 2.
[100] Fee 2007: 515; see also Gaffin 2010.

The church is the firstfruits of the ultimate new creation that is still to come. As firstfruits we are both the genuine reality of the new creation and the foretaste of more to come. Thus as the church we are the new humanity, a new society, the new temple and a new creation. We are a foretaste of heaven on earth, a genuine embodiment of the kingdom, a glimpse of the way things are supposed to be and the way the cosmos ultimately will be. We are a showcase of God's eternal plan of cosmic unity.

God creates the church to display and glorify himself

God not only creates the church as one new humanity to display his eternal plan of cosmic reconciliation but also creates the church to display himself and thus glorify himself. We previously stressed that God's ultimate end is his glory. We also learned that God acts 'to the praise of his glorious grace' (Eph. 1:6) and 'to the praise of his glory' (1:12, 14) and that he acts to display himself, particularly his love, mercy, grace, kindness, creative work and wisdom (2:4–10; 3:8–10). When we connect the dots, we find that God has eternally planned to glorify himself through displaying himself through the church. In other words, God creates the church in order to display his greatness, and as he does so he glorifies himself.

In the creation of the cosmos God communicated himself. Psalm 19 makes this plain:

> The heavens declare the glory of God,
>   and the sky above proclaims his handiwork.
> Day to day pours out speech,
>   and night to night reveals knowledge.
> (19:1–2)

Even more, in the new creation, which is the church, God also communicates himself.

In the formation of Israel God displayed himself. Israel was called to embody God's holiness. The holiness of the people of Israel was essential not only to their proper worship of God but also to their mission: they accurately reflected the true God to the nations only as they lived in a way that reflected him (Exod. 19:5–6; Deut. 28:9–10). As a kingdom of priests Israel was to be committed to the ministry of God's presence throughout the earth. And as a holy nation the Israelites were 'to be a people set apart, different from all other people by what they [were] and [were] becoming – a display people, a showcase to the world of how being in covenant with Yahweh changes a people'.[101] Even more, in the new creation of the church God also displays himself. The church too is rightly described as 'a display people, a showcase to the world of how being in covenant with Yahweh changes a people'.

In Ephesians Paul often teaches that God saves and creates the church to display himself. Examples of this include the following:

so that in the coming ages he might show the immeasurable riches of his grace in kindness towards us in Christ Jesus. (2:7)

we are his workmanship, created in Christ Jesus for good works, which God prepared beforehand, that we should walk in them. (2:10)

so that through the church the manifold wisdom of God might now be made known to the rulers and authorities in the heavenly places. (3:10)

Ephesians reveals how the church showcases God in several ways. Even in the basic structure of the exhortations in Ephesians Paul calls attention to how God's people are to 'walk' (*peripateō*), as Baugh shows. The Old Testament commonly uses 'to walk in' as an image of daily conduct. This idea occurs in Ephesians 2:2, 10 and thus forms an inclusio around verses 1–10. Whereas they formerly walked in sin, the believers in Ephesus now are to walk in the good works of the new creation, as God planned.[102]

Before knowing Christ we walked according to the world, the flesh and Satan (2:1–3). But God graciously stepped in and rescued us through the saving work of Christ. Through uniting us to Christ God made us alive (2:4–7). In turn, our entire walk has been transformed (2:10). We used to resemble the way of the world, but now we walk in good works, in a way that resembles our good God. We have been recreated by God to display

---

[101] Durham 1987: 263. We first noticed this quote in Cole (2009: 94).
[102] Baugh 2015: 148, 164–165.

his goodness to the world. This is all according to his eternal plan (2:10). Indeed, we are now exhorted to walk in ways that reflect God and his purposes. We are to walk in unity, in a manner worthy of our calling (4:1). We are to walk in holiness (4:17), reflective of being created anew as God's image. We are to walk in love, as Christ loves us (5:2). We are to walk in truth and holiness, as children of light (5:8). We are to walk wisely as we understand the times (5:15).

Paul also describes several specific ways in which God's people are a 'display people'. First, our salvation glorifies God by displaying his grace. Throughout the coming ages God's saving us displays the inexhaustible nature of his grace (Eph. 2:7). Recreating dead, enslaved, condemned sinners into living, active image-bearers points to the invincible power of God's grace as well as to its boundless supply. Our election, adoption, redemption, unity, inheritance and sealing in Christ all result in the praise of the glory of his grace (1:6) and lead to the praise of his glory (1:12, 14). Bruce tells that God's purpose in lavishing grace on the undeserving is that 'they should serve as a demonstration of his grace to all succeeding ages . . . the masterpiece of his goodness'.[103]

Second, our very existence as the church glorifies God by displaying his wisdom. As we saw previously, through the church the infinite multidimensional wisdom of God is being made known to the rulers and authorities in the heavenly places (3:10). Thielman instructs us concerning this wisdom revealed as Paul preaches to make something known, 'Paul thinks of "the beautifully complex wisdom of God" as especially evident in the unity of Jewish and Gentile believers in the church (v. 6).'[104]

Third, our unity glorifies God by displaying his oneness (4:1–6). That God is one and not many means he is the only God and is alone worthy to receive worship (Deut. 6:4–5). Being the only God also means he deserves to be worshipped universally. The sheer diversity of people makes it seem unlikely that unity would characterize God's people. But in God's eternal plan he actually displays his oneness through the unity of his church. Paul lists the basis for church unity:

There is one body and one Spirit – just as you were called to the one hope that belongs to your call – one Lord, one faith, one baptism,

---

[103] Bruce 1984: 288.
[104] Thielman 2010: 215–216.

one God and Father of all, who is over all and through all and in all.
(Eph. 4:4–6)

The Christian view of God's oneness jars with paganism. The New Testament contains the raw materials from which the Spirit led the church historic to confess the Holy Trinity. Scripture repeatedly sets this against a backdrop of paganism's many gods. The Christians confessed that 'there is one God, and there is one mediator between God and men, the man Christ Jesus' (1 Tim. 2:5). This is 'in distinction from the myriads (*sic*) gods they formerly worshiped', as Baugh reminds us.[105]

Fourth, our love glorifies God by displaying his love. God's love for us not only inspires him to save us (Eph. 1:3–6) but also manifests itself in the church (3:14–19; 4:11–16; 1 John 4:7–12). Paul prays that God would enable the Ephesians to join other believers in understanding the 'boundless, inscrutable character of Christ's love'.[106]

> For this reason I bow my knees before the Father, from whom every family in heaven and on earth is named, that according to the riches of his glory he may grant you to be strengthened with power through his Spirit in your inner being, so that Christ may dwell in your hearts through faith – that you, being rooted and grounded in love, may have strength to comprehend with all the saints what is the breadth and length and height and depth, and to know the love of Christ that surpasses knowledge, that you may be filled with all the fullness of God.
> (Eph. 3:14–19)

Calvin meditates on God's love and wants us to do the same:

> The second fruit is that the Ephesians should perceive the greatness of Christ's love to men . . . This is the most excellent blessing that can be obtained in the present life . . . it is the highest wisdom, to which all the children of God aspire . . . By these dimensions Paul means nothing other than the love of Christ, of which he speaks

---

[105] Baugh 2015: 305–306.
[106] Ibid. 277.

afterwards . . . The love of Christ is held out to us to meditate on day and night and to be wholly immersed in. He who holds to this alone, has enough.[107]

As we walk in love we reflect the love of Christ, who loved us and gave himself for us (Eph. 5:2). As husbands love their wives they embody Christ's love for his church (5:22–33).

Fifth, our holiness glorifies God by displaying his holiness. God chose to save and create the church that we should be holy and blameless before him (1:4). Our election is not only for salvation but also for the creation of a holy people. In addition, Christ's husband-like self-sacrifice was not only for our salvation but also for the creation of a holy bride. As God's new creation the holy people of God are to put on the new self, created after the likeness of God in true righteousness and holiness (4:24). Further, the church is not only characterized by holiness now but will be presented to Christ as perfectly holy on the final day (5:25–27). Baugh explains:

Christ's loving self-sacrifice (v. 25) sanctifies [the church] for access (2:18; 3:12) into the very presence of God to dwell with him forever . . . In Eph 5:26–27 the church is 'resplendent' (ἔνδοξος, *endoxos*) in utter purity – not of her own making – in preparation for the wedding feast at her entrance into eternal glory (Rev 7:14; 19:7–9; 21:2, 9–11).[108]

Conclusion

The church has its origin in the eternal purposes of God, its basis in the saving work of Christ, its life from union with Christ and its end as the glory of God. The church is God's showcase for his eternal plan of bringing forth cosmic reconciliation and highlighting Christ as the focal point of all history. The church is also God's 'display people', showcasing not only God's purposes but even God himself. In and through the church God shows his grace, wisdom, love, unity and holiness. And as God displays himself he glorifies himself. It is no wonder Paul proclaims:

---

[107] Calvin 1965: 168–169.
[108] Baugh 2015: 489.

Now to him who is able to do far more abundantly than all that we ask or think, according to the power at work within us, to him be glory in the church and in Christ Jesus throughout all generations, for ever and ever. Amen.
(Eph. 3:20–21)

God's ultimate goal for the church is to glorify himself in his people and in his Son. As God has many goals, so does the church. But it has no higher goal than this: to glorify God for his person and mighty deeds. Stott speaks wisely:

> The power comes from him; the glory must go to him. To him be glory *in the church and in Christ Jesus*, in the body and in the Head, in the bride and in the Bridegroom, in the community of peace and in the Peacemaker, *to all generations* (in history), *for ever and ever* (in eternity), *Amen.*[109]

---

[109] Stott 1979: 140–141; emphases original.

7

The glory of God and eschatology: 2 Thessalonians 1

'At the parousia of Christ the bodies of all believers will be transformed so that they will be like the glorious, resurrected body of Jesus himself.'[1] Thielman is correct: Christ's resurrected body is glorious, and he will make our resurrected bodies glorious too (Phil. 3:21). In fact, the glory of God and Christ glows in Paul's vision of last things. He puts Christ where he belongs – in the centre of eschatology – and shows that Christ will manifest his glory in many ways. Christ displays his glory in his character and in sharing his glory with believers, both now and in the future, and in both salvation and judgment.

- Christ's glory at his return (2 Thess. 1:5–12)
- The context for Christ's glory (Acts 17:1–9)
- The revelation of Christ's glory (2 Thess. 1:5–12)
- Exclusion from Christ's glory (2 Thess. 1:8–9)
- Seeing and sharing Christ's glory (2 Thess. 1:10)
- Christ's glory in his people now (2 Thess. 1:11–12)
- Believers will gain Christ's glory (2 Thess. 2:13–15)

Christ's glory at his return (2 Thess. 1:5–12)

Paul and his partners, writing to the church they planted in Thessalonica, begin with thanksgiving to God for the believers' multiplying faith and love. The missionaries have boasted to other churches about the Thessalonians' perseverance and faithfulness. These are noteworthy

---

[1] Thielman 2005: 454.

because of the circumstances – Paul praises their steadfastness 'in all your persecutions and in the afflictions that you are enduring' (v. 4). These persecutions are Paul's launching pad to a treatment in verses 5–12 of Christ's return to condemn his foes and glorify his people.

The context for Christ's glory (Acts 17:1–9)

Becoming familiar with the Thessalonians' sociocultural situation helps us better understand their persecution. As usual, Paul had visited the city's synagogue and taken advantage of his opportunity to preach Jesus from the Old Testament (Acts 17). Reacting to Paul's evangelistic success,

> the Jews were jealous, and taking some wicked men of the rabble, they formed a mob, set the city in an uproar, and attacked the house of Jason [apparently a Jewish convert], seeking to bring them out to the crowd.
> (v. 5)

After false accusations of insurrection by the Jews disturbed 'the people and the city authorities' (v. 8), Jason posted bond for the missionaries, who escaped at night to Berea.

Culture in Thessalonica

Besides Judaism, Paul faced other competing religions in Thessalonica, as Wanamaker makes clear:

> That Thessalonica was also rich in pagan religious cults is revealed even by his claim that the majority of his converts had been pagan worshippers (1 Thess. 1:9). Archaeological and inscriptional evidence indicates that Thessalonica had the usual complement of mystery cults, including those that had Dionysus, Sarapis, and Cabirus as their tutelary deities ... The Dionysian and Cabirian cults were state-sponsored, as the likenesses of their deities on coins minted by the city indicate.[2]

---

[2] Wanamaker 1990: 4–5.

Living in countries with legalized religious pluralism hinders us from understanding the pressure believing Thessalonians felt from local officials, fellow citizens and relatives. Rome made Thessalonica a free city in 42 BC, with a measure of political autonomy and reduced taxes. As was customary in the ancient world, religion and politics were fused to promote peace and prosperity.[3] Citizens were expected to respect the imperial cult and offer incense to the emperor. Christians who refused to perform these duties were looked upon unfavourably by officials.

In addition, fellow citizens and relatives looked down on believers as unfaithful to the state and the family gods. Shogren explains:

> Religion existed on two levels, the civic and the domestic. To be a good citizen meant to pay respects to the patron deities. This included participation in feasts, sacrifices, celebrations, games, and other public events. Every occasion had its religious turn, from banquets to games to business transactions.
>
> Domestic religion involved women more than did the public; it was their temple, although the male head of the family was the titular priest. There were household shrines to Hestia, goddess of the hearth. Banquets were dedicated to the gods. Births, marriages, rites of passage, and funerals all included their religious element.[4]

Persecution in Thessalonica

In the light of the intertwining of state, religion and family, Shogren offers insight: 'Persecutions may have been economic, familial, social, or physical. The persecution seems to have begun with the arrest of Jason (Acts 17:6) and been ongoing.'[5] Persecution should not have surprised churches, since Jesus (Matt. 5:12) and his apostles (Acts 14:21–22; 1 Peter 4:12–17) warned of it, but it is grievous to experience nevertheless, as the Thessalonians knew.

After commending the Thessalonian church for its faith, love and steadfastness in affliction Paul writes, 'This is evidence of the righteous judgement of God, that you may be considered worthy of the kingdom of God, for which you are also suffering' (2 Thess. 1:5). Thankfully, 'to Paul's

---

[3] Ibid. 3–4.
[4] Shogren 2012: 19.
[5] Ibid. 26.

deep pleasure, the Thessalonians not only acted on the gospel, but they held on to it despite fierce trials'.[6] Moreover, this perseverance during persecution was 'evidence of the righteous judgement of God'.

It is not obvious how this is so. In fact, at first it appears that believers' suffering persecution at the hands of unbelievers contradicts the 'righteous judgement of God'. Paul, however, assumes here what he spells out elsewhere: believers are God's children 'provided we suffer with him in order that we may also be glorified with him' (Rom. 8:17). Through suffering God was preparing the Thessalonians for future glory. Stott asserts, 'Their suffering was itself evidence of the justice of God, because it was the first part of the equation which guaranteed that the second part (glory) would follow.'[7] As the next verses bear out, God will vindicate his righteous judgment by delivering his persecuted people and condemning their oppressors.

Paul expresses a similar thought in Philippians 1:27–28:

let your manner of life be worthy of the gospel of Christ, so that . . . I may hear of you that you are standing firm in one spirit, with one mind striving side by side for the faith of the gospel, and not frightened in anything by your opponents. This is a clear sign to them of their destruction, but of your salvation, and that from God.

Although God does not appear to distinguish and separate the good from the evil when his people suffer, he knows and even feels what his saints endure (Acts 9:4) and will one day set matters right.[8] In the meantime, Christians' 'standing firm' despite external opposition is a 'clear sign' of salvation to believers and of condemnation to their enemies. It shows that God is indeed already making a distinction between them. And this is a harbinger of his final distinction and separation between the saved and the lost.

The Philippians passage cited shares something else with 2 Thessalonians 1:5: both speak of believers being or being counted 'worthy' of the gospel or the kingdom. Both bring to mind Jesus' statement:

---

[6] Ibid. 351.
[7] Stott 1994: 145.
[8] Hiebert 1996: 307.

those who are considered worthy to attain to that age and to the resurrection from the dead neither marry nor are given in marriage, for they cannot die any more, because they are equal to angels and are sons of God, being sons of the resurrection.
(Luke 20:35–36)

Do these texts teach a merit theology? Beale answers in the negative with an illustration of going to a professional football game. Both money and the ticket purchases are needed to gain admittance. But they are not equal 'causes' of admittance. The money is the chief cause, but one must possess a ticket as evidence of having paid.

> Likewise, true Christians are those on behalf of whom Christ has paid the penalty of sin, but they must have the badge of good works as evidence that Christ paid their purchase price in order to be considered worthy of passing through final judgment and entering the kingdom . . . Part of the *evidence* for God passing a favorable verdict on behalf of the readers is their persevering faith in the midst of persecution (1:4–5). Such ongoing faith until Christ comes is what will cause the readers to *be counted worthy of the kingdom of God.*[9]

The revelation of Christ's glory (2 Thess. 1:5–12)

God's justice

Paul expands on the righteous judgment of God:

> since indeed God considers it just to repay with affliction those who afflict you, and to grant relief to you who are afflicted as well as to us, when the Lord Jesus is revealed from heaven with his mighty angels.
> (vv. 6–7)

What God considers just *is* just, for justice is one of his divine attributes. Green marshals an impressive array of biblical and extrabiblical texts affirming that

---

[9] Beale 2003: 185; emphases original.

God's judgment is in accordance with his justice (Gen. 18.25; 1 Kings 8.31–32; 2 Chr. 6.22–23; Pss. 7.8–9, 11 [7.9–10, 12]; 9.4, 8 [9.5, 9]; 35.24 [34.24]; Tob. 3.2; 2 Macc. 12.6; Sir. 35.18; 2 Tim. 4.8; Rev. 18.6–7; 19.1–2).[10]

God will justly relieve persecuted believers on that day, and will justly condemn the wicked, as verses 7–10 disclose more clearly than anywhere else in Paul.

Evident here is the classic reversal-of-fortunes motif, prominent in the parable of the rich man and Lazarus. '[A] poor man named Lazarus, covered with sores,' who 'desired to be fed with what fell from the rich man's table . . . died and was carried by the angels to Abraham's side' (Luke 16:20–22). By contrast, a heartless, unrepentant rich man died and went to Hades, where he was 'in torment' (v. 23). Father Abraham, speaking for God, declared to him, 'Child, remember that you in your lifetime received your good things, and Lazarus in like manner bad things; but now he is comforted here, and you are in anguish' (v. 25).

Similarly, 'Because *God is just*, he will vindicate [the persecuted believers] publicly one day. He will reverse the fortunes of both groups, the persecutors and the persecuted, when Christ comes.'[11] With the words 'as well as to us' Paul includes the apostles among those who will find relief from persecution at Christ's return.

God's vengeance

This brings to mind an important biblical principle: believers are not to take repayment for evil into their own hands but are to leave it to God, who alone judges rightly:

> 'Vengeance is mine, and recompense,
>   for the time when their foot shall slip;
> for the day of their calamity is at hand,
>   and their doom comes swiftly.'
> For the LORD will vindicate his people
>   and have compassion on his servants,

---

[10] Green 2002: 286.
[11] Stott 1994: 146; emphasis original.

when he sees that their power is gone
> and there is none remaining, bond or free.
(Deut. 32:35–36)

Repay no one evil for evil, but give thought to do what is honourable in the sight of all. If possible, so far as it depends on you, live peaceably with all. Beloved, never avenge yourselves, but leave it to the wrath of God, for it is written, 'Vengeance is mine, I will repay, says the Lord.' . . . Do not be overcome by evil, but overcome evil with good.
(Rom. 12:17–21)

we know him who said, 'Vengeance is mine; I will repay.' And again, 'The Lord will judge his people.' It is a fearful thing to fall into the hands of the living God.
(Heb. 10:30–31)

Marshall notes that this reference to God's character ('God is just', 2 Thess. 1:6) has

the effect of removing the right to inflict punishment and vengeance from the individual, who may easily act unjustly or be motivated by vindictiveness against his persecutors. When Paul takes up the theme in Romans he emphasises that believers must not avenge themselves but rather return good for evil. They can do so in the confidence that where vengeance is necessary, God himself will take care of it (Rom. 12:17–21).[12]

Christ's person

Second Thessalonians 1:7 speaks of 'the Lord Jesus . . . revealed from heaven'. The passage does not focus on God's blessing his people and judging his enemies, though it includes those topics. Rather, the focus is on a person, the Lord Jesus, as Green explains in the light of the Thessalonians' cultural situation:

This affirmation was of great importance for these Christians who had neither a temple nor a visible god as did their pagan contemporaries. He whom neither they nor their pagan persecutors could see

---

[12] Marshall 1983: 174; cited in Hiebert (1996: 309).

will be revealed in all his glory and power, and on that day all will see him (Matt. 24:30; cf. 1 Pet. 1:8).[13]

Paul speaks of the revelation of Christ. In his previous letter he had taught about the 'coming of the Lord':

the Lord himself will descend from heaven with a cry of command, with the voice of an archangel, and with the sound of the trumpet of God. And the dead in Christ will rise first. Then we who are alive, who are left, will be caught up together with them in the clouds to meet the Lord in the air, and so we will always be with the Lord. (1 Thess. 4:16–17)

Stott helpfully compares and contrasts the two statements. Both depict Christ's coming as personal, visible and glorious. But different details emerge:

Instead of the loud command, the voice of the archangel and the trumpet call of God, we now read of *blazing fire*, a regular biblical symbol of the holy, consuming nature of God's presence. And the retinue which will accompany the descending Lord, which in 1 Thessalonians was the Christian dead (4:14), is now *his powerful angels* . . . (1 Thess. 3:13).[14]

Bruce explores the 'revelation of the Lord Jesus from heaven' as a revelation of glory:

The Parousia of Christ is called his ἀποκάλυψις in 1 Cor 1:7 (also in 1 Pet 1:7, 13; 4:13, 'the revelation of his glory') . . . It is the occasion when 'the glory is to be revealed' (ἀποκαλυφθῆναι) to those who suffer with Christ at present (Rom 8:18); it is accordingly called the 'revealing (ἀποκάλυψις) of the sons of God' – i.e. their being revealed *as* the sons of God, invested with his glory (Rom 8:19). The OT promise that 'the glory of the LORD shall be revealed' (Isa 40:5) takes on fuller significance in the light of the work of Christ.[15]

---

[13] Green 2002: 288–289.
[14] Stott 1994: 147–148.
[15] Bruce 1982: 150.

Christ's return

When will this occur? '[W]hen the Lord Jesus is revealed from heaven with his mighty angels in flaming fire' (2 Thess. 1:7–8). Although God sometimes brings relief to his persecuted people now, full deliverance awaits Jesus' return. Paul combines three prepositional phrases to heighten his words' force: Jesus will come again 'from heaven with his mighty angels in flaming fire'. The first phrase shows that ultimate justice will come from God, not humans. The second phrase presents Jesus as a triumphant warrior-king alongside the 'mighty angels' (cf. Ps. 103:20) – his angelic army. The third phrase portrays Christ's coming in vengeance against his foes.

Investigating Paul's Old Testament allusions to the end of Isaiah increases our understanding of these verses.

> The sound of an uproar from the city!
>> A sound from the temple!
> The sound of the LORD,
>> rendering recompense to his enemies!
> (Isa. 66:6)

> behold, the LORD will come in fire,
>> and his chariots like the whirlwind,
> to render his anger in fury,
>> and his rebuke with flames of fire.
> For by fire will the LORD enter into judgement,
>> and by his sword, with all flesh;
>> and those slain by the LORD shall be many.
> (Isa. 66:15–16)

Isaiah 66:6 tells of the Lord's 'rendering recompense to his enemies', citing the principle of retributive justice, *lex talionis* ('an eye for an eye', Exod. 21:23–25). Paul puts Jesus in the place of Yahweh in Isaiah's prophecy, for 'God considers it just to repay' the persecutors 'with affliction . . . when the Lord Jesus' returns to inflict 'vengeance' on God's foes (2 Thess. 1:6–8). In Isaiah 66:15–16 the LORD comes 'in fire' to render 'his rebuke with flames of fire' and to enter into 'judgement' with humanity. Again the apostle puts Jesus in Yahweh's place, for Jesus comes 'from heaven . . . in flaming fire', bringing the fire of judgment on those who reject the gospel (2 Thess. 1:7–8).

The message of verses 7–8 should have a powerful effect on the persecuted Thessalonian believers, as Hiebert, focusing on 'angels of his power' (his translation), explains:

> The 'power' belongs to Christ, and the angels will be the executors of His commands. This mention of power is part of the consolation offered to the readers; now 'power' belongs to the persecutors, but when Jesus returns, this will be the attribute of the one who will punish the persecutors.[16]

Exclusion from Christ's glory (2 Thess. 1:8–9)

Whom will Jesus condemn when he comes again? Paul's immediate concern is to comfort the persecuted Thessalonians with the knowledge that Christ will punish their persecutors.[17] But he enlarges the recipients of the divine wrath: Christ will inflict 'vengeance on those who do not know God and on those who do not obey the gospel of our Lord Jesus' (v. 8). Though some have argued that this refers to two different groups, it is better to see the two descriptions as referring to the same group.[18] Green responds to Marshall's arguments for two groups, the Gentiles (*those who do not know God*) and the Jews (those who *do not obey the gospel of our Lord Jesus*):

> Although Marshall is correct in pointing out that sometimes the Gentiles are described as those who are ignorant of God (see 1 Thess. 4:5; and Ps. 79:6 [78:6]; Jer. 10:25) and the Jews as those who are disobedient (Isa. 66:4; Acts 7:39; Rom. 10:16), Paul also accuses both groups of being disobedient (Rom. 11:30–32). Also, both the OT and the NT occasionally describe the Jews as those who are ignorant of the true God (Jer. 4:22; 9:3, 6; Hos. 5:4; John 8:55).[19]

---

[16] Hiebert 1996: 311.
[17] Skaug 2020a; see also his 2020b.
[18] Marshall (1983: 177–178) thinks Paul describes two different groups. Those favouring one group include Wanamaker (1990: 227), Green (2002: 290), Stott (1994: 148) and Bruce (1982: 151).
[19] Green 2002: 290.

We agree with Green that Paul describes one group in two ways – they reject both the knowledge of God and the gospel of Christ. First, they reject God's knowledge revealed in creation and conscience. God revealed 'his eternal power and divine nature' in his creation. That knowledge reaches everyone, but,

> although [unbelievers] knew God, they did not honour him as God or give thanks to him, but they became futile in their thinking, and their foolish hearts were darkened. Claiming to be wise, they became fools, and exchanged the glory of the immortal God for images [idols].
> (Rom. 1:20–23)

God likewise revealed his holiness and justice to every person when he wrote 'the law ... on their hearts, while their conscience also bears witness, and their conflicting thoughts accuse or even excuse them' (Rom. 2:15). God, then, finds unbelievers inexcusable for their rejection of divine revelation in creation and conscience.

Second, the returning Christ will condemn sinners because they 'do not obey the gospel of our Lord Jesus' (2 Thess. 1:8). The gospel is a command to believe in Jesus, and faith and unbelief are therefore sometimes expressed in terms of the 'obedience of faith' (Rom. 1:5; 16:26) or of not obeying the gospel (Rom. 10:16; 2 Thess. 1:8), respectively.

What punishment will the lost endure? 'They will suffer the punishment of eternal destruction, away from the presence of the Lord and from the glory of his might' (2 Thess. 1:9). When we commonly define hell as eternal separation (banishment) from God, we are correct but incomplete. As Morgan has previously shown, hell involves three major themes, all of which appear in our passage:[20] punishment ('They will suffer the punishment'), destruction ('of eternal destruction') and banishment ('away from the presence of the Lord and from the glory of his might').

Hell as punishment

First, the lost will suffer eternal punishment at the hands of almighty God.[21] This theme is repeated in our passage:

---

[20] Morgan and Peterson 2004: 135–151.
[21] The biblical picture of eternal punishment also appears most clearly in Matt. 25:31–46; Rev. 20:10–15.

- The righteous judgment of God (v. 5).
- God considers it just to repay with affliction (v. 6).
- When the Lord Jesus is revealed, vengeance will be inflicted (vv. 7–8).
- They will suffer the punishment (v. 9).

Hell as destruction

Second, the lost will suffer 'eternal destruction' (v. 9). This concept has spawned debate on at least two issues. How long is 'eternal'? Does it mean 'age-long', or 'everlasting'? Peterson gives the parameters for the use of the Old Testament word *'ôlām*:

> In Daniel 12:2 the word 'everlasting' (Heb. *'ôlām*) is used to describe the fates of the just and unjust. This word . . . does not always mean 'everlasting.' It is an adjective signifying long duration with limits set by the context. For example, Exodus 21:6 describes the period of time a willing bondslave could choose to serve his master: 'Then he will be his servant for *life*.' When used of God, however, as in Psalm 90:2 ('from *everlasting* to *everlasting* you are God') *'ôlām* means 'eternal.' In this case the limits of long duration indicated by *'ôlām* are set by the eternal life of God himself. That happens frequently in the Old Testament . . . As we will see when we study the New Testament, the state of affairs after the resurrection of the dead is characterized by the life of God himself; the age to come lasts as long as he does – forever.[22]

Shogren extends our study of words translated 'eternal' into the New Testament:

> A study of the use *aiōnios* in the NT shows that it patently takes the meaning of 'eternal' (see 2 Thess 2:16; Heb 5:9; 1 Pet 5:10; 2 Pet 1:11) . . . That it means everlasting is particularly apparent when used in the phrase 'eternal life' (2 Tim 1:9), which in Paul's letters signifies not 'future life for a very long time' but 'the unending resurrection life of the world to come.'[23]

---

22 R. A. Peterson 1995: 34–35; emphases original.
23 Shogren 2012: 252.

Another issue regards whether the fate of the lost as 'eternal destruction' (2 Thess. 1:9) means everlasting ruin in hell, or irreversible annihilation.[24] Annihilationists claim that 'eternal destruction' means extinction of being, with no possibility of recreation. In a word, it means extermination. Although this is how they interpret death or destruction in hell texts, Moo reaches a different conclusion based on a study of the vocabulary of destruction in the New Testament:

> The words need not mean 'destruction' in the sense of 'extinction.' In fact, leaving aside for the moment the judgment texts, none of the key terms usually has this meaning in the Old and New Testaments. Rather, they usually refer to the situation of a person or object that has lost the essence of its nature or function . . . The key words for 'destroy' and 'destruction' can also refer to land that has lost its fruitfulness (*olethros* in Ezek. 6:14; 14:16); . . . to a coin that is useless because it is lost (*apollymi* in Luke 15:9); or to the entire world that 'perishes,' as an inhabited world, in the Flood (2 Pet. 3:6). In none of these cases do the objects cease to exist; they cease to be useful or to exist in their original, intended state.[25]

Morris turns his attention to 'eternal destruction' in 2 Thessalonians 1:9:

> The noun is used in I Cor. 5:5 of the destruction of the flesh with a view to the saving of the spirit. In that passage Paul clearly does not view destruction as annihilation, for there is no likelihood that he thought of such a one being saved in a disembodied state. This has relevance to the verse we are discussing, for it indicates that the word does not signify so much annihilation as the loss of all that is worthwhile, utter ruin . . . 'Eternal life' is that life which belongs to the age to come. Therefore it has no end. At the same time 'eternal' is a quality of life. It is not only that life in the age to come will be longer than life here: it will also be of a different quality. All of this has to be borne in mind when we consider the other expression

---

[24] Evangelicals arguing for eternal conscious punishment include the nine contributors to Morgan and Peterson 2004. Those arguing for annihilationism include Stott in Stott and Edwards 1989; Wenham 1985; Fudge 1994.

[25] Moo in Morgan and Peterson (2004: 105).

'eternal destruction.' It is the opposite of eternal life. It is the end of all that is worthwhile in life.[26]

Beale concurs:

This understanding of *everlasting destruction* is supported also by noting that Paul derives the phrase 'in a blazing fire, giving vengeance' . . . from Isaiah 66:15 . . . the only place in the Old Testament where this combination of terms is found. This is noteworthy because only nine verses later comes the well-known depiction of those who have been judged – 'their worm will not die, nor will their fire be quenched' (Is 66:24) – a clear reference to an unending punishment of conscious beings.[27]

Hell as banishment

Third, the lost 'will suffer the punishment of eternal destruction, away from the presence of the Lord and from the glory of his might' (2 Thess. 1:9). This is the judgment theme of banishment from God's gracious and glorious presence. Others have noted that Paul here uses the language of Isaiah 2.[28] Fee shows this convincingly in the LXX and then draws sound conclusions:

Paul – who . . . from the face of   the Lord
                   and from the glory of his might.

Isaiah – Hide from the face of the fear of the Lord
                   and from the glory of his might.

Here Paul has not only brought language straight across from the Septuagint but has also kept the sense of Isaiah's text, which appears in a 'day of the Lord' oracle of judgment against Judah. In Isaiah that judgment has to do with Israel's being cut off from the divine

---

[26] Morris 1959: 205–206.
[27] Beale 2003: 189; emphasis original.
[28] Beale (ibid.) notes, 'The phrase *from the presence of the Lord and from the majesty of his power* comes from Isaiah 2:10, 19, 21, where the same phrase is repeated three times (Isaiah adds "the fear of" before "the Lord"), though it appears nowhere else in the entire Old Testament'; emphasis original.

Presence; in Paul's use of this language 'the Lord' is now assumed to be Christ himself . . . Paul considers the nature of the judgment to be twofold . . . eternal loss – to be cut off forever from the divine presence . . . For beings created in the divine image this is the ultimate desolation. Second, it means to miss out on 'the glory of his might,' both now and forever. For him eternal glory has to do with being in the presence of the Father and the risen Lord. The eternal judgment of the wicked is the absolute loss of such glory.[29]

With these strong words Paul assures his readers that their persecutors' victories are short-lived and that those persecutors will pay bitterly in the end. Morris agrees: 'Paul is turning their eyes away from the troubles through which they are passing to remind them that the power of their oppressors is as nothing to the might of the glorious Lord who is to be revealed.'[30]

In Paul's Old Testament allusions in 2 Thessalonians 1 he consistently put Jesus in the place of Yahweh. He also does so with reference to God's glory, as Shogren explains:

Now when the Lord comes, he comes in glory, but in the glory that is associated with the epiphany of Yahweh in the OT. For example, when Yahweh met with Moses on Sinai, 'To the Israelites the glory of the LORD looked like a consuming fire on top of the mountain' (Exod 24:17). 'The LORD came from Mount Sinai. From Edom, he gave light to his people, and his glory was shining from Mount Paran . . .' (Deut 33:2). Now it is the Lord Jesus who comes with the Shekinah glory that reveals his divine 'might.'[31]

Seeing and sharing Christ's glory (2 Thess. 1:10)

After saying that the lost will be excluded from 'the glory of [Christ's] might' at his second coming, Paul proclaims that this will occur 'when he comes on that day to be glorified in his saints, and to be marvelled at

---

[29] Fee 2009: 259.
[30] Morris 1959: 206.
[31] Shogren 2012: 253.

among all who have believed, because our testimony to you was believed' (v. 10). 'That day' is the 'day of the Lord', on which, according to the Old Testament, God will primarily judge his enemies but also deliver his people (Joel 2:30–32; Acts 2:20–21). The day of the Lord is now the 'day of our Lord Jesus Christ' (1 Cor. 1:8). When Paul speaks of Jesus' being 'glorified in his saints' and 'marvelled at among' believers, he again appropriates Old Testament texts – Psalm 89:7 (LXX 88:8) and 68:35 (LXX 67:36), respectively – and puts Jesus in the place of God.[32] Christ's glory will be broadcast when he returns and his people, including the Thessalonians, give him glory and worship him. Stott aptly summarizes Paul's portrayal of heaven's glories:

> When Christ *comes*, he . . . will also *be glorified in his holy people and . . . be marvelled at among all those who have believed . . .* (10). That is to say, not only will the Lord Jesus be 'revealed' objectively in his own splendour (7), so that we see it, but his splendour will be revealed in us, his redeemed people, so that we will be transformed by it and will become vehicles by which it is displayed.[33]

Paul's words remind us of Romans 8: '[W]e are children of God, and if children, then heirs – heirs of God and fellow heirs with Christ, provided we suffer with him in order that we may also be glorified with him' (vv. 16–17). The Thessalonians are currently suffering persecution, but when Jesus comes again they will see and share his glory and forget their suffering for ever. Paul's words are designed to encourage them to live for Christ, even under severe persecution.

Christ's glory in his people now (2 Thess. 1:11–12)

Paul rounds off verses 3–12 by returning to the place he began – prayer. Instead of a thanksgiving report (v. 3) he gives a prayer report telling what he, Silvanus and Timothy regularly pray for the Thessalonian church: 'To this end we always pray for you, that our God may make you worthy of his calling and may fulfil every resolve for good and every work of faith

---

[32] So Fee (2009: 260–262).
[33] Stott 1994: 149–150; emphasis original.

by his power' (v. 11). Paul's focus is on God's working in the Thessalonians 'by his power'. Paul and his companions ask God to count the believers worthy of his calling them to salvation – a high standard indeed (cf. Eph. 4:1). Further, Paul asks God to bring to fruition their good intentions so that good deeds will result. Bruce is succinct: 'If their Lord is to be glorified in them at his Advent, he must be glorified in their present way of life.'[34] And Paul knows that will happen only by God's power (2 Thess. 1:11).

Paul next states the end to which he and his colleagues pray for the Thessalonians: 'so that the name of our Lord Jesus may be glorified in you, and you in him, according to the grace of our God and the Lord Jesus Christ' (v. 12). The goal of Paul's prayer for the believers' pleasing God, growing and serving is that Christ and they would be mutually glorified, and this by the enabling grace of the Father and the Son. Once more Bruce warrants quotation:

> The consummation of glory on the Day of the Lord is closely related to holy living here and now. For holiness now and glory hereafter God has called them (cf. 1 Thess 2:12; 4:7; 5:24) . . . 'that the name of our Lord Jesus may be glorified in you.' It has been stated in v 10 that Christ at his coming will be glorified in his people. But there is no difference in principle between his being glorified in them then and his being glorified in them now. His 'name' – i.e. his reputation – is 'glorified' when those who bear that name bring credit to it by their lives.[35]

Conclusion

Stott is correct: 'The most striking feature of this chapter is its recurring references to the glory of Christ.'[36] This feature unfolds in four stages, all related to the second coming:

> a. *The Lord Jesus will be revealed in his glory (1:7).* The Parousia will be . . . an event of awe-inspiring, cosmic splendour (like lightning flashing across the whole sky, Jesus said).

---

[34] Bruce 1982: 157.
[35] Ibid. 156–157.
[36] Stott 1994: 151.

b. The Lord Jesus will be glorified in his people (1:10). This will entail a complete transformation into Christ's image. Our bodies will become at the Resurrection 'like his glorious body.'

c. Those who reject Christ will be excluded from his glory (1:8–9). By being separated from the glory of Christ, the condemned will be alienated from their own true identity as human beings.

d. Meanwhile Jesus Christ must begin to be glorified in us (1:12). The glorification of Jesus in his people, and their consequent glorification, are not a transformation which is entirely reserved for the last day. The process begins now.[37]

Believers will gain Christ's glory (2 Thess. 2:13–15)

Paul, Silvanus and Timothy begin in 2:1–12 by differentiating the Thessalonian believers from the unsaved people deceived by the antichrist. These rebels act like those persecuting his readers; so, by foretelling their condemnation, Paul encourages the saints in Thessalonica. He contrasts the rebels' and believers' lifestyles, assessment of the gospel, influences and destinies. The rebels' lifestyle is such that they 'had pleasure in unrighteousness' (v. 12). By contrast, the believers seek 'sanctification' (v. 13). The rebels 'refused to love the truth and so be saved' (v. 10). By contrast, the readers believe 'in the truth' (v. 13). Beale cites powerful yet different influences upon the two groups:

> While 2:11 says that 'God sends [unbelievers] a powerful delusion so that they will believe the lie,' 2:13 says that God sends the Spirit to others to set them apart from falsehood so that they have faith *in the truth.*[38]

Finally, the two groups have opposite destinies. The rebels 'are perishing' (v. 10) and will be 'condemned' (12). By contrast, the believers will 'obtain the glory of our Lord Jesus Christ' (v. 14).

---

[37] Ibid. 152–155; emphases original.
[38] Beale 2003: 228; emphasis original.

Thanksgiving for salvation (2 Thess. 2:13)

Paul and his companions must offer continual thanksgiving to God for the salvation of the Thessalonians, their brothers in Christ. '[W]e ought always to give thanks to God for you, brothers beloved by the Lord, because God chose you as the firstfruits to be saved, through sanctification by the Spirit and belief in the truth' (v. 13). Bruce correctly observes that this thanksgiving is the 'resumption of the introductory thanksgiving of 1:3'.[39] As often in Scripture,[40] God's love for and election of his people go hand in hand. 'God's election of Christians is an explanation of what it means that they have been loved by God,' as Beale says.[41] The Thessalonians are 'beloved by the Lord', which, as Fee reminds us, means the Lord Jesus. God set his love on them and chose them for salvation.

Two possibilities obtain: 'God chose you as the firstfruits to be saved,' or 'God chose you from the beginning to be saved.' The textual tradition divides into two readings: 'from the beginning' or 'firstfruits', respectively (v. 13).[42] We follow Metzger,[43] the NIV and the ESV and favour 'firstfruits'. The apostle thanks God because he elected Thessalonians 'as the firstfruits to be saved'. Fee notes that Paul thereby encourages his readers in two ways. First, he distinguishes them from those who persecute them and are heading for condemnation (vv. 11–12). Second, Paul calls them God's 'firstfruits, as it were, of a great eschatological harvest'.[44] This heartens his readers because it means God has chosen to save others in Thessalonica.

Paul expresses salvation here in terms of sanctification and faith. As mentioned earlier, sanctification in Paul is initial, progressive and final. Initial or definitive sanctification is the Holy Spirit's work of setting apart sinners to God and holiness once and for all. It is also called definitive sanctification because God defines those initially sanctified as his saints (1:2). Progressive sanctification is the Spirit's working practical holiness into believers' lives (1 Thess. 4:3–5). The Spirit works progressive holiness into believers, using the Word and prayer (John 17:17). Final sanctification

---

[39] Bruce 1982: 189.
[40] See Deut. 4:37; 7:7; 10:15; Eph. 1:4–5; 2 Tim. 1:9.
[41] Beale 2003: 225.
[42] For discussion see Fee (2009: 301–302), who supports 'firstfruits', and Beale (2003: 226–227), who prefers 'from the beginning'.
[43] Metzger 1968: 636.
[44] Fee 2009: 302.

is the Holy Spirit's work of perfecting the saints in holiness at Christ's return (Eph. 5:27; 1 Thess. 5:23–24).[45]

In verse 13 'Spirit' and 'truth' are both in the genitive case but are used differently. 'Spirit' is a subjective genitive: the Spirit produces sanctification as its prime mover. 'Truth' is an objective genitive: it receives the action of 'belief', or 'faith'. Thus the ESV translates this as 'through sanctification by the Spirit and belief in the truth'.

Paul combines sanctification and faith so as to highlight God's grace while also affirming human responsibility. Green strikes the proper balance:

> In 1 Thessalonians Paul exhorted the believers again and again to dedicate themselves to sanctification (1 Thess. 4:3, 4, 7), reminding them that sanctification was God's will for them and that God called them to the same. But he also assured the Thessalonians that sanctification was a work of God (1 Thess. 5:23) that he effects through the agency of the Holy Spirit (1 Thess. 4:8) . . . Far from its being auxiliary to their salvation, the apostle understands the *sanctifying work* as the action *of the Spirit* of God that brings about salvation . . . These Christians entered into the realm of salvation *through belief in the truth*, that is, through their faith in the gospel that was proclaimed to them (see vv. 10, 12). Although the divine decision and activity in bringing about salvation are the primary focus, the apostle does not lose sight of human responsibility in this process, which is indicated by the word *belief*.[46]

Paul writes, 'To this he called you through our gospel, so that you may obtain the glory of our Lord Jesus Christ' (2 Thess. 2:14). Stott steers us correctly: '*To this* must mean "to this salvation just mentioned."'[47] Paul now speaks of salvation in terms of calling. Calling is God's work of summoning people to himself through gospel preaching. It includes God's sovereign and mysterious inner call and his universal, outward gospel call. God worked in the Thessalonians when they heard the gospel, and they believed and were saved. God's purpose for his people is that they 'obtain the glory of our Lord Jesus Christ'.

---

[45] See Morgan with Peterson 2020: 465.

[46] Green 2002: 326–327; emphasis original.

[47] Stott 1994: 176.

Paul follows these amazing words with an exhortation for his readers to persevere amid trials: 'So then, brothers, stand firm and hold to the traditions that you were taught by us, either by our spoken word or by our letter' (2 Thess. 2:15). The Thessalonians are 'not to be quickly shaken in mind or alarmed' (v. 2) but are to stand firm, keeping a firm grasp on the apostolic 'traditions'. Stott observes: '[These] are not the later traditions of the church, but the original teachings or traditions of the apostles ... while subsequent ecclesiastical traditions are the superstructure which the church has erected on [them].'[48] The readers must be steadfast and firmly committed to the apostles' words, both preached and written (such as 1 Thessalonians).

Obtaining the 'glory of our Lord Jesus Christ' (2 Thess. 2:14)

We return to Paul's marvellous telling of Christians' obtaining the 'glory of our Lord Jesus Christ' (2 Thess. 2:14). The New Testament speaks of believers' final salvation in a number of ways, including the new heavens and new earth, sabbath rest, God's kingdom, God's presence, seeing God and God's glory.[49] Paul's preferred way of speaking of final salvation is in terms of glory. He anticipates God's people being glorified (Rom. 8:17, 30), sharing in glory, being raised in glory (1 Cor. 15:43) and obtaining the glory of the Father or the Son. Paul speaks of an eternal weight of glory (2 Cor. 4:17), glory revealed to us (Rom. 8:18), our hope of glory (5:2), our being called to God's kingdom and glory (1 Thess. 2:12), our appearing with Christ in glory (Col. 3:4) and our obtaining salvation with eternal glory (2 Tim. 2:10).

From these passages we draw the following conclusions. First, glory has to do chiefly with God's own character, and then it has to do with humans' final salvation. Knight, commenting on 2 Timothy 2:10, links God's intrinsic glory and the glory he shares with his people:

Since δόξα ... is used normally in the NT of God's glory, majesty, and sublimity, it is natural that it also be used of the future eternal state (αἰώνιον) and realm of existence in which his splendor is everywhere and immediately present and, as here, of that in which

---

[48] Ibid. 178.
[49] See Peterson 2014a.

the redeemed participate in a marvelous and endless way as they behold his splendor in a full and direct way.[50]

Second, glory as final salvation is eschatological, as Campbell says:

There is something all-consuming about the glory of God in the eschaton. It is the ultimate end of everything from Paul's perspective. The highest goal of life, of humanity, of creation is the glory of God in Christ. It is true to say that everything exists to serve this eternal glory in the end.[51]

The accent is almost always on the future state of affairs to accompany the consummation of salvation. But, as with every other major eschatological theme, glory is 'already' and 'not yet'. God has already given believers a taste of final glory. It is astounding that Paul could say that we, already indwelt by Christ, the 'hope of glory' (Col. 1:27), behold his glory and 'are being transformed into the same image from one degree of glory to another' (2 Cor. 3:18). Yet overwhelmingly glory is not yet, for 'we rejoice in *hope* of the glory of God' (Rom. 5:2). And only when Christ our life appears will we 'appear with him in glory' (Col. 3:4). As Bruce succinctly says, 'The glory of Christ which his people are to obtain [2 Thess. 2:24] is their sharing in his glory at the Parousia.'[52]

Third, final glory is holistic, involving body and soul. Although some evangelicals protest, Scripture teaches an intermediate state in which a human's immaterial part ('soul' or 'spirit') departs the body at death and goes into Christ's presence in heaven. Thus Paul speaks of believers at death being 'away from the body and at home with the Lord' (2 Cor. 5:8). But this is not God's ultimate destiny for his people. Instead, the returning Christ will 'transform our lowly body to be like his glorious body' (Phil. 3:21). Thiselton correctly labels this holistic resurrection of believers a 'resurrection to glory into full characterization by the image . . . of Christ, fully shaped by the Holy Spirit'.[53]

Fourth, glory as ultimate salvation is Christological: it entails sharing in Christ's glory. Paul contrasts present suffering and future glory (Rom. 8:18),

---

[50] Knight 1992: 400.
[51] Campbell 2020: 460.
[52] Bruce 1982: 191.
[53] Thiselton 2000: 245.

and Moo compares Jewish and Christian views of this contrast: 'Judaism also contrasted present suffering and future glory. But, since the Christian's glory is a partaking of Christ's own glory ("glorified with him"), Paul puts more stress than does Judaism on the righteous person's participation in this glory.'[54]

It is well known that when Paul affirms union with Christ, he speaks of believers' participation in Christ's redemptive deeds: we died with him (Rom. 6:8), were raised with him and are seated at God's right hand with him (Eph. 2:6). It is not as well known that in two places Paul teaches that in a sense we will come again with Christ. '[T]he creation waits with eager longing for the revealing of the sons of God' (Rom. 8:19). The word translated 'revealing' is *apokalypsis*, which means 'revelation', and which the New Testament uses of Christ's return (1 Peter 1:7, 13; Rev. 1:1). Paul says the creation waits for believers' second coming, so to speak.

Paul also uses the word 'appear' within a single verse to speak of the return both of Christ and of his people: 'When Christ who is your life appears, then you also will appear with him in glory' (Col. 3:4). Paul is not confusing Christ and believers with such language; rather, he is showing how closely identified believers are with their Saviour. Now we belong to God, but our full identity will be made known only when Jesus comes again. John agrees: 'Beloved, we are God's children now, and what we will be has not yet appeared; but we know that when he appears we shall be like him, because we shall see him as he is' (1 John 3:2). Moo, referring to this text, says it well: 'The believer's appearance "in glory," or "in a state of glory," will mean a final transformation into the "image" of Christ . . . by means of resurrection.'[55]

Fifth, believers' final glory involves God's creation:

I consider that the sufferings of this present time are not worth comparing with the glory that is to be revealed to us . . . [T]he creation itself will be set free from its bondage to corruption and obtain the freedom of the glory of the children of God.
(Rom. 8:18, 21)

---

[54] Moo 1996: 512.
[55] Moo 2008: 251.

Once more, Moo's words are apt: 'It is only with and because of the glory of God's children that creation experiences its own full and final deliverance.'[56]

Sixth, after all these words describing Christians' glory as final salvation, we must admit that in the end glory is indescribable. Seifrid comments on 2 Corinthians 4:17 ('[T]his light momentary affliction is preparing for us an eternal weight of glory beyond all comparison'):

> The momentary weight of affliction ... works an eternal weight *(baros)* of glory for Paul. It does so in a manner that is so surpassing that it can hardly be described: it surpasses even that which is surpassing *(kath' hyperbolēn eis hyperbolēn)* ... 'Glory' remains the glory of God alone. Nevertheless, the human being, who is called into a saving relationship of communication with God, paradoxically shares in it ... Likewise Paul here emphatically underscores the 'how much more,' that is, the transcendence, of that glory (3:9–11).[57]

Seventh and most important, believers' final glory redounds to God alone. The following passages combine references to ultimate salvation with praise to God:

> it is all for your sake, so that as grace extends to more and more people it may increase thanksgiving, to the glory of God.
> (2 Cor. 4:15)

> Grace to you and peace from God our Father and the Lord Jesus Christ, who gave himself for our sins to deliver us from the present evil age, according to the will of our God and Father, to whom be the glory for ever and ever. Amen.
> (Gal. 1:3–5)

> In him we have obtained an inheritance, having been predestined according to the purpose of him who works all things according to the counsel of his will, so that we who were the first to hope in Christ might be to the praise of his glory.
> (Eph. 1:11–12)

---

[56] Moo 1996: 517.
[57] Seifrid 2014: 218.

I received mercy for this reason, that in me, as the foremost, Jesus Christ might display his perfect patience as an example to those who were to believe in him for eternal life. To the King of ages, immortal, invisible, the only God, be honour and glory for ever and ever. Amen. (1 Tim. 1:16–17)

Called into God's own kingdom and glory (1 Thess. 2:12)

Paul's reference to believers gaining 'the glory of our Lord Jesus Christ' (2 Thess. 2:14) recalls his earlier words '[W]e exhorted each one of you and encouraged you and charged you to walk in a manner worthy of God, who calls you *into his own kingdom and glory*' (1 Thess. 2:12). This passage combines the main theme of our study, God's glory, with another key biblical theme – the kingdom of God.

When preaching the gospel to them, Paul did not ask the Thessalonians to support him. Rather, he worked hard for long hours to support himself: '[Y]ou remember, brothers, our labour and toil: we worked night and day, that we might not be a burden to any of you, while we proclaimed to you the gospel of God' (v. 9). Not only so, but Paul also underscores the godly conduct of himself, Silvanus and Timothy toward the Christians: 'You are witnesses, and God also, how holy and righteous and blameless was our conduct towards you believers' (v. 10).

Having used a maternal image to describe his ministry among the Thessalonians (1 Thess. 2:7–8), Paul now shifts to a paternal one: 'For you know how, like a father with his children, we exhorted each one of you and encouraged you and charged you to walk in a manner worthy of God' (vv. 11–12). Like a good father caring for his children, Paul encouraged, comforted and urged them to please God in their daily lives.[58] Green comments on the three verbs:

> These three together summarize the exhortation, persuasion, and insistence with which the apostolic team delivered the moral instruction to *each one* of the members of this church . . . The strong language of this instruction was borne (*sic*) out of their fatherly concern.[59]

---

[58] Beale 2003: 74.
[59] Green 2002: 136; emphasis original.

The apostle expects his readers to live 'in a manner worthy of God'. Paul sets a high standard, and it is possible to misunderstand him as teaching merit theology. But Beale offers a corrective. Walking worthy does not earn admittance into God's kingdom but shows outwardly that Christ has truly saved someone. 'Since those whom God *calls* he also enables to believe and do works of sanctification (1 Thess. 5:23–24), all the glory at the end of the ages' belongs to him alone.[60]

Paul has been scaling a mountain and now reaches the peak when he writes of 'God, who calls you into his own kingdom and glory' (v. 12). God effectively summoned the Thessalonians to himself through the gospel. Here Paul sets forth God's goal for them and all believers: to enter his eschatological kingdom and to see and partake of his divine glory. God's kingdom is his reign, his dominion. Paul declares that God 'has delivered us from the domain of darkness and transferred us to the kingdom of his beloved Son, in whom we have redemption, the forgiveness of sins' (Col. 1:13–14).

Bruce helpfully connects kingdom and glory:

The kingdom of God is held out as something which his children are to inherit – an inheritance from which evildoers are excluded (1 Cor 6:9, 10; Gal 5:21; Eph 5:5). The manifestation of the kingdom of God will coincide with the revelation of his glory, in which his children will share.[61]

Although Paul does not emphasize the kingdom of God as much as Jesus does, he does have a theology of the kingdom. Beale summarizes:

Paul sometimes refers only to the present phase of the kingdom (Rom 14:17; 1 Cor 4:20; 15:24; Col 1:13) and other times to its future, consummate reality (1 Cor 6:9–10; 15:50; Gal 5:21; 2 Thess 1:5; 2 Tim 4:1, 18). Both aspects may be included here, though the future is likely at the forefront, given the futuristic references elsewhere in the epistle (see 1:10; 2:19; 3:13; 4:13–17; 5:1–7).[62]

---

[60] Beale 2003: 75; emphasis original.
[61] Bruce 1982: 37.
[62] Beale 2003: 75.

We agree that Paul's emphasis here is on the future fullness of the kingdom, when God's glory will be revealed (Rom. 5:2; 8:17–18; Col. 1:27; 2 Thess. 2:14).[63] This entails resurrected, transformed and glorified bodies, as Wanamaker reminds us:

> Elsewhere Paul teaches that the Christian is to participate 'physically' in the glory of God when salvation has been fully realized in the future through the resurrection of the dead and the transformation of the body (cf. Rom. 8:18–23; 1 Cor. 15:42–44; Phil. 3:20f.).[64]

---

[63] Green 2002: 138.
[64] Wanamaker 1990: 108.

8
The glory of God
and systematic theology

We have explored the glory of God in Paul's epistles in relation to other theological themes highlighted in those epistles:

- The glory of God and salvation (Romans)
- The glory of God and the resurrection (1 Corinthians)
- The glory of God and the new covenant (2 Corinthians)
- The glory of God and the church (Ephesians)
- The glory of God and eschatology (2 Thessalonians)

In doing so we have touched on many areas of systematic theology. It is time to expand those findings toward a summary of the glory of God and systematic theology in Paul:

- God and his Word
- Humanity and sin
- Christ's person and work
- The Holy Spirit and the new covenant
- Salvation
- The church
- The future
- Ministry

God and his Word

God
Paul has much to say about God and his glory. God is glorious, and his glory permeates the Trinity and God's presence, attributes, works and purposes.

Glory marks each member of the Trinity. Paul writes of the 'Father of glory' (Eph. 1:17), and calls Jesus the 'Lord of glory' (1 Cor. 2:8). Although Paul does not call the Holy Spirit the 'Spirit of glory and of God', as Peter does (1 Peter 4:14), he associates the Spirit and glory (1 Cor. 15:44; 2 Cor. 3:18).

God's glory also communicates God's presence. This is evident in both Testaments. We see God's glorious presence in the following:

- The glory cloud (Exod. 16:7, 10; 40:34–35; 1 Cor. 10:1)
- The manifestations to Moses (Exod. 33:18, 22; 2 Cor. 3:7)
- The temple (1 Kgs 8:10–11; 2 Chr. 7:1–3; 1 Cor. 3:16–17)
- The birth of Christ (Isa. 9:2–7; Luke 2:9–11)
- The person of Christ (John 1:14; 2 Cor. 4:4; Col. 1:27)
- The return of Christ (2 Thess. 1:8–10)
- The Holy Spirit (John 16:13–15; 2 Cor. 3:8, 18)
- Heaven itself (2 Cor. 4:17; Rev. 21:11, 23)

God's glory relates to his entire person and correlates with his attributes and works. Glory shapes Paul's images and doxologies, which praise the 'glory of the blessed God' (1 Tim. 1:11) for his attributes and works, including the following:

- Holiness (1 Tim. 1:16)
- Transcendence (1 Tim. 1:16)
- Uniqueness (1 Tim. 1:17)
- Eternity (1 Tim. 1:17)
- Majesty (1 Tim. 1:11; 6:15)[1]
- Grace (2 Cor. 4:15)
- Veracity (Rom. 3:7)
- Creation, providence and consummation (Rom. 11:36)
- Wisdom (Rom. 16:27)
- Sovereignty (1 Tim. 1:17; 6:16)
- Power (Eph. 3:20–21)
- Goodness (Phil. 4:19–20)
- Justice (2 Thess. 1:5–12)
- Preservation (2 Tim. 4:18)

[1] When Paul speaks of the 'glory of the blessed God', he 'points to God in his ineffable splendor' (Yarbrough 2018: 118).

The fundamental theological distinction concerning the glory of God is that between his intrinsic (internal) glory and his extrinsic (revealed) glory. God's extrinsic glory is thus the manifestation of his intrinsic fullness. As noted in chapter 1, Scripture, including Paul, links the extrinsic display of God's glory to a variety of his attributes, such as the following:

- Holiness (Titus 1:11–14)
- Immortality (Rom. 1:23)
- Sovereignty (1 Cor. 2:7; 2 Cor. 4:6; Gal. 1:4–5; Eph. 1:11–12)
- Power (Rom. 6:4, 22; Eph. 3:20–21)
- Righteousness (Rom. 3:21–26; 2 Cor. 3:9)
- Wisdom (Rom. 16:27; Eph. 3:10–11)
- Grace (Eph. 1:6, 12, 14; 2 Thess. 1:12)
- Love (Eph. 3:14–19)
- Mercy (Rom. 9:23)
- Kindness (Eph. 2:4–10)
- Patience (Rom. 9:22)
- Justice (2 Thess. 1:8–9)

God's glory also drives his goals. At present he wills for believers to 'worship by the Spirit of God and glory in Christ Jesus' (Phil. 3:3). He desires them to cause other believers also to glory in Christ (Phil. 1:26). God's ultimate goals include the exaltation of his Son, so that 'every tongue [should] confess that Jesus Christ is Lord, to the glory of God the Father' (Phil. 2:9–11). This will occur when God fulfils his plan to unite in Christ all things in heaven and on earth (Eph. 1:10). According to his 'eternal purpose' (Eph. 3:11) God will glorify himself by displaying his wisdom in the church as his showcase to the heavenly realms (Eph. 3:9–12)! Not surprisingly, God ends this chapter of Ephesians thus: '[T]o him be glory in the church and in Christ Jesus throughout all generations, for ever and ever. Amen' (Eph. 3:21). Louis Berkhof summarizes:

> The Church of Jesus Christ found the true end of creation, not in anything outside of God, but in God Himself, more particularly in the external manifestation of His inherent excellency. This does not mean that God's receiving glory from others is the final end. The receiving of glory through the praises of His moral creatures, is an end included in the supreme end, but is not itself that end. God

did not create first of all to receive glory, but to make his glory extant and manifest. The glorious perfections of God are manifested in His entire creation; and this manifestation is not intended as an empty show, a mere exhibition to be admired by the creatures, but also aims at promoting their welfare and perfect happiness. Moreover, it seeks to attune their hearts to the praises of the Creator, and to elicit from their souls the expression of their gratefulness and love and adoration. The supreme end of God in creation, the manifestation of His glory, therefore, includes, as subordinate ends, the happiness and salvation of His creatures, and the reception of praise from grateful and adoring hearts.[2]

His Word

We found one reference to the glory of God and Scripture in Paul. After Paul's enemies accuse him of vacillation in ministry and message because he has altered his plans to visit Corinth, he responds with denial and defence: 'As surely as God is faithful, our word to you has not been Yes and No' (2 Cor. 1:18). Paul's steadfastness and reliability are based on that of God and Christ, who are utterly reliable (vv. 18–19). Indeed, '[A]ll the promises of God find their Yes in him. That is why it is through him that we utter our Amen to God for his glory' (v. 20). Christ faithfully fulfilled Old Testament promises. Therefore, his undergirding Paul's message and conduct produces stability in life and ministry. Moreover, God the Father establishes Paul and the Corinthian church by giving them the Holy Spirit as anointing, seal and guarantee (vv. 21–22). Paul, Silvanus and Timothy say 'Amen' to the gospel of Christ that they preached and the Corinthians believed. And this redounds 'to God for glory' (lit.), 'possibly . . . a further liturgical interjection following the "Amen."'[3] Regardless, Paul's preaching of the gospel from Scripture and the Corinthians' faith promote God's glory in worship.

Humanity and sin

Humanity

Paul writes of humanity in relation to God. God created humans in his image and likeness, dependent on him. God made us to glorify him by

---

[2] Berkhof 1941: 136.
[3] Barnett 1997: 109, n. 38.

knowing, loving and serving him as his creatures. Therefore, although sin could be defined in many ways, essentially it is creaturely rebellion against the Creator. In the fall Adam and Eve asserted their independence from God. Despite the fact that God revealed his glory in his creation of the world (Ps. 19:1–6) and of humanity (Rom. 1:19–20; 2:14–15), our first parents and all their descendants refused to give God the glory he deserves.

God's revelation in creation left humans without excuse for their unbelief. Nevertheless, '[T]hey neither glorified him as God nor gave thanks to him' (Rom. 1:21, NIV). Humans did not lose the image of God in the fall, but the image was distorted, so that we give glory to ourselves or other idols instead of the One who made us for himself.[4] Paul is blunt: '[T]hey became futile in their thinking, and their foolish hearts were darkened. Claiming to be wise, they became fools, and exchanged the glory of the immortal God for images resembling mortal man and birds and animals and creeping things' (vv. 21–23). Shockingly, rebellious humans exchanged God's glory, his divine magnificence, for idols!

Sin

As we have seen, at its heart sin is failure to glorify God: '[A]ll have sinned and fall short of the glory of God' (Rom. 3:23). In the light of his flow of thought in Romans, Paul likely means 'all have sinned' in Adam (Rom. 5:12–19) and 'fall short' of God's glory in their daily lives. Sin is universal, for

> None is righteous, no, not one;
>> no one understands;
>> no one seeks for God.
> All have turned aside; together they have become worthless;
>> no one does good,
>>> not even one.
> (Rom. 3:10–12)

Sin is complex: it is violation of God's law, is personal and social, includes guilt and pollution and involves thoughts, words and actions. Perhaps most importantly, sin had a beginning in history and will have an end.[5]

---

[4] We acknowledge help from Gaffin (2010: 147).
[5] For biblical exposition of these points and more see Morgan with Peterson 2020: 194–200.

Our sin keeps us from believing the gospel. Even worse, Satan blinds 'the minds of the unbelievers, to keep them from seeing the light of the gospel of the glory of Christ' and believing it for salvation (2 Cor. 4:4). Sin is a deceitful and cruel master for those outside Christ (Jer. 17:9; Eph. 2:1–3).

In sum, sin is depicted as exchanging the glory of the incorruptible God for something less, such as idols (Rom. 1:23; cf. Ps. 106:20; Jer. 2:11–12). Sin is falling short of the glory of God (Rom. 3:23) and brings disrepute on his name (2:24). The irony of all this is striking: as humans we all refused to acknowledge God's glory and instead sought our own glory. In so doing we forfeited the glory God intended for us as his image-bearers. Thankfully, God's grace is greater than all our sin (Eph. 2:4–10) and leads to God's glory (Rom. 16:25–27).

Christ's person and work

Christ's person

Paul frequently connects Christ's person and God's glory. In a confession of faith the apostle spans the Son of God's incarnation to his ascension:

> He was manifested in the flesh,
> vindicated by the Spirit,
> seen by angels,
> proclaimed among the nations,
> believed on in the world,
> taken up in glory.
> (1 Tim. 3:16)

Paul proclaims Christ's deity: this age's rulers, though claiming to be wise, displayed their folly when they 'crucified the Lord of glory' (1 Cor. 2:8). Believers have a hope that fills them with joy, for they wait for 'the appearing of the glory of our great God and Saviour Jesus Christ' (Titus 2:13).

Three times Paul speaks of the revelation of God's mystery in Colossians, and its epitome occurs in 1:27, when he declares to Gentile believers the 'glory of this mystery, which is Christ in you, the hope of glory'.

Christ, the crucified One, in his resurrection became the 'firstfruits of those who have fallen asleep', whose resurrection guarantees theirs. He is the second Adam, who brings life where our first father brought death: '[A]s in Adam all die, so also in Christ shall all be made alive' (1 Cor. 15:20, 22). Adam by his primal trespass corrupted and condemned his descendants. Christ, the second Adam, by his 'one act of righteousness', his obedience to death on the cross, brings justification and eternal life to all believers (Rom. 5:18–19).

Paul presents Christ as the glory and image of God, especially in his exaltation. Gaffin aids us: 'The gospel-glory of "Christ, who is the image of God" (2 Cor. 4:4), is specifically the glory he possesses as the "heavenly" image bearer,' who has risen and ascended.[6] God the Creator brings supernatural illumination when he causes the 'light of the gospel of the glory of Christ, who is the image of God', to shine on his people (2 Cor. 4:4). This divine illumination overcomes Satan's blinding of sinners, with the result that believers gain the 'light of the knowledge of the glory of God in the face of Jesus Christ' (v. 6).

The results of Christ's death and resurrection extend to the end, for at his return Christ will raise believers and 'transform our lowly body to be like his glorious body' by his omnipotent power (Phil. 3:21). When Christ appears in glory, he will inflict vengeance on unbelievers (2 Thess. 1:7–9) and glorify his people (Col. 3:4).

Christ's work

Paul views Christ's work of salvation from at least six angles. Each reveals God's glory and results in final glory for believers, which results in eternal glory to God.

First, Christ's death is a propitiation. Humans were guilty before a holy and just God (Rom. 1:18) and had no way to erase their guilt. On the cross, Christ propitiated the Father by suffering the penalty that sinners deserved – the wrath of God (1 John 4:10). God thereby promoted his glory by demonstrating his righteousness in Christ's cross (Rom. 3:25–26). God thus showed his righteousness 'so that he might be just and the justifier of the one who has faith in Jesus' (Rom. 3:26). Therefore, this excludes all boasting in human effort for salvation (vv. 27–31) and results instead in believers' boasting in Christ's cross (Gal. 6:14).

Second, Christ's death and resurrection accomplished reconciliation (Rom. 5:10). Humans were estranged from God because of their sin and

---

[6] Gaffin 2010: 137–138.

enmity (Col. 1:21). Graciously, Jesus our peacemaker died in our place to reconcile God to us and us to God. This magnifies God's grace and promotes his glory. Christ's atonement also makes peace between previously estranged believers, causing them to worship God (Eph. 2:13–22). Christ's work of reconciliation is so effective that it reconciles 'to himself all things, whether on earth or in heaven, making peace by the blood of his cross' (Col. 1:20). This fulfils God's plan to broadcast his 'grace', 'wisdom' and 'insight' when in the 'fullness of time' he unites all things in Christ (Eph. 1:7–10). Consequently, reconciliation brings believers joy and moves them to exult in God (Rom. 5:11).

Third, Christ's death is a redemption. Humans were slaves to sin and unable to free themselves (Rom. 6:17, 20). Christ dies an accursed death (Gal. 3:13) to liberate the slaves so that they experience forgiveness of sins (Col. 1:14), adoption (Gal. 4:5) and the freedom of God's children (Gal. 4:7; 5:1). Moreover, Christ's work is so great that it will accomplish the redemption of the cosmos (Rom. 8:19–21). God has sealed believers with the Holy Spirit 'for the day of redemption' (Eph. 4:30), and they therefore anticipate their final 'adoption as sons, the redemption of [their] bodies' (Rom. 8:23), which is glorification (1 Cor. 15:43). Indeed, the 'glory that is to be revealed to us' is so great that it makes present sufferings seem unimportant (Rom. 8:18). It does not surprise us, then, that believers in final glory sing this song to their Redeemer, who ransomed them with his blood: 'Worthy is the Lamb who was slain, to receive power and wealth and wisdom and might and honour and glory and blessing!' (Rev. 5:12).

Fourth, Christ's death is a sacrifice that glorifies God. Humans are unclean in God's sight and in need of purification. Paul urges his readers to imitate God the Father as his 'beloved children' and to 'walk in love, as Christ loved us and gave himself up for us, a fragrant offering and sacrifice to God' (Eph. 5:1–2). The apostle thus calls Christians to show love as the Father and Son have done for them. Specifically, Christ voluntarily became our substitute as a 'fragrant offering and sacrifice to God'. Baugh reminds us that even as 'OT animal and grain sacrifice . . . gave off a pleasing aroma to God . . . this sacrifice pleases God in fulfillment of his commands and satisfies his justice'.[7] Christ's saving accomplishment thus glorifies God as it pleases him and demonstrates his righteousness. As a result, the Son

---

[7] Baugh 2015: 404–405.

deserves honour because he 'loves us and has freed us from our sins by his blood' (Rev. 1:5).

Fifth, Christ's death achieves a huge victory. Humans have enemies much stronger than they. These include Satan, his demons, the world as a system hostile to God and his church, human enemies, death and hell. In grace God sent a mighty champion, Jesus Christ, who in his death and resurrection defeated our foes. For this he deserves worldwide glory and honour.

God's victory is already and not yet. Already because of his Son's propitiatory death, God got glory for himself when he 'disarmed the rulers and authorities and put them to open shame, by triumphing over them in him' (Col. 2:15). But a greater revelation of God's glory awaits, for not yet has he cast these foes into the lake of fire. Already the Father has 'delivered us from the domain of darkness and transferred us to the kingdom of his beloved Son' (Col. 1:13), but not yet has the kingdom of God come in its final form on the new earth.

Already Christ has been exalted and glorified (Eph. 1:21), but not yet has he come 'in his glory and the glory of the Father and of the holy angels' (Luke 9:26). Already the Father has 'highly exalted [the Son] and bestowed on him the name that is above every name' (Phil. 2:9), but not yet has every name bowed 'in heaven and on earth and under the earth' and not yet has every tongue confessed 'that Jesus Christ is Lord, to the glory of God the Father' (Phil. 2:10–11).

Sixth, Christ's death sanctified, sanctifies and will yet sanctify his church. In love he died to 'sanctify' the church, to make it holy (Eph. 5:26). God has made believers saints, continues to work continuing holiness into them and will perfect them in holiness when Jesus comes again. Christ's goal in giving himself for the church is to 'present the church to himself in splendour, without spot or wrinkle or any such thing, that she might be holy and without blemish' (Eph. 5:27). Christ's effective atonement will result in the perfect sanctification of his bride, the church. This is why the announcement of the wedding supper of the Lamb resounds to the glory of God:

Hallelujah!
For the Lord our God
   the Almighty reigns.
Let us rejoice and exult
   and give him the glory,

for the marriage of the Lamb has come,
    and his Bride has made herself ready.
(Rev. 19:6–7)

God glorifies himself in Christ's death and resurrection that accomplished propitiation, reconciliation, redemption, sacrifice, victory and sanctification. Although Paul is speaking of reconciliation, his response applies to all six pictures of Christ's saving work: 'More than that, we also rejoice in God through our Lord Jesus Christ, through whom we have now received reconciliation' (Rom. 5:11).

The Holy Spirit and the new covenant

The Holy Spirit

Paul links the Holy Spirit and God's glory in at least three ways. He tells how the three trinitarian persons are involved in sealing believers: 'In him you also . . . were sealed with the promised Holy Spirit' (Eph. 1:13). The Father seals (a divine passive; see 2 Cor. 1:21–22), believers are sealed in union with Christ and the seal is the Holy Spirit. The Spirit is the 'Holy Spirit of God, by whom you were sealed for the day of redemption' (Eph. 4:30). The Spirit is seal and 'guarantee of our inheritance until we acquire possession of it, to the praise of [God's] glory' (v. 14).

Paul joins worship in the Spirit and glorying in Christ. In opposition to the Judaizers, who boast in physical circumcision, Paul declares, '[W]e are the circumcision, who worship by the Spirit of God and glory in Christ Jesus and put no confidence in the flesh' (Phil. 3:3). The three ideas are connected, for worship in the Spirit leads to glorying in Christ, which is incompatible with trusting human effort ('the flesh') for salvation.

Christian theology correctly regards glorification as a future blessing for God's people. Astonishingly, however, Paul teaches that there is a sense in which glorification is also present: '[W]e all, with unveiled face, beholding the glory of the Lord, are being transformed into the same image from one degree of glory to another' (2 Cor. 3.18). Paul connects this present growth in glory to the Holy Spirit: 'For this comes from the Lord who is the Spirit' (v. 18). It is important to keep in mind that this amazing work of the Spirit in believers now is the 'triumph of the glory of God'.[8] Michael Horton captures how the Spirit's uniting us to Christ effects our glory:

> Through the Spirit, all that is done by Christ for us, outside of us and in the past, is received and made fruitful within us in the present. In this way, the power that is constitutive of the consummation (the age to come) is already at work now in the world. Through the Spirit's agency, not only is Christ's past work applied to us but his present status of glory in glory penetrates our own existence in a semirealized manner. The Spirit's work is what connects us here and now to Christ's past, present, and future ... [T]he Spirit shapes creaturely reality according to the archetypal image of the Son.[9]

The new covenant

In his key passage on the new covenant Paul shows how much more glorious it is than the old covenant (2 Cor. 3:4–18). The old covenant did not lack glory, for it was God's gracious gift given exclusively to his people Israel (Exod. 20:2; Deut. 7:6–8). The old covenant had gracious purposes, for God desired obedient Israel to be his 'treasured possession among all peoples ... a kingdom of priests and a holy nation' (Exod. 19:5–6). It clearly revealed God's character as a 'jealous God', who hates sin, and as overflowing with 'steadfast love' to those who love and obey him (Exod. 20:5–6). God graciously made the old covenant the core of biblical ethics (Deut. 5:6–21).

The face of Moses, the mediator of the old covenant, glowed with glory when he returned from meeting with God. But new covenant glory is superior even to that of Moses (2 Cor. 3:7). Paul labels the old covenant the 'ministry of death' (v. 7) and 'of condemnation' (v. 9) because the Ten Commandments laid bare Israel's inability to keep the covenant. By contrast 'the Spirit' who gives 'life' (v. 6) fulfils Old Testament predictions and regenerates new covenant believers, enabling them to obey God. The 'new covenant' of the Spirit abounds in glory (vv. 7–11). The old covenant did not lack glory in itself, but compared to the glory of the new covenant

---

[8] Barnett 1997: 209.
[9] Horton 2008: 21; cf. his 'God did not become human so that humans might become God, or even supernatural, but so that humans who had fallen into sin and death could be redeemed, reconciled, justified, renewed, and glorified as the humanity that we were created to become' (2007: 302).

the old covenant had no glory! 'Indeed, in this case, what once had glory has come to have no glory at all, because of the glory [of the new covenant] that surpasses it' (v. 10).

Salvation

Election

'Blessed be the God and Father of our Lord Jesus Christ', Paul writes, because the Father chose people for salvation 'before the foundation of the world', and '[i]n love he predestined us for adoption' (Eph. 1:3–5). Indeed, God 'saved us . . . not because of our works but because of his own purpose and grace, which he gave us in Christ Jesus before the ages began' (2 Tim. 1:9). All this contributes to the 'praise of [God's] glorious grace' (Eph. 1:6).

We do not understand all there is to know about God's mysterious election, but we do know that God displays his glory in election. In his longest treatment of election Paul tells of God's dealings with Pharaoh before the exodus: '[T]he Scripture says to Pharaoh, "For this very purpose I have raised you up, that I might show my power in you, and that my name might be proclaimed in all the earth"' (Rom. 9:17). Paul testifies that God chose to 'make known the riches of his glory for vessels of mercy, which he has prepared beforehand for glory' (Rom. 9:23). So, in glory God chooses people for glory, all of which redounds to God's glory.

Grace and faith

God manifests his glory in both grace and faith.

Grace

Paul extols the Trinity for salvation: the Father for choosing, the Son for redeeming and the Spirit as God's seal on his people (Eph. 1:3–4). Fittingly, he praises God's grace and glory in this salvation 'to the praise of his glorious grace' (v. 6) and twice 'to the praise of his glory' (vv. 12, 14). After mentioning God's rich mercy and great love Paul sets forth the epitome of grace – God's saving us when we were spiritually dead and unable to help ourselves (2:4–5). God's purpose? '[S]o that in the coming ages he might show the immeasurable riches of his grace in kindness towards us in Christ Jesus' (v. 7).

Faith

Faith glorifies God because it refuses to trust in human credentials or achievement but trusts Christ instead as he is offered in the gospel: believers 'glory in Christ Jesus and put no confidence in the flesh' (Phil. 3:3). Paul explains:

> I count everything as loss because of the surpassing worth of knowing Christ Jesus my Lord. For his sake I have suffered the loss of all things and count them as rubbish, in order that I may gain Christ and be found in him, not having a righteousness of my own that comes from the law, but that which comes through faith in Christ, the righteousness from God that depends on faith.
> (vv. 8–9)

May our testimony be that of Abraham and Paul, who both contributed to God's glory:

> No distrust made him waver concerning the promise of God, but he grew strong in his faith as he gave glory to God.
> (Rom. 4:20)

> far be it from me to boast except in the cross of our Lord Jesus Christ.
> (Gal. 6:14)

Union with Christ

God glorifies himself in all aspects of salvation, including union with Christ. Union with Christ is the most comprehensive way of speaking of God's applying salvation to believers. God joins to Christ those who believe the gospel, and they receive all of his saving benefits. As we have seen (pp. 151–163), union with Christ is personal (Eph. 1:3–14; 2:1–10), communal (2:11–22) and cosmic (1:9–10). At creation Adam and Eve reflected the glory of God as his image-bearers, but in the fall they and their descendants forfeited God's glory, so that the image was defaced. In grace God restores and perfects that marred image in Christ and those in union with him.

> In response to human sinfulness and the loss of image-bearing glory, God displays his glory specifically in his saving grace . . . by

his gospel-glory, preeminently and especially 'the glory of God in the face of Jesus Christ' (2 Cor. 4:6).[10]

Justification

God glorifies himself in the salvation of the lost, including their justification. Justification uniquely reveals God's justice and love in the cross of Christ. The cross is the greatest manifestation of God's love:

> God shows his love for us in that while we were still sinners, Christ died for us.
> (Rom. 5:8)

> In this is love, not that we have loved God but that he loved us and sent his Son to be the propitiation for our sins.
> (1 John 4:10)

As the second quotation shows, it is precisely in Christ's propitiation of God's justice that his love is pre-eminently displayed. Paul teaches that God set forth his Son 'as a propitiation by his blood . . . to show God's righteousness . . . at the present time, so that he might be just and the justifier of the one who has faith in Jesus' (Rom. 3:25–26).

Schreiner ties these truths together:

> God's justice is satisfied because Christ bore the full payment for sin. But God is also the justifier, because on the basis of the cross of Christ sinners receive forgiveness through faith in Jesus. In the cross of Christ the justice and mercy of God meet. God's holiness is satisfied by Christ's bearing the penalty of sin, and God's saving activity is realized in the lives of those who trust in Christ.[11]

God is glorified in justifying lost persons who believe in Jesus, because so doing magnifies his grace.

Adoption

Like justification, adoption is by God's grace through faith in Christ. Like justification, adoption displays God's glory by promising his people glory,

---

[10] Gaffin 2010: 147.
[11] Schreiner 2008: 360.

in this case a glorious inheritance. The two aspects of salvation are both legal, but here they also differ, for justification occurs in a criminal court while adoption occurs in a family court. Adoption is God's placing into his family as adult sons all who trust his unique Son Jesus as Redeemer. All needed adoption, because we 'were enslaved to the elementary principles of the world', the demonic realm standing behind Gentile paganism and Jewish legalism (Gal. 4:3). Further, as lawbreakers we were 'under a curse' (3:10). Mercifully, 'Christ redeemed us from the curse of the law by becoming a curse for us' in crucifixion (v. 13). The Lord of glory became our legal substitute. The result? Every believer is 'no longer a slave, but a son, and if a son, then an heir through God' (4:7). As God's children we are 'heirs of God and fellow heirs with Christ, provided we suffer with him in order that we may also be glorified with him' (Rom. 8:17). Our Father will thus bring 'many sons to glory' (Heb. 2:10), for 'all things are [ours], whether . . . the world or life or death or the present or the future – all are [ours], and [we] are Christ's, and Christ is God's' (1 Cor. 3:21–23).

Adoption is past, present and future. The Father has adopted believers as his children, and we now enjoy Christian freedom as his sons and daughters (Gal. 5:1), even as we suffer (Rom. 8:18). And we, having the 'Spirit of adoption' in our hearts (v. 15), eagerly await our 'adoption as sons, the redemption of our bodies', which is glorification (v. 23). The creation also longs to 'be set free from its bondage to corruption and obtain the freedom of the glory of the children of God' (v. 21). Burke's words bear repeating: 'These sufferings cannot be compared to the eternal joys and glory that will ensue . . . Creation one day will indeed be liberated from its present bondage and brought into the glorious freedom of the children of God.'[12]

Sanctification, suffering and persecution

Sanctification

Paul connects progressive sanctification and the glory of God. He is insistent that God's grace promotes holiness, not sin. Paul is angry at some who, extrapolating from his gospel of grace, conclude that he teaches that our continuing to sin 'abounds to [God's] glory' (Rom. 3:7). He turns such people over to God's judgment (v. 8).

---

[12] Burke 2006: 186–187.

Paul views the Christian life as a battle against the devil, the world and the flesh that the churches (Eph. 6:10–19), his disciples (e.g. Timothy, 1 Tim. 1:18) and he himself (Rom. 7:23) must fight. This does not mean that Paul is defeatist, because even as he struggles he exclaims, 'Thanks be to God through Jesus Christ our Lord!' (v. 25). And in the next chapter Paul declares that our future glorification is certain (8:30).

Although Christians struggle, their ultimate victory is assured, and they can know real victory in the Christian life. God in Christ has freed believers from sin's domination (Rom. 6:17–18). Believers have been saved from sin's penalty, but they still struggle to overcome its power. '[A]ll have sinned and fall short of the glory of God' (Rom. 3:23). God created us to attain glory but we all have failed. Thankfully, because of the work of the Spirit the outcome is certain and results in glory. Scripture links 'image' with 'glory'. God created humans to reflect God's glory. The Holy Spirit sanctifies believers, restoring some of God's distorted image so they partially reflect his glory now. The struggle is real and the growth gradual. Ultimate victory is assured, however, because of the work of the Spirit, as Ferguson explains:

The mark we were created to reach, but have missed, was glory. We have sinned and failed to attain that destiny. Against this background, the task of the Spirit may be stated simply: to bring us to glory, to create glory within us, and to glorify us together with Christ. The startling significance of this might be plainer if we expressed it thus: the Spirit is given to glorify us; not just to 'add' glory as a crown to what we are, but actually to transform the very constitution of our being so that we become glorious . . . In the New Testament, this glorification is seen to begin already in the present order, in believers. Through the Spirit they are already being changed from glory to glory, as they gaze on/reflect the face of the Lord (2 Cor. 3:17–18). But the consummation of this glorification awaits the eschaton and the Spirit's ministry in the resurrection. Here, too, the pattern of his working is: as in Christ, so in believers.[13]

Suffering and persecution

Paul has a theology of suffering that informs his view of the Christian life. He ministers to suffering believers by combining suffering and hope.

---

[13] Ferguson 1996: 139–140, 249–250.

Because Jesus has delivered them, they 'rejoice in hope of the glory of God' (Rom. 5:2), the hope of a glorious resurrection. Surprisingly, Paul next writes, 'More than that, we rejoice in our sufferings, knowing that suffering produces endurance, and endurance produces character, and character produces hope' (Rom. 5:3–4). Paul depicts links in a chain: trusting God while suffering builds steadfastness, which over time builds steadfast character. And this breeds hope, because seeing God at work in our lives now to make us into steady people gives us hope of glory in the next life.

The Spirit testifies within believers that they are God's children (Rom. 8:16). And because they are his children, they are also his heirs, 'and fellow heirs with Christ, provided [they] suffer with him in order that [they] may also be glorified with him' (v. 17). Paul adds a qualification that assumes that God unites to Christ his true children and heirs. This involves union with Christ in his death, which means suffering now, and union with him in his resurrection, which means future glory. Gaffin observes:

> This present glory of the church, paradoxically and parallel to the experience of its Lord prior to his resurrection, is veiled by afflictions and adversity. Sharing in 'the fellowship of his sufferings' is the way believers experience 'the power of his resurrection' (Phil. 3:10; cf. 2 Cor. 1:5); the condition for those who aspire to be glorified with Christ is that for now 'we suffer with him' (Rom. 8:17).[14]

In Romans 8:18 Paul helps Christians gain a proper perspective on suffering: 'I consider that the sufferings of this present time are not worth comparing with the glory that is to be revealed to us.' Throughout history the prospect of great future glory has strengthened God's people to cope with terrible suffering in this life. Schreiner is right: 'Paul dazzles his readers with the attractiveness and beauty of the future glory.'[15] The apostle weighs present suffering against future glorification: '[T]his light momentary affliction is preparing for us an eternal weight of glory beyond all comparison' (2 Cor. 4:17).

---

[14] Gaffin 1993: 349.
[15] Schreiner 1998: 434.

God calls believers not only to suffer but sometimes to endure persecution for his name's sake and glory. Paul's most famous list of things he suffered is found in 2 Corinthians 11:23–29, where he defends his apostleship against the accusations of the false apostles. Among the many things Paul 'boasts' of are those involving persecution:

> far more imprisonments, with countless beatings, and often near death. Five times I received at the hands of the Jews the forty lashes less one. Three times I was beaten with rods. Once I was stoned . . . danger from my own people, danger from Gentiles . . . danger from false brothers . . .
> (vv. 23–26)

Why does Paul then say, 'If I must boast, I will boast of the things that show my weakness' (2 Cor. 11:30)? He does so, as Hughes explains, to show 'on the one hand the emphasis on the utter weakness of the human instrument and, on the other hand and in consequence, the magnification of the glorious grace and power of Almighty God'.[16]

Preservation and assurance

Preservation

Paul teaches that God not only graciously saves us but also graciously keeps us: 'There is therefore now no condemnation for those who are in Christ Jesus' (Rom. 8:1). God the Judge will not condemn us but will save us to the end, displaying his great glory, for which we will in turn give him glory. Paul makes four arguments for preservation in Romans 8. First, in his sovereignty God foreknew (loved before time), predestined (chose to be saved), called to Christ, justified and glorified us (8:29–30). Paul puts glorification, still future, in the past tense, for in his sovereign plan believers will not fail to be glorified. God will share his glory with his people.

Second, Paul asks, 'If God is for us, who can be against us?' (v. 31). The Lord of all shows that he is on our side supremely by giving his beloved Son to die for us. No one will ever take us away from the Almighty, who has promised to 'graciously give us all things' (v. 32). One

---

16 Hughes 1962: 418.

of those things is resurrection bodies, raised from the dead in glory (1 Cor. 15:43).

Third, Paul asks who will bring a successful accusation against God's people. The answer is no one, for God, who knows all sins, has declared us righteous (Rom. 8:33). Paul then asks who will condemn us and mentions Christ, who with the Father is the Judge. Will Christ condemn us? No, he will save us, for he is our Saviour, who died, rose and intercedes for us (v. 34).

Fourth, Paul bases our preservation on God's love in Christ. The apostle asks what can separate God's people from Christ's love (v. 35). He cites seven threats, including 'sword' (death), and concludes, 'No, in all these things we are more than conquerors through him who loved us' (v. 37). He concludes that nothing at all will ever 'be able to separate us from the love of God in Christ Jesus our Lord' (v. 39). God's overcoming love will replace our sin and shame with salvation and glory.

In many other places Paul teaches that God will preserve his people for final salvation. Here are a few more:

[God] will sustain you to the end, guiltless in the day of our Lord Jesus Christ.
(1 Cor. 1:8)

I am sure of this, that he who began a good work in you will bring it to completion at the day of Jesus.
(Phil. 1:6)

Now may the God of peace himself sanctify you completely, and may your whole spirit and soul and body be kept blameless at the coming of our Lord Jesus Christ. He who calls you is faithful; he will surely do it.
(1 Thess. 5:23–24)

Paul's response after this next text forms a fitting end to our treatment of God's preservation of his people: 'The Lord will rescue me from every evil deed and bring me safely into his heavenly kingdom. To him be the glory for ever and ever. Amen' (2 Tim. 4:18). Because the Lord of glory loved us and gave himself for us, we will not fail to obtain glory (2 Thess. 2:14), and this will lead to God's eternal praise and glory.

Assurance

God desires believers to have confidence of final salvation, as 1 John 5:13 says: 'I write these things to you who believe in the name of the Son of God, that you may know that you have eternal life.' God assures us in three ways: by his Word, by his Spirit's witness within our hearts and by changing our lives. All three ways reveal his glory, give glory to his people and redound to his glory.

The most important way in which God assures his people is through his Word, the gospel. He promises salvation to all who believe. The preservation texts above belong here as well, as do many other Pauline texts. In Romans Paul declares:

> God shows his love for us in that while we were still sinners, Christ died for us. Since, therefore, we have now been justified by his blood, much more shall we be saved by him from the wrath of God. (Rom. 5:8–9)

God's Word assures us of our finally receiving 'an eternal weight of glory beyond all comparison' (2 Cor. 4:17).

God also assures us within by his Spirit: 'The Spirit himself bears witness with our spirit that we are children of God' (Rom. 8:16). Chiefly, God assures his children by the promises of his Word. But he confirms that message by testifying within their hearts that he belongs to them and they to him. The Holy Spirit testifies within believers that God is their Father and they are his beloved children. Although we must endure suffering, God's 'hope does not put us to shame, because God's love has been poured into our hearts through the Holy Spirit who has been given to us' (Rom. 5:5). At times we groan within as we wait for the 'redemption of our bodies' (Rom. 8:23). The Spirit loves us and also groans (v. 26), assuring us that what lies ahead for us is the 'freedom of the glory of the children of God' (v. 21).

God also assures us by changing Christians' lives. The Spirit produces fruit (Gal. 5:22–23) in the lives of all who 'belong to Christ Jesus' and 'have crucified the flesh with its passions and desires' (v. 24). Those whom God saves freely by his grace apart from works (Eph. 2:8–9) are 'his workmanship, created in Christ Jesus for good works, which God prepared beforehand, that we should walk in them' (v. 10). God works in our lives to strengthen our assurance. We 'work out [our] own salvation with fear and trembling' only because 'it is God who works in [us], both to will and to work for his good pleasure' (Phil. 2:12–13). Astoundingly, although final glorification is still future, even now God grants glory to believers: '[W]e all, with unveiled face, beholding the glory of the Lord, are being transformed into the same image from one degree of glory to another' (2 Cor. 3:18).

In amazing grace, then, God grants assurance of salvation to his people. God assures us that we will 'obtain the glory of our Lord Jesus Christ' (2 Thess. 2:14), because Christ 'gave himself for our sins to deliver us from the present evil age', and this moves us to praise the 'Father, to whom be the glory for ever and ever. Amen' (Gal. 1:4–5).

The church

Israel

In response to the bold request of Moses, the mediator of the old covenant, God revealed his glorious presence to him and proclaimed his name (Exod. 33:18–23; 34:5–8). In a passage exalting new covenant glory Paul asserts that his new covenant ministry is much more glorious than that of Moses (2 Cor. 3:7–18). The second time Moses carried the two tablets of the law down the mountain from God's presence, 'the skin of his face shone' with God's glory (Exod. 34:29). It shone so much that the people were afraid to approach him (v. 30). In fact, whenever Moses came out from the Lord to speak to the people, they would see his face shining, and he would veil his face (vv. 34–35).

Paul contrasts the glory of the death-dealing old covenant with the greater glory of the life-giving Spirit in the new covenant (2 Cor. 3:7–8). The old covenant had glory in condemnation, but the new covenant has far greater glory in justification (v. 9). Finally, Paul says that, compared to the brilliant glory of the new covenant, the old covenant's glory is 'no glory at all' (v. 10). New covenant glory arrested Saul of Tarsus on his way to Damascus and now validates his apostolic ministry to the Corinthians.

Paul's message concerning first-century Israel contains condemnation and hope. He condemns the Jews' rebellion against God: 'You who boast in the law dishonour God by breaking the law' (Rom. 2:23). He admits that they are zealous but is saddened that it is for the wrong reason:

'[B]eing ignorant of the righteousness of God, and seeking to establish their own, they did not submit to God's righteousness' (10:2–3). Still, he loves the Israelites and prays earnestly for their salvation (9:2–3). He records eight blessings given only to Israel (vv. 4–5), including 'the glory', which in context points to worship of God's glorious presence in tabernacle and temple. God has an ambiguous relationship to the Israelites: 'As regards the gospel, they are enemies of God for your sake. But as regards election, they are beloved for the sake of their forefathers. For the gifts and the calling of God are irrevocable' (11:28–29). Paul is convinced that God is not finished with ethnic Israel and yearns for the day when 'all Israel will be saved' (v. 26).

The church as 'one new man'

God's ultimate purpose for the church is his own glory. He gets glory by uniting believing Jews and Gentiles in 'one new man' (Eph. 2:15). Paul depicts the spiritual disadvantages of Gentiles compared to Jews, groups at enmity (2:11–12). Paul lists circumcision and five other religious hurdles: they were 'separated from Christ, alienated from the commonwealth of Israel and strangers to the covenants of promise, having no hope and without God in the world' (2:12). Most importantly, they were 'separated from Christ' and thus did not know the living God. In addition, they had no hope and were without God in the world, for they lacked Scripture and God's promises of a Redeemer.

Then Paul says, 'But now in Christ Jesus you who once were far off have been brought near by the blood of Christ' (Eph. 2:13). God did this 'in Christ Jesus', in union with him, and 'by the blood of Christ', his atoning sacrifice. Christ has unified believing Jews and Gentiles by his death, thereby making peace between them (v. 14). His crucified body broke down the 'dividing wall of hostility', the law that separated Jews from Gentiles.

Incredibly, Christ created 'in himself one new man in place of the two, so making peace' (Eph. 2:15). Paul applies the new creation theme to the church. Jesus Christ is the second Adam (1 Cor. 15:45–47), who by his death and resurrection brings eternal life. When the Holy Spirit spiritually unites believers to Christ, he also unites them to one another in one body, the church, constituting a new race, all of which brings glory to the triune God.

Paul tells of benefits of Christ's work of recreation: '[T]hrough him we both have access in one Spirit to the Father' (v. 18). Paul ends the passage

(Eph. 2:11–22) by declaring, 'So then you are no longer strangers and aliens, but you are fellow citizens with the saints and members of the household of God' (v. 19). What a contrast with Paul's description of the Gentiles in verse 12!

God's new creation – the church – relates to all three spheres of God's plan for cosmic unity. The church is linked to the personal dimension, for it is composed of individuals, formerly alienated from God but now through Christ united to him (Eph. 2:1–10). Second, the church is also linked to the communal dimension, as the people of God reconciled to one another (2:11–22). Third, often overlooked is the church's role in the cosmic dimension. As the people reconciled to God and to one another, the church showcases God's plan of cosmic reconciliation. It is God's will 'that through the church the manifold wisdom of God might now be made known to the rulers and authorities in the heavenly places' (Eph. 3:10).

The reality of the unity of Jews and Gentiles together as one new humanity is an incredible testimony to God's broader purposes. The intended audience of this showcase is here described as the rulers and authorities in the heavenly realms. God will bring together in Christ all things in heaven and on earth (Eph. 1:10); all things will highlight Christ as the focal point of the cosmos. The church preaches Christ not only to humanity in the verbal proclamation of the gospel, but also to the entire cosmos through the visible display of unity.

The church as God's display people

God also creates the church in order to display his greatness, and as he does so he glorifies himself. Examples of this in Ephesians include his showing the 'immeasurable riches of his grace in kindness towards us in Christ Jesus' (2:7) and his making known the 'manifold wisdom of God . . . to the rulers and authorities in the heavenly places' (3:10).

Paul offers at least five ways in which believers are a 'display people'. First, our salvation glorifies God by displaying his grace (2:7). Second, our very existence as the church glorifies God by displaying his wisdom (3:10). Third, our unity glorifies God by displaying his oneness (4:1–6). Fourth, our love glorifies God by displaying his love (Eph. 5:2). Fifth, our holiness glorifies God by displaying his holiness (4:24).

The church is God's showcase for his eternal plan of bringing forth cosmic reconciliation and highlighting Christ as the focal point of all history. The church is also God's 'display people', showcasing God's purposes and even God himself. In and through the church God shows his grace, wisdom, love, unity and holiness. And as God displays himself he glorifies himself. That is why Paul proclaims:

> Now to him who is able to do far more abundantly than all that we ask or think, according to the power at work within us, to him be glory in the church and in Christ Jesus throughout all generations, for ever and ever. Amen.
> (Eph. 3:20–21)

The future

The second coming

Although the second coming will mean blessing and judgment, its focus is on a person – 'the Lord Jesus', who will be 'revealed from heaven' (2 Thess. 1:7). Unlike his humble first coming to be crucified, his return will be his glorious revelation 'with his mighty angels in flaming fire' (vv. 7–8) as a warrior-king. While Christ will bring relief to persecuted believers, he will inflict 'vengeance on those who do not know God and on those who do not obey the gospel of our Lord Jesus' (v. 8). His return will be the 'day of wrath' marked by 'God's righteous judgement' (Rom. 2:5) for foes but is the 'blessed hope, the appearing of the glory of our great God and Saviour Jesus Christ' (Titus 2:13) for his people. In retributive justice he will bring to the wicked the 'punishment of eternal destruction, away from the presence of the Lord and from the glory of his might', but to his own he will come 'to be glorified in his saints, and to be marvelled at among all who have believed' (2 Thess. 1:9–10).

Believers, then, are to love Jesus' appearing and its attendant blessings (2 Tim. 4:8). Paul helps the Thessalonians who feared that deceased Christians would miss out at Christ's future coming:

> the Lord himself will descend from heaven with a cry of command, with the voice of an archangel, and with the sound of the trumpet of God. And the dead in Christ will rise first. Then we who are alive, who are left, will be caught up together with them in the clouds to

meet the Lord in the air, and so we will always be with the Lord. Therefore encourage one another with these words.
(1 Thess. 4:16–18)

The Old Testament day of the Lord is now 'the day of our Lord Jesus Christ' (1 Cor. 1:8). Christ's glory will be broadcast when he returns, in both judgment and blessing. As a result, his people will give him glory and worship him.

The resurrection

The Old Testament infrequently looked forward to the resurrection of the dead (Dan. 12:2; cf. Isa. 26:19). In his first coming 'our Saviour Christ Jesus . . . abolished death and brought life and immortality to light through the gospel' (2 Tim. 1:10). Jesus did this through his teaching (John 5:28–29) and especially through his own resurrection. Christ's resurrection is an essential part of the gospel (1 Cor. 15:3–4) and is the basis for our resurrection.

The risen Christ is the 'firstfruits of those who have fallen asleep' (1 Cor. 15:20). As 'firstfruits' he is the pioneer in eschatological resurrection and the guarantee of the resurrection of all believers to eternal life. Paul contrasts Christ's and Adam's effects on humanity: '[A]s by a man came death, by a man has come also the resurrection of the dead' (v. 21).

Paul contrasts believers' earthly bodies with their resurrection bodies. First, fallen earthly bodies are 'perishable', subject to decay and decomposition. By contrast, resurrection bodies are imperishable or immortal, not subject to decay or death (v. 42). Second, earthly bodies are 'sown in dishonour', while resurrection bodies are 'raised in glory' (v. 43). All humans experience dishonour in life and especially in death. By contrast the resurrection body is a glorious body, far surpassing the present body. Third, earthly bodies are 'sown in weakness', while resurrection bodies are 'raised in power' (v. 43). Fourth, earthly bodies are 'natural', and resurrection bodies are 'spiritual' (v. 44). Natural bodies animated by the soul are fitted for ordinary human life on earth, but spiritual bodies animated by the Spirit are transformed and fitted for eternal life on the new earth.

The believing dead are raised and transformed because 'flesh and blood cannot inherit the kingdom of God, nor does the perishable inherit the imperishable' (v. 50). This transformation affects the living and the deceased

(v. 51) and marks death's ultimate demise (vv. 54–57). Believers now have normal bodies like Adam's after the fall, but when Christ returns, they will have resurrection bodies like his (v. 49). Paul makes his most concise statement of believers' hope of resurrection in Philippians 3:20–21:

> our citizenship is in heaven, and from it we await a Saviour, the Lord Jesus Christ, who will transform our lowly body to be like his glorious body, by the power that enables him even to subject all things to himself.

When Christ comes again, he and those who bear his image will be unified, for they 'will appear with him in glory' (Col. 3:4). Ferguson is succinct: 'We are raised in Christ, with Christ, by Christ, to be like Christ.'[17]

Heaven

'Through him we have also obtained access by faith into this grace in which we stand, and we rejoice in hope of the glory of God' (Rom. 5:2). God has saved us by grace through faith in Christ, we now live by grace through faith and we have joy and hope as we long for the final heavenly revelation of God's glory.

Christ's death and resurrection are so magnificent and efficacious that they not only defeat our spiritual adversaries and redeem God's people (Col. 2:13–15) but also deliver creation:

> For the creation was subjected to futility, not willingly, but because of him who subjected it, in hope that the creation itself will be set free from its bondage to corruption and obtain the freedom of the glory of the children of God.
> (Rom. 8:20–21)

Sometimes, therefore, Paul uses 'glory' to speak of heaven; that is, the final salvation of believers and the whole creation.

Many Christians long for the intermediate state without giving much thought to the final state. This is a mistake. Scripture teaches the blessing of the intermediate state for believers, who prefer to be 'away from the body and at home with the Lord' (2 Cor. 5:8). Paul even calls the

---

[17] Ferguson 1996: 251.

intermediate state 'far better' than knowing Christ in this life (Phil. 1:23) because it means being in Christ's immediate presence without sin. But the intermediate state is not the best of salvation, for we go there as spirits or souls without our bodies. God made Adam and Eve as holistic beings, united in body and soul. That is how we live now, and that is how we will live in the eternal state. The best situation is God's raising us from the dead, transforming our earthly bodies into bodies fitted by the Spirit for eternal life (spiritual bodies) with God and all the saints on the new earth.

Over and over Paul uses the word 'glory' to describe the final salvation God's children will inherit. This is true from beginning to end. '[B]efore the ages' God decreed a 'secret and hidden wisdom . . . for our glory' (1 Cor. 2:7). In fact, in mercy he chose his people to be 'prepared beforehand for glory' (Rom. 9:23). In addition, 'When Christ who is your life appears, then you also will appear with him in glory' (Col. 3:4). We are so bound to Christ that only at his return will our true identity be revealed.

The Redeemer is 'Christ in' believers, their 'hope of glory' (Col. 1:27), and therefore they will not fail to 'obtain the salvation that is in Christ Jesus with eternal glory' (2 Tim. 2:10). Paul anticipates glory being revealed to God's people (Rom. 8:18) and their being glorified (vv. 17, 30).

Christ, the 'Lord of glory' (1 Cor. 2:8), moves believers to hope confidently for 'an eternal weight of glory beyond all comparison' (2 Cor. 4:17). 'God, who calls [us] into his own kingdom and glory' (1 Thess. 2:12), will enable us to 'obtain the glory of our Lord Jesus Christ' (2 Thess. 2:14) and raise our bodies 'in glory' (1 Cor. 15:43).

Hell

Although not receiving the attention it deserves, one important picture of hell is exclusion from Christ's glory, as 2 Thessalonians 1:8–9 shows. In his epistles Paul does not use the words translated 'hell' but depicts the fate of the wicked through terms such as 'wrath', 'death', 'condemnation' and 'curse', as Moo teaches.[18]

> Because of your hard and impenitent heart you are storing up *wrath* for yourself on the day of *wrath* when God's righteous judgement will be revealed.
> (Rom. 2:5)

---

[18] Moo in Morgan and Peterson 2004: 92, 93.

the wages of sin is *death*, but the free gift of God is eternal life in
Christ Jesus our Lord.
(Rom. 6:23)

There is therefore now no *condemnation* for those who are in Christ
Jesus.
(Rom. 8:1)

all who rely on works of the law are under a *curse*; for it is written,
'Cursed be everyone who does not abide by all things written in the
Book of the Law, and do them' . . . Christ redeemed us from the
curse of the law by becoming a *curse* for us – for it is written, 'Cursed
is everyone who is hanged on a tree.'
(Gal. 3:10, 13)

As Moo writes, '[Paul] agrees with that larger New Testament witness in
portraying hell as an unending state of punishment and exclusion away
from the presence of the Lord.'[19] In his major passage on hell Paul warns
that the returning Jesus will inflict 'vengeance on those who do not know
God and on those who do not obey the gospel of our Lord Jesus' (2 Thess.
1:8). They 'will suffer the punishment of eternal destruction, away from
the presence of the Lord and from the glory of his might' (v. 9). Hell
contains three major themes, all of which occur in this text: punishment,
destruction and banishment.[20]

Hell involves punishment

In hell the unsaved 'will suffer . . . punishment' (2 Thess. 1:9). God will afflict
the lost with eternal punishment. This theme recurs in our passage, which
tells of the 'righteous judgement of God' (v. 5), the fact that 'God considers
it just to repay with affliction those who afflict' his people (v. 6) and that
Christ will inflict 'vengeance' (vv. 7–8). God is the just Judge who gives the
righteous 'eternal life' and the wicked 'eternal punishment' (Matt. 25:46).

Hell involves destruction

The lost will suffer 'eternal destruction' in hell (2 Thess. 1:9). Two issues
are debated. First, does 'eternal' mean 'age-long', or 'everlasting'? Paul uses

---

[19] Ibid. 109.
[20] Morgan in Morgan and Peterson 2004: 135–151.

the word *aiōnios* to signify 'everlasting': 'eternal life' (Rom. 6:23), 'the eternal God' (16:26), 'eternal comfort' (2 Thess. 2:16) and in our text 'eternal destruction' (1:9). Second, does 'eternal destruction' mean everlasting ruin in hell, or irreversible annihilation? Annihilationists claim that 'eternal destruction' means extinction of being, with no possibility of recreation – namely, extermination. Pointing to the Old Testament background, Beale argues for endless ruin. He says Paul draws the words 'in flaming fire, inflicting vengeance' from Isaiah 66:15, where uniquely in the Old Testament these words occur. Beale notes that an unambiguous reference to eternal conscious punishment follows a few verses later: 'their worm shall not die, their fire shall not be quenched' (Isa. 66:24)[21] – words Jesus used to portray everlasting suffering of the lost in hell (Mark 9:42–48).

Hell involves banishment

In hell the lost 'will suffer the punishment of eternal destruction, away from the presence of the Lord and from the glory of his might' (2 Thess. 1:9). This is judgment as banishment from God's gracious and glorious presence. Paul here uses the language of Isaiah 2, as Fee presents cogently from the LXX, and then concludes correctly, 'In Isaiah that judgment has to do with Israel's being cut off from the divine Presence; in Paul's use of this language "the Lord" is now assumed to be Christ himself.' Fee says that Paul gives two aspects to divine judgment:

> eternal loss – to be cut off forever from the divine presence . . . and to miss out on 'the glory of his might,' both now and forever. For him eternal glory has to do with being in the presence of the Father and the risen Lord. The eternal judgment of the wicked is the absolute loss of such glory.[22]

Paul's contrast between the fates of the righteous and of the unrighteous is arresting. Heaven means eternally dwelling in and enjoying God's glorious presence. Hell means enduring eternal punishment, ruin and exclusion from God's grace and glory.

---

21 Beale 2003: 189.
22 Fee 2009: 259.

Ministry

Glory and global missions

Romans promotes God's glory in its salutation, purpose statement and concluding doxology. And Paul ties each of these sections to missions. Already in his salutation Paul shows concern for God's glory and the gospel. God commissioned the apostle Paul to preach the gospel 'for the sake of his name among all the nations', including in Rome (Rom. 1:5–6). Often in Scripture God's 'name' refers to his person, and here it refers to the person of Christ. Paul's utmost reason for preaching was the glory of God, as Stott explains from Romans 1:

> The highest of missionary motives is neither obedience to the Great Commission (important as that is), nor love for sinners who are alienated and perishing (strong as that incentive is, especially when we contemplate the wrath of God, verse 18), but rather zeal – burning and passionate zeal – for the glory of Jesus Christ.[23]

Gospel preaching, pursued with proper motives, is done to glorify God. At the same time the gospel manifests God's glory. Paul explains that believers see God's glory in the 'gospel of the glory of Christ, who is the image of God' (2 Cor. 4:4). When Paul calls Christ God's image, he is saying both that Christ is God and that he reveals God. Harris is correct: 'As God's εἰκών, Christ both shares and expresses God's nature. He is the precise and visible representation of the invisible God (Col. 1:15).' This is because in gospel proclamation Christ's person and work are exalted as God's only remedy for sin. Harris is pithy: 'It is Christ's own glory that is proclaimed in the gospel.'[24]

Paul's famous thematic statement furthers God's glory by implication:

> I am not ashamed of the gospel, for it is the power of God for salvation to everyone who believes, to the Jew first and also to the Greek. For in it the righteousness of God is revealed from faith for faith, as it is written, 'The righteous shall live by faith.'
> (Rom. 1:16–17)

---

[23] Stott 1995: 53.
[24] Harris 2005: 330.

Romans is concerned about missions in the articulation and furtherance of the gospel. Romans 1:18 – 4:25 constitutes Scripture's most important words on free justification. God declares sinners who believe in Jesus to be righteous to glorify his name.

Paul's last words in Romans resonate with the church's mission:

> Now to him who is able to strengthen you according to my gospel and the preaching of Jesus Christ, according to the revelation of the mystery that was kept secret for long ages but has now been disclosed and through the prophetic writings has been made known to all nations, according to the command of the eternal God, to bring about the obedience of faith – to the only wise God be glory for evermore through Jesus Christ! Amen.
> (Rom. 16:25–27)

Paul praises God's power and wisdom in revealing the 'mystery' contained in the Old Testament prophets but not fully revealed until the Holy Spirit broadcast it in Paul's 'gospel and the preaching of Jesus Christ' (v. 25). This mystery concerns Romans' theme of the 'obedience of faith' (v. 26); namely, the spread of the gospel to Jews and Gentiles that leads to godly living. Paul's doxology thus fittingly ends Romans, for it shows that the whole Christian mission redounds to the 'glory' of the 'only wise God . . . for evermore through Jesus Christ! Amen' (v. 27).

Glory and new covenant ministry

At first blush, Paul's words seem strange: 'Now I am speaking to you Gentiles. Inasmuch then as I am an apostle to the Gentiles, I magnify my ministry' (Rom. 11:13). The word translated 'magnify' is δοξάζειν, which is usually translated 'to glorify'. Paul glorifies his ministry? Yes, as the words that immediately follow explain: 'I magnify my ministry in order somehow to make my fellow Jews jealous, and thus save some of them' (Rom. 11:13–14). Paul's ministry focuses on the Word of God, Christ and the gospel. And he leaves no doubt that his major concern in all his ministry is the glory of God.

In 2 Corinthians 3:7–18 Paul acclaims the glory of new covenant ministry that reflects the glory of the Trinity. The historical context of 2 Corinthians helps us understand his words on the old and new covenants and their respective ministries. Hughes is correct:

Certain false teachers, who claimed to be apostles, had infiltrated the ranks of the Corinthian church, and in promoting their own claims they had gone out of their way to discredit Paul and to call in question the genuineness of his apostleship.[25]

Second Corinthians is Paul's defence against charges aimed at his person, apostleship and ministry, for the sake of the gospel and God's glory.

Moses, the mediator of the old covenant, had the audacity to ask God to show him his glory (Exod. 33:18). And he did! God promised to make his goodness pass in front of Moses and to proclaim his name to him (v. 19). But, God warned, 'you cannot see my face, for man shall not see me and live' (v. 20). The Lord would allow Moses to see a small portion of his glory as God passed by (vv. 21–23). The next day God proclaimed his name, his character as a personal being, to Moses, who responded with worship. Further, Moses' face shone when he came out from the presence of the Lord to meet the Israelites, so that they were afraid of him (Exod. 34:29–30). As a result, Moses would put a veil on his face.

Paul insists that he and the other apostles are not, 'like so many, peddlers of God's word', but instead are 'men of sincerity, [who] as commissioned by God, in the sight of God . . . speak in Christ' (2 Cor. 2:17). The apostles' qualifications, argues Paul, are 'from God, who has made us sufficient to be ministers of a new covenant, not of the letter but of the Spirit. For the letter kills, but the Spirit gives life' (2 Cor. 3:5–6). Paul argues that, as great as the glory of the old covenant was, it is eclipsed by the glory of the new covenant and its ministry. The ministry of the new covenant has 'even more glory' than and 'far exceed[s]' that of the old (vv. 8–9). 'Indeed, in this case, what once had glory has come to have no glory at all, because of the glory that surpasses it' (v. 10).

Therefore, new covenant ministry, suffused with God's glory, is great indeed! By God's mercy Paul, contrary to his detractors' charges, eschews 'disgraceful, underhanded ways' and refuses to 'practise cunning' (2 Cor. 4:1–2). Rather, as a minister of the glorious new covenant he openly proclaims the truth of the 'light of the gospel of the glory of Christ' (v. 4). Paul and the other apostles proclaim not themselves but

---

[25] Hughes 1962: xvi.

'Jesus Christ as Lord', as they are 'servants for Jesus' sake' (v. 5). The reason? God, the Creator of light (Gen. 1:3), illumined their hearts 'to give the light of the knowledge of the glory of God in the face of Jesus Christ' (2 Cor. 4:6).

Glory and gospel preaching

The chief goal of Paul's preaching was to bring glory to God through the salvation of sinners. This involved both his message and his manner, as he clarifies: Christ sent him 'to preach the gospel, and not with words of eloquent wisdom, lest the cross of Christ be emptied of its power' (1 Cor. 1:17). This strategy was countercultural, as Ciampa and Rosner explain:

> He eschewed the neatly packaged eloquence and wit of the orator, who sought glory from the crowds . . . Such speakers put more stock in winning arguments and impressing an audience than in actually saying something of consequence. Paul distanced himself from this model of speaking.[26]

Instead of majoring on aesthetic rhetoric, as the sophists did, Paul came to Corinth 'not . . . proclaiming to you the testimony of God with lofty speech or wisdom. For I decided to know nothing among you except Jesus Christ and him crucified' (2:1–2). This was very unlike most orators' first visit to a city:

> In the ancient world a public speaker's initial visit to a city was critical to establishing their reputation. Orators would compete for applause and offer entertainment to diners in between courses at the best banquets. Competitive showmanship was the order of the day.[27]

Plainly, Paul wanted no part of showmanship. His preaching avoided sophistic attempts to gain glory for himself and focused instead on the message of 'Jesus Christ and him crucified' (1 Cor. 2:2). Moreover, we must appreciate how countercultural was the *content* of Paul's message.

---

[26] Ciampa and Rosner 2010: 86.
[27] Ibid. 112.

Thiselton informs us, 'It is little wonder that the proclamation of the cross of Christ, entailing the shameful death of a person marginalized from society as an alleged criminal, was perceived by many as an affront (σκάνδαλον) and sheer folly (μωρία, 1:23).'[28]

Paul deliberately turned the spotlight away from himself and on to Christ. The question is why – it was so that God might get the glory. Paul preached Christ in simple words as a 'demonstration of the Spirit and of power, so that [his hearers'] faith might not rest in the wisdom of men but in the power of God' (1 Cor. 2:4–5). Paul's homiletics glorified God by extolling his power and wisdom.

The results of Paul's preaching in the composition of the churches also glorified God. Here again, contrary to worldly wisdom, God humbled the proud and exalted the lowly. His strategy was to reach few of those who were well educated, influential in society or of high social standing and instead to reach many who were in society's lower classes. Paul did not beat around the bush:

> consider your calling, brothers: not many of you were wise according to worldly standards, not many were powerful, not many were of noble birth. But God chose what is foolish in the world to shame the wise; God chose what is weak in the world to shame the strong; God chose what is low and despised in the world, even things that are not, to bring to nothing things that are.
> (1 Cor. 1:26–28)

God's purpose in doing this is crucial to our argument. God rejected the high and chose the lowly 'so that no human being might boast in the presence of God' (v. 29). Twice Paul writes that God's purpose was to 'shame' the wise and influential and once to 'bring to nothing' societal conventions. Paul contrasts God's 'shaming' the high and mighty with 'boast[ing] in the Lord' (v. 31). Shame and glory (boasting) are antithetical. God will not share his glory with human beings. He has reserved his glory for himself, and receives it even in the make-up of the churches as a result of the apostolic preaching.

Paul quotes Jeremiah, '[A]s it is written, "Let the one who boasts, boast in the Lord"' (1 Cor. 1:31, citing Jer. 9:24). Those whom God unites to

---

28 Thiselton 2000: 21.

Christ (1 Cor. 1:30) may boast, but only 'in the Lord'. Jeremiah's context influences Paul's words leading up to 1 Corinthians 1:31:

> Thus says the LORD: 'Let not the wise man boast in his wisdom, let not the mighty man boast in his might, let not the rich man boast in his riches, but let him who boasts boast in this, that he understands and knows me, that I am the LORD who practises steadfast love, justice, and righteousness in the earth. For in these things I delight, declares the LORD.'
> (Jer. 9:23–24)

There is another sense in which the content of Paul's preaching contributes to our study of glory. He proclaims the profound and eternal glory that awaits those who know Christ. Paul rejects worldly wisdom but does teach a 'secret and hidden wisdom of God, which God decreed before the ages for our glory' (1 Cor. 2:7). As evidence of the world rulers' ignorance of God's wisdom, Paul says, 'None of the rulers of this age understood this, for if they had, they would not have crucified the Lord of glory' (v. 8). Then the apostle, relying on Isaiah 64:4, rhapsodizes concerning believers' future glory:

> But, as it is written,
>
>> 'What no eye has seen, nor ear heard,
>>   nor the heart of man imagined,
>> what God has prepared for those who love him' –
>
> these things God has revealed to us through the Spirit.
> (1 Cor. 2:9–10)

Our eternal life in resurrected bodies will be wonderful, but at present many details elude us. So Paul elsewhere describes our end as an 'eternal weight of glory beyond all comparison' (2 Cor. 4:17).

Paul does not hide his goal in ministry. He preaches Jesus' death and resurrection 'so that as grace extends to more and more people it may increase thanksgiving, to the glory of God' (2 Cor. 4:15). Tasker's words aptly conclude this section:

The more people who come to know the grace of God through the gospel Paul preaches, the more numerous will be the thanksgivings that will be evoked, and the greater the praise that will be offered to God. In a word, that God may be increasingly glorified, not that he himself may be exalted, is Paul's supreme ambition.[29]

---

[29] Tasker 1958: 76.

9

The glory of God
and the Christian life

Scripture paints many pictures of the Christian life. Believers are stewards, pilgrims, farmers, runners, victors, lovers, overcomers and more. A neglected picture of the Christian life is that of believers as recipients of God's glory both now and in the future. God gradually transforms us 'from one degree of glory to another' as we behold 'the glory of the Lord' (2 Cor. 3:18) until he confirms us in final resurrection glory (1 Cor. 15:43). God intends for his glory to have an impact on many areas of our lives. Here we investigate six such areas from passages we have not previously explored in depth:

- Glory and love (Phil. 1:3–11)
- Glory and provision (Phil. 4:10–20)
- Glory and hope (Col. 3:4)
- Glory and mystery (Col. 1:27)
- Glory and boasting (Gal. 6:14)
- Glory and worship (1 Tim. 1:17; 6:15–16)

Glory and love (Phil. 1:3–11)

Paul's opening prayer for the Philippians overflows with warmth, love in Christ and God's glory. After his salutation Paul tells that he gives joyous thanks to God whenever he thinks of the dear Philippians. The reason? Because of their fellowship (*koinōnia*) in the gospel they have shared from the beginning (vv. 3–5). Paul is confident in God's faithfulness that God will never abandon the Philippians but will continue his good work in them until Christ returns (v. 6).

Paul writes, 'It is right for me to feel this way about you all, because I hold you in my heart, for you are all partakers with me of grace' (v. 7). Paul holds the Philippians in his heart; that is, he cares deeply for them. Together they have partaken of God's grace in the gospel, and as a result the Philippians have stood with him while he was in prison for the gospel. 'The closeness of fellow-feeling is based upon a common participation (*koinōnia*) in the grace of God, and a deep sense of oneness even though the apostle and the church are separated', as Martin asserts.[1]

'God is my witness, how I yearn for you all with the affection of Christ Jesus' (v. 8). To show how strongly he feels, Chapman explains, Paul 'invokes God as his witness over his heart'.[2] His love for the Philippian church is not merely his own personal love. It is his love suffused with Christ's love, as Hawthorne explains:

> Paul loves them as Christ loves them and because Christ loves them through him . . . So Paul is saying, in effect: '. . . I wish to assure you that I long for you. I hold you in the heart of Christ Jesus! This is the measure and meaning of my affection for you.' Surely this astonishing metaphor powerfully drove home to the Philippians the depth and reality of Paul's love for them?[3]

Paul wants his readers to excel in love: 'And it is my prayer that your love may abound more and more' (v. 9). Paul desires their love for God and one another to brim and overflow. He specifies 'with knowledge and all discernment, so that you may approve what is excellent' (vv. 9–10). The Philippians' 'ever-increasing love is also to be a discriminating love',[4] so that they will be 'pure and blameless for the day of Christ' (v. 10). Paul desires their progressive sanctification until Christ's second coming.

Paul powerfully rounds out his prayer: his goal is that they be 'filled with the fruit of righteousness that comes through Jesus Christ, to the glory and praise of God' (v. 11). Paul's prayer includes vital aspects of the Christian life: his readers are to abound in love combined with wise judgment so as to approve only the best things. Love and discernment are the means to the end of being 'pure and blameless' and 'filled with the fruit of righteousness' until Jesus returns. The ultimate goal of all this? 'The glory and praise of God' (v. 11).

---

[1] Martin 1959: 63.
[2] Chapman 2012: 49.
[3] Hawthorne 1983: 25.
[4] Ibid. 26.

Chapman accurately captures Paul's flow of thought:

> We conduct ourselves here in this life by letting our love for God,
> educated in the excellent things of God's Word, spill out into pure
> conduct in eager expectation of Christ's return. Moreover, Paul's
> perspective reaches out more broadly than our own human sphere
> of interest. Ultimately he is concerned for God's glory and praise. In
> the end, as those who love God, we are to conduct our lives with the
> goal of bringing praise, glory, and honor to Him.[5]

In sum, Paul begins by thanking God and ends by praying for the
Philippians' love to redound to the glory of God. He rejoices in their warm
friendship and gospel fellowship. He holds the church in his heart and
dearly loves them – with the affection of Jesus himself. Out of this God-
given love he prays for the church's love to abound, to overflow. The
apostle's prayer for them is not for love of a generic sort but for true love,
a love tied to knowledge, wisdom, holiness and righteousness. As God's
people flourish in this kind of love, they glorify God, by both reflecting
and praising him.

Glory and provision (Phil. 4:10–20)

Paul's affection for the Philippians is obvious from the beginning to the
end of his letter. He says, concerning those whom he twice calls 'my
beloved' (2:12; 4:1):

> I hold you in my heart.
> (1:7)

> I yearn for you all with the affection of Christ Jesus.
> (1:8)

> my brothers, whom I love and long for, my joy and crown.
> (4:1)

One reason Paul feels this way about them is their giving to support his
ministry:

---

[5] Chapman 2012: 52.

You Philippians yourselves know that in the beginning of the gospel, when I left Macedonia, no church entered into partnership with me in giving and receiving, except you only. Even in Thessalonica you sent me help for my needs once and again.
(Phil. 4:15–16)

Now in prison Paul praises Epaphroditus, a servant of the Philippian church, whom the Philippians sent to Paul to minister to him financially and spiritually (2:25, 30). Paul acknowledges their support: 'I rejoiced in the Lord greatly that now at length you have revived your concern for me. You were indeed concerned for me, but you had no opportunity' (4:10).

Paul explains that while he appreciates the Philippians' gift ('it was kind of you', v. 14), he has learned not to depend on such gifts. Rather, he has learned how to be content living both with plenty and with little (vv. 11–12). His secret? 'I can do all things through him who strengthens me' (v. 13). Interpreting 'all things' in context points to Paul's circumstances of abundance and need (v. 12). He is grateful for Christians' provisions for his needs, but his greater dependence is on his provider Christ: 'I can do all things through him who strengthens me' (v. 13). Hawthorne translates and exegetes this verse:

'in union with the one who infuses me with strength' ... The secret of Paul's independence is his dependence upon Another ... He whose life was seized by Christ; he who gladly gave up all for Christ; he who paradoxically gained all by losing all for Christ; he who longed to know Christ and the power of his resurrection (3:7–10), and so on, could only envision Christ as his true source of inner strength.[6]

Viewing life spiritually, Paul seeks the fruit of the Philippians' ministry to him to accrue to them spiritually even more so than their generous gifts through Epaphroditus, which he regards as sacrificial offerings to God (vv. 17–18). He rejoices that they are storing up treasures in heaven, as Jesus taught (Matt. 6:19–20). Chapman hits the right note: 'In the midst of thanking them for their gift, Paul also desires to model contentment in the Lord's provision throughout life.'[7]

---

[6] Hawthorne 1983: 201.
[7] Chapman 2012: 263.

Paul's words in several places in Philippians, especially in 4:10–20, clash with Greco-Roman social conventions concerning giving and receiving. Fowl points to the overriding difference between the two approaches: 'Paul and the Philippians share a friendship founded, directed, and sustained by Christ. Their giving and Paul's receiving happens in and through Christ.'[8] Summarizing the work of Peterman, Fowl lists six ways in which Paul's words subvert Greco-Roman ideas of giving and receiving:

> First, there is no notion of debt. Paul never acknowledges a debt to the Philippians either for this gift or for past ones. Second, there is no hint of repayment (if there is no debt, how could there be repayment?). God repays. Third, the Philippians will reap spiritual benefits from their giving. God will give these benefits. Greco-Roman conventions allowed for non-material repayment in terms of honor given to the benefactor by the recipients. Fourth, the Philippians' gift brings them into solidarity with Paul's affliction. Fifth, this partnership furthers the gospel. Sixth, their gift is a spiritual sacrifice pleasing to God.[9]

Receiving gifts in Greco-Roman culture involved the obligation of giving back. Paul does not give back but declares that God will do so: '[M]y God will supply every need of yours according to his riches in glory in Christ Jesus' (Phil. 4:19). The Philippians have provided for Paul's physical needs; he promises that God will provide for all of their needs, physical and spiritual, according to his unlimited heavenly supply. Hawthorne agrees: 'In return for supplying his needs out of their poverty (cf. 2 Cor. 8:2), he asks God to meet all their needs out of his riches, in accordance with his vast assets, "on a scale worthy of his wealth."'[10]

Paul concludes his treatment of God's great provision for his people by giving credit where credit is due: 'To our God and Father be glory for ever and ever. Amen' (Phil. 4:20). Chapman's words form a fitting end to our treatment of glory and provision:

> Having just mentioned God's glory in verse 19, Paul here offers up this doxology to God . . . This verse invokes the mystery of worship.

---

8 Fowl 2009: 197.
9 Ibid., citing Peterman 1997: 149–511.
10 Hawthorne 1983: 211.

God already possesses untold glory (4:19), yet Paul calls for glory to be ascribed to Him (4:20) . . . The reality of Paul's heartfelt cry is that God be recognized as the Glorious One for all eternity. This forms a fitting response in light of God's provision for His people mentioned in verse 19. Moreover, it also represents the proper Christian exaltation of the almighty God of the Universe, and it conveys the heartfelt praise within every Christian act of worship.[11]

Glory and hope (Col. 3:4)[12]

Christ, the 'Lord of glory' (1 Cor. 2:8), causes justified believers to 'rejoice in hope of the glory of God' (Rom. 5:2). This hope entails an 'eternal weight of glory beyond all comparison' (2 Cor. 4:17), such that we will 'obtain the glory of our Lord Jesus Christ' (2 Thess. 2:14), with even our bodies being 'raised in glory' (1 Cor. 15:43).

In Colossians Paul fosters hope by teaching that we will appear with Christ in glory (Col. 3:4). Paul has denounced the false teachers and their asceticism (2:8–23). Now he shifts his focus, speaks positively and points his readers heavenward: '[S]eek the things that are above . . . Set your minds on things that are above' (3:1–2). He points them to 'where Christ is, seated at the right hand of God', for Christ is the antidote to both the poisonous instruction and the vain asceticism of the false teachers (2:8–23).

Paul motivates believers to seek Christ by speaking of them as participants in his story. He tells them, '[Y]ou have died' (3:3), meaning 'with Christ' (cf. 2:20), and speaks of their union with Christ in his resurrection (3:1). Due to the believers' union with Christ in his death and resurrection, Paul says, '[Y]our life is hidden with Christ in God' (v. 3). Many things of God exist in heaven now but have not yet been revealed. Moo explains that Paul refers to a basic hidden–revealed theme of a Jewish apocalyptic world view:

> But the apocalyptic seer is given a vision of these things, things that will one day be revealed as they come to pass and are seen by people

---

[11] Chapman 2012: 271–272.
[12] This section relies on Peterson 2014b: 162–164.

242

on earth. So, Paul suggests, at the present time our heavenly identity is real, but it is hidden . . . In the meantime our true status is veiled and, though we may not look any different than those around us, Paul's point is that we certainly need to behave differently.[13]

Contrary to the false teachers' ascetic doctrine, God's people are to pursue Christ, who is above. This does not involve the denial of bodily appetites as a means to spirituality but requires focusing on Christ in heaven and drawing strength from union with him for everyday life on earth.

Amazingly, Paul takes our involvement in Christ's narrative further. We died with him, were buried with him, arose with him, ascended with him and sat down in heaven with him, and in a sense we will even come again with him! 'When Christ who is your life appears, then you also will appear with him in glory' (v. 4). Using the word 'appears', Paul speaks of Jesus' second coming and in the same sentence says that we will 'appear' too. In what sense do we have a second coming in union with Christ? Moo answers correctly:

> When he appears in glory at the time of his return, believers will appear with him. Our identification with Christ, now real but hidden, will one day be manifest . . . Because Christ is now 'in us,' we have 'the hope of glory' (Col. 1:27), and it is that same union, expressed in the other direction – we 'in Christ' – that will bring hope to its certain accomplishment.[14]

Our union with Christ is so inclusive that Paul says we will 'return' with him. Paul means that only at Christ's return will our true identity in him be disclosed.[15] Paul teaches the same truth in Romans 8:18–19: 'I consider that the sufferings of this present time are not worth comparing with the glory that is to be revealed to us. For the creation waits with eager longing for the revealing of the sons of God.' The word translated 'revealing' is *apokalypsis*, more literally rendered 'revelation'. This word

---

[13] Moo 2008: 250.
[14] Ibid. 251–252.
[15] John agrees: 'Beloved, we are God's children now, and what we will be has not yet appeared; but we know that when he appears we shall be like him, because we shall see him as he is' (1 John 3:2).

frequently refers to Jesus' return, and in Romans 8:19 refers to our 'return', so to speak. How is this possible? Because of union with Christ, as Bruce explains:

> That glorious liberty [of the children of God] will be manifested on the day of their revelation, for the revelation of the Son of God in glory carries with it the revelation of the sons and daughters of God in that same glory – the glory which is his by right and theirs by the grace which unites them to him.[16]

All in all, believers' lives are so tethered to the Son of God that by virtue of union with him Paul could refer to 'Christ who is your life' (Col. 3:4). In context he is countering the claims of the false teachers that the Colossian Christians are deficient. To the contrary, he insists, they have all they need in union with the Son and are therefore secure. Indeed, now their lives are 'hidden with Christ in God' (v. 3). He is 'Christ in' them, their 'hope of glory' (Col. 1:27), and therefore they will not fail to 'obtain the salvation that is in Christ Jesus with eternal glory' (2 Tim. 2:10).

Glory and mystery (Col. 1:27)

Moo is insightful: the word '"mystery" (*mysterion*) . . . is one of the most interesting in Paul's theological vocabulary. It is particularly prominent in Ephesians and Colossians, where half of the twenty Pauline occurrences are found.'[17] We saw in Ephesians[18] the incredible mystery of Christ's future cosmic rule over all things (1:9–10). Here we turn to the three Colossians passages and their connection to glory:

> the mystery hidden for ages and generations but now revealed to his saints. To them God chose to make known how great among the Gentiles are the riches of the glory of this mystery, which is Christ in you, the hope of glory.
> (Col. 1:26–27)

---

[16] Bruce 1984: 136.
[17] Moo 2008: 155.
[18] See pp. 160–163.

to reach all the riches of full assurance of understanding and the knowledge of God's mystery, which is Christ, in whom are hidden all the treasures of wisdom and knowledge.
(Col. 2:2–3)

At the same time, pray also for us, that God may open to us a door for the word, to declare the mystery of Christ, on account of which I am in prison.
(Col. 4:3)

Colossians 1:26–27

Paul rejoices that he suffers (non-redemptively, of course) for Christ and the church to help complete the suffering God has allotted believers in union with Christ (Col. 1:24; Rev. 6:9–11). God commissioned Paul as a minister of the Word, whose job it was to proclaim the gospel, which includes the 'mystery hidden for ages and generations but now revealed to his saints' (Col. 1:26). In Ephesians Paul had written of 'my insight into the mystery of Christ, which was not made known to the sons of men in other generations as it has now been revealed to his holy apostles and prophets by the Spirit' (Eph. 3:4–5). The idea of mystery here involves truths revealed partially in the Old Testament and more fully in the New Testament, especially pertaining to Christ, the last days and unity between Jews and Gentiles.[19]

Colossians includes the Gentiles in the concept of mystery, for to the saints 'God chose to make known how great among the Gentiles are the riches of the glory of this mystery' (Col. 1:27). But Colossians lacks the ideas prominent in Ephesians that the mystery involves God's bringing together Jews and Gentiles in one worldwide church and that God continues to herald his wisdom and glory to the universe by making known his plan to do so (Eph. 3:8–10). Colossians' emphasis is broader, as is characteristic of the term's overall Pauline use. Moo states:

Nor should we feel any compulsion to come up with a single referent for Paul's 'mystery.' He uses the term in a functional more than a topical manner, applying it to a number of different, albeit usually related, aspects of God's climactic work in Christ.[20]

---

[19] Beale and Gladd 2014: 20, 321–322.
[20] Moo 2008: 158.

Paul uses extravagant language, speaking of the 'riches of the glory of this mystery' (Col. 1:27), so that 'the glory of God's rich grace thus lavishly dispensed may move them to grateful adoration', as Bruce asserts.[21] The apostle then comes to the heart of the first mention of mystery in Colossians: 'Christ in you, the hope of glory' (Col. 1:27). Moo is helpful: 'Paul's focus here is on how God's new covenant people are completely identified with their representative, Christ, and how that new identity gives hope for the future.'[22] God's amazing grace and glory blessed the believing Gentiles with salvation, and Christ now lives in them.

Indwelling is a key Pauline theme:

> In at least sixteen texts Paul teaches the Trinity makes his home in and with God's people as individuals and as the church. Paul usually ascribes indwelling to the Spirit, but does so six times to the Son (Rom. 8:10; 2 Cor. 13:5; Gal. 2:20; Eph. 3:17; Col. 1:27; 3:11), and twice to the Father (2 Cor. 6:16; Eph. 2:22). Christians, then, are indwelt by the Father, Son, and Holy Spirit.[23]

Christ in believers is the 'hope of glory' (Col. 1:27). '[Christ] is, in his person, the hope that points to glory and the hope that is headed to glory'.[24] Thus their salvation is secure (cf. Rom. 8:11), as Bruce avows: because by grace through faith 'they have his risen life within them, [this] affords them a stable basis for confidence that they will share in the fullness of glory' when he returns.[25]

Colossians 2:2–3

Paul shares his struggles not only for churches he planted but also for ones, like those in Colossae and Laodicea, that he never visited. For them too 'Paul expends his energies – by his care, his prayers . . . and by his letters', as Martin summarizes.[26] Paul wants his readers to be encouraged and unified in love so they will enjoy great assurance of salvation. Assurance is tied to knowing 'God's mystery, which is Christ' (Col. 2:2).

---

[21] Bruce 1984: 85.
[22] Moo 2008: 159.
[23] Peterson 2014b: 412.
[24] Campbell 2020: 310.
[25] Bruce 1984: 86.
[26] Martin 1973: 74.

This knowledge is not merely intellectual but is also personal; it is knowledge of God's mystery, which is a person; namely, Christ. This knowledge is essential and sufficient for salvation and Christian living, for 'all the treasures of wisdom and knowledge' are hidden in him alone (Col. 2:3). Paul counters the false teachers' claims to special knowledge apart from Christ. This is impossible, as Moo shows. Although 1:15–20 uses more elevated language to exalt Christ, Paul here crisply summarizes his overriding concern – to present Christ as the answer to all human needs for knowledge and life.[27]

Colossians 4:3

After exhorting the Colossians to pray with perseverance, alertness and thanksgiving (4:2), Paul, who prays for them (1:3, 9), asks them to pray for him and his ministry (4:3). He wants them to uphold him in prayer, asking God to provide opportunity for him to preach the Word with clarity. He expresses the content of his preaching as the 'mystery of Christ' and says it is why he is in prison (v. 3).

Scholars have put forth various interpretations of the meaning of 'mystery of Christ'. Moo argues for an interpretation, correctly in our estimation, that is consistent with Paul's teaching on the 'mystery' throughout Colossians:

The focus in Colossians, in a manner wholly distinctive to this letter, is christological. The mystery, Paul said earlier, is 'Christ in you, the hope of glory' (1:27) or, simply, 'Christ' (2:2). These texts suggest that we should understand 'the mystery of Christ' not as 'the mystery that Christ proclaims' (taking *Christou* as a subjective genitive) or even 'the mystery about Christ' (objective genitive; see NLT) but 'the mystery which is Christ' (an epexegetic genitive). God is therefore here once again defined in christological terms: God opens the door for the mystery of Christ to be proclaimed.[28]

Therefore, Paul's teaching in Colossians about the mystery God entrusted to him centres on the person and work of Christ, who apprehended him on the Damascus road to change his life for ever. The apostle

---

[27] Moo 2008: 169.
[28] Ibid. 323.

explains, '[H]e who had set me apart before I was born, and who called me by his grace, was pleased to reveal his Son to me, in order that I might preach him among the Gentiles' (Gal. 1:15–16). Bruce's words form a fitting summary: 'For Paul, to preach the gospel was to preach Christ, and so to make known the "hidden wisdom" of God, which was "decreed before the ages" for his people's glory' (1 Cor. 2:7).'[29]

Paul's response to God in Ephesians belongs here too: '[T]o him be glory in the church and in Christ Jesus throughout all generations, for ever and ever. Amen' (Eph. 3:21).

Glory and boasting (Gal. 6:14)

'Boasting' constitutes a significant theme for the apostle. He uses the verb 'to boast' and the nouns 'boast' and 'boasting' in both negative and positive ways. By 'boasting' Paul means 'taking pride in', 'glorying in' and then 'having confidence in'.[30] Herman Ridderbos gets to the heart of negative boasting:

> What is most deeply at stake in the concept of 'boasting' is the question as to what it is in which man places his trust . . . In this manner man becomes confident and strong against God, the flesh boasts in itself instead of boasting in God (cf. 1 Cor. 1:29ff.). Boasting is therefore not a phenomenon restricted to the Jews. It is equally characteristic of the Greeks, who glory in their wisdom (1 Cor. 1:19–31). It is the natural impulse of every man, against which even the Christian must continue to be warned (Gal. 6:4; Rom. 11:17ff.).[31]

Ridderbos captures Paul's idea of the evil of boasting in humans instead of God. Paul gives many positive reasons for boasting. These positive reasons are best viewed against Paul's reasons *not* to boast. Humans should not boast or glory in the following:

- The law (Rom. 2:23)
- Men (1 Cor. 3:21)
- Outward appearance (2 Cor. 5:12)

---

[29] Bruce 1984: 173.
[30] See Ciampa and Rosner 2010: 492.
[31] Ridderbos 1975: 141.

- The flesh (2 Cor. 11:18)
- Others' flesh (Gal. 6:13)
- Works (Eph. 2:9)

In sum, Paul asserts that God's will is that 'no human being [should] boast in the presence of God' (1 Cor. 1:29). More concisely, father Abraham exemplifies the fact that no one should boast 'before God' (Rom. 4:2). In fact, faith excludes all negative boasting (Rom. 3:27).

While Paul excludes some boasting, he delights to speak of the positive grounds for boasting. Taking his cue from Jeremiah 9:23–24, Paul twice says simply, 'Let the one who boasts, boast in the Lord' (1 Cor. 1:31; 2 Cor. 10:17; Jer. 9:22–23, LXX). In terms of the gospel, '[W]e also boast in God through our Lord Jesus Christ' (Rom. 5:11, NIV). Another way of saying this is that we and our converts 'glory in Christ Jesus' (Phil. 1:26; 3:3). Silva defines 'glory' here as 'joyful pride and exultant boasting'.[32]

Paul speaks against his opponents and their boasting. They not only fail to keep the law themselves, 'but they desire to have you circumcised that they may boast in your flesh' (Gal. 6:13). His opponents brag about their devotion to the law, and they urge the Galatian Gentiles to be circumcised, that there may be further cause for boasting. In contrast to those who put confidence in the flesh and want to boast in others' flesh, Paul is resolute: '[F]ar be it from me to boast except in the cross of our Lord Jesus Christ' (Gal. 6:14). Longenecker sets the cross in its historical context:

> Today, after almost two millennia of viewing the cross as a sacred symbol, it is difficult for Christians to appreciate the repugnance and horror with which the cross was viewed among Jews and Gentiles in the first century . . . The only things comparable in our day would be venerating an electric chair or wearing a hangman's noose around our necks as a symbol of religious devotion.[33]

And Ridderbos starkly contrasts two views of boasting or glorying:

> The real motive of these Judaistic zealots is selfish pride . . . They want to glory in the Galatian Gentiles before others . . . But this

---

[32] Silva 2005: 149.
[33] Longenecker 1990: 294.

thing in which [Paul] glories constitutes a threat to those who seek themselves. The cross of Christ is his glory ... Paul, however, presents this glory of the cross by naming it with the fulness and richness of Christ's names ... *The world* as used here is an epitome of everything outside of Christ in which man seeks his glory and puts his trust ... Their glory, Paul says in effect, is worldly, godless, vain, however religious it may seem to be ... Because of the cross this whole world has been crucified for Paul. He has written it off as a basis for glorying and trust.[34]

Boasting in the cross transforms Paul's view of life, as he says in Galatians 6: '[F]ar be it from me to boast except in the cross of our Lord Jesus Christ, by which the world has been crucified to me, and I to the world' (v. 14). Paul means that Jesus' atoning death has brought about a big separation between Paul, and all believers for whom he speaks, and the sinful world system. Paul no longer belongs to the world. Rather, he and all Christians are a part of God's 'new creation' (v. 15). As a result, 'All "simply human" factors [such as circumcision or uncircumcision] become meaningless in the face of God's world-transforming work in his Son Jesus Christ. The old state of affairs has ended.'[35]

As a result, Paul boasts in his weaknesses (2 Cor. 11:30; 12:5, 9) and sufferings for Christ (Rom. 5:3, NIV). He is concerned not with outward appearances but with what is in the heart (2 Cor. 5:12). In Christ, Paul boasts of his work for God (Rom. 15:17, NIV) and successful ministry (Phil. 2:16, NIV). By God's grace in Christ Paul boasts in others (1 Cor. 15:31, NIV).

Paul boasts with an eye on future glory, for 'we boast in the hope of the glory of God' (Rom. 5:2, NIV). Paul's affection for the Thessalonians leads to boasting: '[W]hat is our hope or joy or crown of boasting before our Lord Jesus at his coming? Is it not you?' (1 Thess. 2:19). Paul's confident hope for himself and for those to whom he ministers is that 'on the day of our Lord Jesus you will boast of us as we will boast of you' (2 Cor. 1:14).

Ridderbos ties together Paul's teaching on boasting:

That there is no place for boasting becomes quite clear only from the gospel, in which 'the law of works' has given way to 'the law of

---

[34] Ridderbos 1953: 223–225; emphasis original.
[35] Moo 2013: 397.

250

faith,' that is, in which another order governs. From that other order, as it is evident already in Abraham's life and as it already for him excluded every boast (Rom. 4:2), . . . the mortal peril of . . . trusting in the flesh is manifest: 'that no flesh should boast before God' (1 Cor. 1:29), and that but one possibility and one ground of boasting should remain: boasting in the Lord (1 Cor. 1:31; 2 Cor. 10:17), and in the cross of our Lord Jesus Christ (Gal. 6:14).[36]

Glory and worship (1 Tim. 1:17; 6:15–16)

The primary human response to God's revealed glory is to give him glory in worship. Paul does this at the end of verses 12–17. He thanks Christ for appointing him to gospel ministry (v. 12), gives his testimony as an example of Christ's mercy, grace and patience toward sinners (vv. 13–16), and offers praise to God in a doxology: 'To the King of ages, immortal, invisible, the only God, be honour and glory for ever and ever. Amen' (v. 17).

Doxologies are expressions, often liturgical, of praise to God. Mounce situates their locations in New Testament books:

> Doxologies occur . . . throughout the Pauline literature, sometimes in the opening of a letter (Gal 1:5; cf. Rev 1:6), or the closing (1 Tim 6:16; cf. Phil 4:20; cf. 1 Pet 4:11; 5:11; 2 Pet 3:18; Heb 13:20–21; Jude 24–25), or the middle (Rom 9:5; 11:36; 16:27; Eph 3:20–21; cf. Rev 5:13).[37]

New Testament doxologies are derived from the Old Testament mediated through Jewish synagogue worship.

Knight notes a pattern for New Testament doxologies:

> The doxologies in the NT usually consist, as does this one, of three or four component parts: the person designated and praised (usually in the dative), the statement of praise itself (usually with δόξα), a conclusion indicating the eternal duration of the praise (usually some variant of εἰς τοὺς αἰῶνας), and (in most cases) an ἀμήν.[38]

---

[36] Ridderbos 1975: 141.
[37] Mounce 2000: 48.
[38] Knight 1992: 104.

God is worshipped because of who he is and what he does. Paul combines these and praises him for his attributes of mercy (Rom. 11:32), wisdom, knowledge, justice, inscrutability and grace (vv. 33–35). His works deserving praise include creation, providence and consummation. The apostle rightly says, 'To him be glory for ever. Amen' (v. 36).

God made humans to worship him, which is why Paul is offended at the Gentile folly of exchanging worship of the true God for idols. '[T]hey exchanged the truth about God for a lie and worshipped and served the creature rather than the Creator, who is blessed for ever! Amen' (Rom. 1:25). Paul regards Christ as the proper object of worship along with the Father. The Israelites' greatest benefit 'is the Christ who is God over all, blessed for ever. Amen' (Rom. 9:5). Paul includes the Holy Spirit in worship: 'Through [Christ] we both [Jews and Gentiles] have access in one Spirit to the Father' (Eph. 2:18). Through Jesus, the Mediator, all believers can approach God the Father in worship united in the Holy Spirit.

What is important in indifferent matters, such as the dietary code and Jewish holy days, is to make decisions 'in honour of the Lord' that '[give] thanks to God' (Rom. 14:6). This means that in everyday life we remember Christ's lordship and live for him (vv. 8–9). Paul's goal for an ethnically unified church in Rome is that 'together [all the believers] may with one voice glorify the God and Father of our Lord Jesus Christ' (15:6). Doing so will further the 'glory of God' (v. 7).

Paul teaches that the returning Christ will be the focus of much worship 'when he comes on that day to be glorified in his saints, and to be marvelled at among all who have believed' (2 Thess. 1:10). 'That day' is the Old Testament day of the Lord, which has become the 'day of the Lord Jesus Christ' (1 Cor. 1:8). Jesus' glory will be broadcast when he returns, and his people will give him glory and worship him. Then 'at the name of Jesus every knee [will] bow . . . and every tongue confess that Jesus Christ is Lord, to the glory of God the Father' (Phil. 2:10–11).

In the light of his former persecution of the church Paul regards himself as the worst of sinners. All the more reason, then, for God to display his mercy and overflowing grace to Paul 'as an example to those who were to believe in him for eternal life' (1 Tim. 1:16). As he often does, after speaking of Christ's mercy and grace Paul bursts out in a doxology to God the Father: 'To the King of ages, immortal, invisible, the only God, be honour and glory for ever and ever. Amen' (v. 17).

We will examine the parts of this doxology in turn. As we do, we will compare it to the doxology near the epistle's end:

> he who is the blessed and only Sovereign, the King of kings and Lord of lords, who alone has immortality, who dwells in unapproachable light, whom no one has ever seen or can see. To him be honour and eternal dominion. Amen.
> (1 Tim. 6:15–16)

Paul directs honour and glory to God as 'King'. The Old Testament often refers to God as King. Psalm 47 is one example of many:

> Clap your hands, all peoples!
>   Shout to God with loud songs of joy!
> For the LORD, the Most High, is to be feared,
>   a great king over all the earth . . .
> Sing praises to God, sing praises!
>   Sing praises to our King, sing praises!
> For God is the King of all the earth;
>   sing praises with a psalm!
> God reigns over the nations;
>   God sits on his holy throne.
> (vv. 1–2, 6–8)

Many other Scriptures refer to God as king without using the title, such as

> The LORD has established his throne in the heavens,
>   and his kingdom rules over all.
> (Ps. 103:19)

Paul describes God, the King, with four adjectives. First, God is not just any king but 'King of ages'. Fee interprets, '"The King eternal" (lit., "the King of the ages") picks up the theme of eternal life in [1 Tim. 1] verse 16. God is eternal in that he rules in/over all the ages.'[39] As the eternal King, God deserves eternal glory. The designation 'king' was used also of

---

[39] Fee 1984: 54.

human beings. But the words 'of ages' distinguish divine from human rulers.

In Paul's concluding doxology he calls God 'the blessed and only Sovereign, the King of kings and Lord of lords' (1 Tim. 6:15). Towner correctly says that '"King of kings" repeats but expands the attribution of kingship in 1:17.' Indeed, the full expression makes the 'resounding claim that God's authority and power to rule over all human powers are beyond compare'.[40] Towner also remarks that, intentionally or not, 'King eternal' in 1:17 is polemical, challenging rulers of the pagan world. The doxology of 6:15–16 likewise strikes a 'blow . . . against imperial claims'.[41]

Second, God is 'immortal' (1 Tim. 1:17). This expression, Knight writes, describes 'God as one who is "not perishable," i.e., not subject to destruction and therefore in the most absolute sense of the words "imperishable, incorruptible, and immortal."' Later, when Paul says God 'alone has immortality' (1 Tim. 6:16), he means this attribute is 'intrinsically unique to God'.[42] Paul uses this adjective of God in describing humans' folly of idolatry: 'Claiming to be wise, they became fools, and exchanged the glory of the immortal God for images resembling mortal man and birds and animals and creeping things' (Rom. 1:22–23).

Expressed in positive terms, God's immortality means that he alone '[has] life in himself' (John 5:26; said of both the Father and the Son) and as a result is the 'fountain of living waters' (Jer. 2:13) who 'gives life to all things' (1 Tim. 6:13; cf. Acts 17:25).

Third, God is 'invisible' (1 Tim. 1:17) and 'dwells in unapproachable light, whom no one has ever seen or can see' (6:16). The Old Testament background stresses God's 'blinding glory' that reveals that he is 'so infinitely holy that sinful humanity can never see him and live', as Fee remarks.[43] Thus when Moses boldly asks God to show him his glory, he replies, '"I will make all my goodness pass before you and will proclaim before you my name 'The LORD' . . . But," he said, "you cannot see my face, for man shall not see me and live"' (Exod. 33:19–20). God revealed a fraction of his glory to Moses, but God's glorious essence remained invisible. Marshall sets this attribute in a cultural context: invisibility 'was

---

40 Towner 2006: 420.
41 Ibid. 152, 421.
42 Knight 1992: 105, 270.
43 Fee 1984: 153–154.

a standing attribute of God, especially among the Jews in opposition to pagan idolatry which conceived of the gods as present in images'.[44]

Fourth, God is the 'only God'. Monotheism is found in all parts of the Old Testament:

Hear, O Israel: The LORD our God, the LORD is one.
(Deut. 6:4)

you are great and do wondrous things;
    you alone are God.
(Ps. 86:10)

So now, O LORD our God, save us from his [Sennacherib's] hand, that all the kingdoms of the earth may know that you alone are the LORD.
(Isa. 37:20)

God is one, and he is supreme. This makes the worship of other gods false and in vain.

Both doxologies end with ascriptions of glory to God:

To the King of ages, immortal, invisible, the only God, be honour and glory for ever and ever. Amen.
(1 Tim. 1:17)

I charge you in the presence of God . . . who is the blessed and only Sovereign, the King of kings and Lord of lords, who alone has immortality, who dwells in unapproachable light, whom no one has ever seen or can see. To him be honour and eternal dominion. Amen.
(1 Tim. 6:13–16)

The first doxology ends predictably with 'honour and glory' attributed to God in praise. This combination is not unusual in New Testament doxologies (Rev. 4:9, 11; 5:12, 13; 7:12). Basically synonyms, 'honour' and 'glory' combine to accentuate the respect and praise owed God. The terms are not identical but differ in nuance, as Knight summarizes:

---

44 Marshall 1999: 405.

τιμή . . . refers basically to the 'honor' and 'respect' that one is worth or has earned . . . When used of God, as here, it designates that which rightly belongs to God, which those offering the doxology should recognize about him, so that they should seek to ascribe such honor to him . . . δόξα reflects the OT Hebrew *kābôd* . . . which indicates . . . [God's] glorious revelation of himself . . . Used in a doxology it signifies desire either that God's radiance continue to be seen in its splendor and glory or that appropriate praise be given in response to it.[45]

The second doxology ends unpredictably because Paul adds 'eternal dominion' to his ascription of 'honour' to God. The customary form leads us to expect 'honour and glory', as in 1:16. Why does Paul substitute 'power' for glory? Kelly answers, 'The substitution of power is suggested by the general theme, which stresses God's role as a potentate supreme over all would-be rivals, and to which power is clearly more appropriate.'[46]

The first doxology appropriately ends 'To . . . the only God, be honour and glory *for ever and ever*. Amen' (1 Tim. 1:17). These concluding words elevate the greatness of honour given to God to an even higher level. 'For ever and ever' is a standard ending to doxologies and should not be overinterpreted. Towner speaks wisely:

Neither the plural form (lit. 'for the ages of the ages') nor the repetition in this longer form reflects precise measurements of time. Rather, the Hebrew idiom functions to stretch the praise of the doxology beyond all limits to eternity.[47]

'Amen' invites Timothy and the churches and all subsequent readers to join in the praise of him to whom belongs honour and glory for ever and ever. Amen!

It is good to locate the worship of God along the spectrum of God's great glory. The triune God's glory is one, but as a prism disperses white light into the colours of the rainbow, so the Bible speaks of God's unified glory in several senses to put its beauty on display. God's glory in its first

---

45 Knight 1992: 106.
46 Kelly 1963: 147.
47 Towner 2006: 153–154.

and fundamental sense is unique to him alone. In its second sense God reveals his glory in creation, human image-bearers, providence and salvation. In its third and fourth senses God's people give him glory in worship, which he receives. In its fifth sense God shares his glory with his people in initial, progressive and most of all final salvation. In its sixth and final sense God purposed that all of the above will resound eternally to his infinite glory.

God's glory is thus the following:

- Glory possessed: God's unique glory
- Glory displayed: God's glory partially revealed in creation, image-bearers, providence and salvation
- Glory ascribed and received: the glory that believers give back to God and that he accepts
- Glory shared: the glory that God shares with his people in salvation
- Glory purposed: the glory that will resound to God for ever

God alone is worthy of everlasting praise, for he who is inherently glorious displays his glory, through his creation, image-bearers, providence and redemptive acts. God's people respond by glorifying him, and he receives their glory. By uniting his people to the glorious Christ, he shares his glory with them. All of this will resonate eternally to his glory.

Soli Deo gloria!

Bibliography

Aalen, S. (1971), 'doxa', in *NIDNTTE* 2.44–48.

Allison, G. R. (2011), *Historical Theology: An Introduction to Christian Doctrine*, Grand Rapids: Zondervan.

Allison, G. R., and A. J. Köstenberger (2020), *The Holy Spirit*, TPG, Nashville: B&H Academic.

Arnold, C. E. (2010), *Ephesians*, ZECNT, Grand Rapids: Zondervan.

Balthasar, H. U. V. (1983–91), *Seeing the Form*, in *The Glory of the Lord*, vol. 1, tr. E. Leiva, ed. J. Fessio and J. Riches, San Francisco: Ignatius; New York: Crossroad.

Barber, D. C., and R. A. Peterson (2012), *Life Everlasting: The Unfolding Story of Heaven*, EBT, Phillipsburg: P&R.

Barclay, W. (2002), *The Letters to the Galatians and Ephesians*, NDSB, Louisville: Westminster John Knox.

Barnett, P. (1997), *The Second Epistle to the Corinthians*, NICNT, Grand Rapids: Eerdmans.

Bauckham, R. (2008), *Jesus and the God of Israel: God Crucified and Other Studies on the New Testament's Christology of Divine Identity*, Grand Rapids: Eerdmans.

—— (2015), *The Gospel of Glory: Major Themes in Johannine Theology*, Grand Rapids: Baker.

Baugh, S. M. (2015), *Ephesians*, EEC, Bellingham: Lexham.

Bavinck, H. (2003–8), *Reformed Dogmatics*, ed. J. Bolt, tr. J. Vriend, Grand Rapids: Baker.

Beale, G. K. (1999), *The Book of Revelation*, NIGTC, Grand Rapids: Eerdmans.

—— (2003), *1–2 Thessalonians*, IVPNTC, Downers Grove: InterVarsity Press; Leicester: Inter-Varsity Press.

—— (2004), *The Temple and the Church's Mission: A Biblical Theology of the Dwelling Place of God*, NSBT 17, Leicester: Apollos; Downers Grove: InterVarsity Press.

—— (2008), *We Become What We Worship: A Biblical Theology of Idolatry*, Downers Grove: InterVarsity Press; Nottingham: Inter-Varsity Press.

—— (2011), *A New Testament Biblical Theology: The Unfolding of the Old Testament in the New*, Grand Rapids: Baker.

Beale, G. K., and B. L. Gladd (2014), *Hidden but Now Revealed: A Biblical Theology of Mystery*, Downers Grove: InterVarsity Press; Nottingham: Apollos.

Belleville, L. (1991), *Reflections of Glory: Paul's Polemical Use of the Moses-doxa Tradition in 2 Corinthians 3.1–18*, JSNTSup 52, Sheffield: Sheffield Academic Press.

—— (1993), 'Tradition of Creation? Paul's Use of the Exodus 34 Tradition in 2 Corinthians 3.7–18', in C. A. Evans and J. A. Sanders (eds.), *Paul and the Scriptures of Israel*, JSNTSup 83, Sheffield: JSOT, 165–186.

Berkhof, L. (1941), *Systematic Theology*, Grand Rapids: Eerdmans.

Berquist, M. J. (1942), 'Meaning of Doxa in the Epistles of Paul', PhD diss., Southern Baptist Theological Seminary.

Berry, D. L. (2016), *Glory in Romans and the Unified Purpose of God in Redemptive History*, Eugene: Pickwick.

Blackwell, B. C. (2007), 'The Motif of Glory (Doxa) in Romans', unpublished paper presented at British New Testament Conference, Exeter, 7 September 2007, University of Durham.

—— (2010), 'Immortal Glory and the Problem of Death in Romans 3.23', *JSNT* 32.3: 285–308.

—— (2015), 'The Greek Life of Adam and Eve and Romans 8:14–39: (Re)creation and Glory', in B. C. Blackwell, J. K. Goodrich and J. Maston (eds.), *Reading Romans in Context*, Grand Rapids: Zondervan, 108–114.

Bock, D. L., (1999), *Three Views on the Millennium and Beyond*, Grand Rapids: Zondervan.

—— (2002), *Jesus According to Scripture: Restoring the Portrait from the Gospels*, Grand Rapids: Baker Academic.

Bowling, A. S. V. (1980), 'בּוּט', in *TWOT*, 345–346.

Bowman, R. M., and J. E. Komoszewski (2007), *Putting Jesus in His Place: The Case for the Deity of Christ*, Grand Rapids: Kregel.

Bray, G. (1993), *The Doctrine of God*, CCT, Downers Grove: InterVarsity Press; Leicester: Inter-Varsity Press.

—— (2012), *God Is Love: A Biblical and Systematic Theology*, Wheaton: Crossway.

Bruce, F. F. (1982), *1 and 2 Thessalonians*, WBC, Dallas: Word.

—— (1984), *The Epistles to the Colossians, to Philemon, and to the Ephesians*, NICNT, Grand Rapids: Eerdmans.

Burge, G. M. (1992), 'Glory', in *DJG*, 268–270.

Burke, T. (2006), *Adopted into God's Family*, NSBT, Downers Grove: InterVarsity Press; Nottingham: Apollos.

Byrskog, S. (2008), 'Christology and Identity in an Intertextual Perspective: The Glory of Adam in the Narrative Substructure of Paul's Letter to the Romans', in B. Holmberg and M. Winninge (eds.), *Identity Formation in the New Testament*, WUNT 227, Tübingen: Mohr Siebeck, 1–18.

Caird, G. B. (1969), 'The Glory of God in the Fourth Gospel: An Exercise in Biblical Semantics', *NTS* 15.3: 265–277.

—— (1994), *New Testament Theology*, Oxford: Oxford University Press.

Calvin, J. (1960), *Institutes of the Christian Religion*, ed. J. T. McNeill, tr. F. L. Battles, Philadelphia: Westminster.

—— (1965), *Galatians, Ephesians, Philippians, and Colossians*, CNTC, tr. T. H. L. Parker, Grand Rapids: Eerdmans.

—— (2003), *Commentaries on the Epistles of Paul the Apostle to the Hebrews*, Grand Rapids: Baker.

Campbell, C. R. (2012), *Paul and Union with Christ: An Exegetical and Theological Study*, Grand Rapids: Zondervan.

—— (2020), *Paul and the Hope of Glory: An Exegetical and Theological Study*, Grand Rapids: Zondervan.

Caneday, A. B. (2007), '"They Exchanged the Glory of God for the Likeness of an Image": Idolatrous Adam and Israel as Representatives in Paul's Letter to the Romans', *SBJT* 11.3: 34–45.

Carson, D. A. (1987), *Showing the Spirit: A Theological Exposition of 1 Corinthians 12–14*, Grand Rapids: Baker.

—— (1996), *The Gagging of God: Christianity Confronts Pluralism*, Grand Rapids: Zondervan; Leicester: Apollos.

Carson, D. A., P. T. O'Brien and M. A. Seifrid (eds.) (2001, 2004), *Justification and Variegated Nomism*, Grand Rapids: Baker Academic.

Chapell, B. (2010), 'A Pastoral Theology of the Glory of God', in C. W. Morgan and R. A. Peterson (eds.), *The Glory of God*, TIC 2, Wheaton: Crossway, 189–208.

Chapman, D. (2012), *Philippians: Rejoicing and Thanksgiving*, FTB, Fearn, UK: Christian Focus.

Ciampa, R. E., and B. S. Rosner (2010), *The First Letter to the Corinthians*, PNTC, Grand Rapids: Eerdmans.

Clowney, E. P. (1995), *The Church*, CCT, Downers Grove: InterVarsity Press; Leicester: Inter-Varsity Press.

Cole, G. A. (2007), *He Who Gives Life: The Doctrine of the Holy Spirit*, FOET, Wheaton: Crossway.

—— (2009), *God the Peacemaker: How Atonement Brings Shalom*, NSBT, Downers Grove: InterVarsity Press; Nottingham: Apollos.

Collins, C. J. (1997), 'kābôd', in *NIDOTTE* 2.577–587.

Cook, W. R. (1984), 'The "Glory" Motif in the Johannine Corpus', *JETS* 27.3: 291–297.

Cooper, J. W. (1989), *Body, Soul, and Life Everlasting: Biblical Anthropology and the Monism–Dualism Debate*, Grand Rapids: Eerdmans.

Cranfield, C. E. B. (2004), *A Critical and Exegetical Commentary on the Epistle to the Romans*, ICC, London: T&T Clark.

Davies, G. H. (1962), 'Glory', in *IDB* 2.401–403.

De Vaan, M. (2011), 'The Glory of YHWH in the Old Testament with Special Attention to the Book of Ezekiel', *TynB* 62.1: 151–154.

—— (2012), 'Ezekiel: Prophet of the Name and Glory of YHWH – the Character of His Book and Several of Its Main Themes', *JBPR* 4: 94–108.

—— (2013), 'The Relationship Between the Glory of YHWH and the Spirit of YHWH in the Book of Ezekiel', *JBPR* 5: 109–127.

Demarest, B. A. (1982), *General Revelation: Historical Views and Contemporary Issues*, Grand Rapids: Zondervan.

—— (1997), *The Cross and Salvation: The Doctrine of Salvation*, FOET, Wheaton: Crossway.

Duff, P. B. (2004), 'Glory in the Ministry of Death: Gentile Condemnation and Letters of Recommendation in 2 Cor. 3:6–18', *NT* 46.4: 313–337.

Dunn, J. D. G. (1998), *The Theology of Paul the Apostle*, Grand Rapids: Eerdmans.

Durham, J. I. (1987), *Exodus*, WBC, Waco: Word.

Easley, K. H., and C. W. Morgan (eds.) (2013), *The Community of Jesus: A Theology of the Church*, Nashville: B&H Academic.

Edwards, J. (1989), *Ethical Writings*, WJE 8, New Haven: Yale University Press.

—— (1998), 'The End for Which God Created the World', in J. Piper (ed.), *God's Passion for His Glory*, Wheaton: Crossway, 125–251.

Edwards, T. C. (1979), *A Commentary on the First Epistle to the Corinthians*, Minneapolis: Klock & Klock.

Eichrodt, W. (1967), *Theology of the Old Testament*, vol. 2, tr. J. A. Baker, OTL, Philadelphia: Westminster.

Elwell, W. A. (1991), *Topical Analysis of the Bible*, Grand Rapids: Baker.

Emerson, M. Y., and C. W. Morgan (2015), 'The Glory of God in 2 Corinthians', *SBJT* 19.3: 21–39.

Erickson, M. J. (1981), *The Word Became Flesh: A Contemporary Incarnational Christology*, Grand Rapids: Baker.

Fee, G. D. (1984), *1 and 2 Timothy, Titus*, NIBC, Peabody: Hendrickson.

—— (1987), *The First Epistle to the Corinthians*, NICNT, Grand Rapids: Eerdmans.

—— (1994), *God's Empowering Presence: The Holy Spirit in the Letters of Paul*, Peabody: Hendrickson.

—— (2007), *Pauline Christology: An Exegetical-Theological Study*, Peabody: Hendrickson.

—— (2009), *The First and Second Letters to the Thessalonians*, NICNT, Grand Rapids: Eerdmans.

Feinberg, J. (2001), *No One Like Him: The Doctrine of God*, FOET, Wheaton: Crossway.

Ferguson, S. (1989), *Children of the Living God*, Edinburgh: Banner of Truth.

—— (1996), *The Holy Spirit*, CCT, Downers Grove: InterVarsity Press; Leicester: Inter-Varsity Press.

—— (2014), *The Trinitarian Devotion of John Owen*, Sanford: Reformation Trust.

Fitzmyer, J. A. (1981), 'Glory Reflected on the Face of Christ (2 Cor. 3:7–4:6) and a Palestinian Jewish Motif', *TS* 42: 630–644.

Fowl, S. E. (2009), *Philippians*, THNTC, Grand Rapids: Eerdmans.

Frame, J. (2002), *The Doctrine of God*, Phillipsburg: P&R.

Fudge, E. W. (1994), *The Fire that Consumes: The Biblical Case for Conditional Immortality*, rev. edn, Carlisle: Paternoster.

Gaffin, R. B. (1987), *Resurrection and Redemption: A Study in Paul's Soteriology*, 2nd edn, Phillipsburg: P&R.

—— (1993), 'Glory, Glorification', in *DPL*, 348–350.

—— (1998), '"Life-Giving Spirit": Probing the Center of Paul's Pneumatology', *JETS* 41.4: 573–589.

—— (2000), 'Glory', in *NDBT*, 507–511.

—— (2010), 'The Glory of God in Paul's Epistles', in C. W. Morgan and R. A. Peterson (eds.), *The Glory of God*, TIC 2, Wheaton: Crossway, 127–152.

—— (2013), *By Faith, Not by Sight: Paul and the Order of Salvation*, 2nd edn, Phillipsburg: P&R.

Garland, D. E. (1999), *2 Corinthians*, NAC, Nashville: B&H.

—— (2003), *1 Corinthians*, BECNT, Grand Rapids: Baker.

Garrett, D. A. (2010), 'Veiled Hearts: The Translation and Interpretation of 2 Corinthians 3', *JETS* 53.4: 729–772.

Gathercole, S. J. (2006), *The Preexistent Son: Recovering the Christologies of Matthew, Mark, and Luke*, Grand Rapids: Eerdmans.

Gentry, P. J. (2016), '"The Glory of God" – The Character of God's Being and Way in the World: Some Reflections on a Key Biblical Theology Theme', *SBJT* 20.1: 149–161.

Gentry, P. J., and S. J. Wellum (2012), *Kingdom Through Covenant: A Biblical-Theological Understanding of the Covenants*, Wheaton: Crossway.

George, T. (2007), 'The Nature of God: Being, Attributes, and Acts', in D. L. Akin (ed.), *A Theology for the Church*, Nashville: B&H, 176–241.

Gerstner, J. H. (1993), *The Rational, Biblical Theology of Jonathan Edwards*, Powhatan: Berean.

Gladd, B. (2009), 'The Last Adam as the "Life-Giving Spirit" Revisited: A Possible Old Testament Background of One of Paul's Most Perplexing Phrases', *WTJ* 71: 297–309.

Gorman, M. J. (2015), *Becoming the Gospel: Paul, Participation and Mission*, Grand Rapids: Eerdmans.

Green, G. L. (2002), *The Letters to the Thessalonians*, PNTC, Grand Rapids: Eerdmans.

Grogan, G. W. (1986), *Isaiah*, EBC, Grand Rapids: Zondervan.

Grudem, W. (2020), *Systematic Theology*, 2nd edn, London: Inter-Varsity Press; Grand Rapids: Zondervan.

Guthrie, D. (1981), *New Testament Theology*, Downers Grove: InterVarsity Press; Leicester: Inter-Varsity Press.

Hafemann, S. (1992), 'The Glory and Veil of Moses in 2 Cor 3:7–13: An Example of Paul's Contextual Exegesis of the OT – A Proposal', *HBT* 14: 31–49.

—— (1995), *Paul, Moses, and the History of Israel: The Letter/Spirit Contrast and the Argument from Scripture in 2 Corinthians 3*, Tübingen: Mohr Siebeck.

Hamilton, J. M. (2006a), 'The Glory of God in Salvation Through Judgment: The Centre of Biblical Theology', *TynB* 57.1: 57–84.

—— (2006b), *God's Indwelling Presence: The Holy Spirit in the Old and New Testaments*, NACSBT, Nashville: B&H.

—— (2010), *God's Glory in Salvation Through Judgment: A Biblical Theology*, Wheaton: Crossway.

Hannah, J. D. (2008), *How Do We Glorify God?*, BRF, Phillipsburg: P&R.

Harris, M. J. (1985), *Raised Immortal: Resurrection and Immortality in the New Testament*, Grand Rapids: Eerdmans.

—— (1990), *From Grave to Glory: Resurrection in the New Testament*, Grand Rapids: Zondervan.

—— (1992), *Jesus as God: The New Testament Use of Theos in Reference to Jesus*, Grand Rapids: Baker.

—— (2005), *The Second Epistle to the Corinthians*, NIGTC, Grand Rapids: Eerdmans.

Harrison, E. F. (1982), 'Glory', in *ISBE* 2.477–483.

Harrison, J. R. (2009), 'Paul and the Roman Ideal of Glory in the Epistle to the Romans', in U. Schnelle (ed.), *The Letter to the Romans*, Leuven: Peeters, 329–369.

Hartley, J. E. (2003), 'Holy and Holiness, Clean and Unclean', in *DOTP*, 420–431.

Hawthorne, G. F. (1983), *Philippians*, WBC, Waco: Word.

Hays, R. B. (1989), *Echoes of Scripture in the Letters of Paul*, New Haven: Yale University Press.

Hiebert, D. E. (1996), *1 & 2 Thessalonians*, rev. edn, Winona Lake: BMH.

Hill, C. E., and F. A. James III (eds.) (2004), *The Glory of the Atonement: Biblical, Theological, and Practical Perspectives*, Downers Grove: InterVarsity Press; Leicester: Apollos.

Hodge, C. (2003), *Systematic Theology*, repr., Peabody: Hendrickson.

Hoehner, H. W. (2002), *Ephesians: An Exegetical Commentary*, Grand Rapids: Baker Academic.

Hoekema, A. A. (1979), *The Bible and the Future*, Grand Rapids: Eerdmans.

—— (1986), *Created in God's Image*, Grand Rapids: Eerdmans.

—— (1989), *Saved by Grace*, Grand Rapids: Eerdmans.

Hooker, M. D. (1980), *From Adam to Christ: Essays on Paul*, Cambridge: Cambridge University Press.

Horton, M. S. (2007), *Covenant and Salvation: Union with Christ*, Louisville: Westminster John Knox.

—— (2008), *People and Place: A Covenant Ecclesiology*, Louisville: Westminster John Knox.

House, P. R. (1998), *Old Testament Theology*, Downers Grove: InterVarsity Press.

Hughes, P. E. (1962), *The Second Epistle to the Corinthians*, NICNT, Grand Rapids: Eerdmans.

—— (1989), *The True Image: The Origin and Destiny of Man in Christ*, Grand Rapids: Eerdmans.

Hurst, L. D., and N. T. Wright (eds.) (1987), *The Glory of Christ in the New Testament: Studies in Christology in Memory of George Bradford Caird*, Oxford: Clarendon.

Hurtado, L. (1999), *At the Origins of Christian Worship: The Context and Character of Earliest Christian Devotion*, Carlisle: Paternoster.

—— (2003), *Lord Jesus Christ: Devotion to Jesus in Earliest Christianity*, Grand Rapids: Eerdmans.

—— (2005), *How on Earth Did Jesus Become a God? Questions About the Earliest Devotion to Jesus*, Grand Rapids: Eerdmans.

Huttar, D. K. (1996), 'Glory', in *EDBT*, 287–288.

Jeffery, S., M. Ovey and A. Sach (2007), *Pierced for Our Transgressions: Recovering the Glory of Penal Substitution*, Nottingham: Inter-Varsity Press; Wheaton: Crossway.

Jennings, J. N. (2010), 'A Missional Theology of the Glory of God', in C. W. Morgan and R. A. Peterson (eds.), *The Glory of God*, TIC 2, Wheaton: Crossway, 209–233.

Jensen, P. (2002), *The Revelation of God*, CCT, Downers Grove: InterVarsity Press; Leicester: Inter-Varsity Press.

Kaiser, C. B. (2001), *The Doctrine of God: A Historical Survey*, rev. edn, Eugene: Wipf & Stock.

Kaiser, W. C. (2007), *The Majesty of God in the Old Testament: A Guide for Preaching and Teaching*, Grand Rapids: Baker.

Kelly, J. N. D. (1963), *A Commentary on the Pastoral Epistles*, Grand Rapids: Baker.

Kim, S. (1984), *The Origin of Paul's Gospel*, 2nd edn, WUNT II/4, Tübingen: Mohr Siebeck.

—— (2002), *Paul and the New Perspective: Second Thoughts on the Origins of Paul's Gospel*, Grand Rapids: Eerdmans.

King, J. (2018), *The Beauty of the Lord: Theology as Aesthetics*, SHST, Bellingham: Lexham.

Kirk, D. (2008), *Unlocking Romans: Resurrection and the Justification of God*, Grand Rapids: Eerdmans.

Kittel, G. (1967), 'δόξα, δοξάζω', in *TDNT* 2.235–258.

Kline, M. G. (1977a), 'Creation in the Image of the Glory-Spirit', *WTJ* 39.2: 250–272.

—— (1977b), 'Investiture with the Image of God', *WTJ* 40.1: 39–62.

—— (1980), *Images of the Spirit*, Grand Rapids: Baker.

—— (2001), *Glory in Our Midst: A Biblical-Theological Reading of Zechariah's Night Visions*, Overland Park: Two-Age.

Knight, G. W. (1992), *Commentary on the Pastoral Epistles*, NIGTC, Grand Rapids: Eerdmans.

Köstenberger, A. J. (2010), 'The Glory of God in John's Gospel and Revelation', in C. W. Morgan and R. A. Peterson (eds.), *The Glory of God*, TIC 2, Wheaton: Crossway, 107–126.

Kruse, C. G. (2012), *Paul's Letter to the Romans*, PNTC, Grand Rapids: Eerdmans.

Lane, W. (1974), *The Gospel According to Mark*, NICNT, Grand Rapids: Eerdmans.

Letham, R. (1993), *The Work of Christ*, CCT, Downers Grove: InterVarsity Press; Leicester: Inter-Varsity Press.

—— (2004), *The Holy Trinity: In Scripture, History, Theology, and Worship*, Phillipsburg: P&R.

Lincoln, A. T. (1990), *Ephesians*, WBC, Dallas: Word.

Lioy, D. (2010), *Axis of Glory: A Biblical and Theological Analysis of the Temple Motif in Scripture*, SBL 138, New York: Peter Lang.

Longenecker, R. N. (1990), *Galatians*, WBC, Nashville: Word.

Longman, T. (2010), 'The Glory of God in the Old Testament', in C. W. Morgan and R. A. Peterson (eds.), *The Glory of God*, TIC 2, Wheaton: Crossway, 47–78.

McConville, J. G. (1979), 'God's Name and God's Glory', *TynB* 30: 149–163.

—— (2016), *Being Human in God's World: An Old Testament Theology of Humanity*, Grand Rapids: Baker.

Macleod, D. (1998), *The Person of Christ*, CCT, Downers Grove: InterVarsity Press; Leicester: Inter-Varsity Press.

McNeile, A. H. (1908), *Book of Exodus*, WC, London: Methuen.

Mahony, J. W. (2013), 'A Theology of Sin for Today', in C. W. Morgan and R. A. Peterson (eds.), *Fallen: A Theology of Sin*, TIC 5, Wheaton: Crossway, 131–162.

Marshall, I. H. (1983), *1 and 2 Thessalonians*, NCBC, Grand Rapids: Eerdmans.

—— (1990), *Jesus the Saviour: Studies in New Testament Theology*, Downers Grove: InterVarsity Press.

—— (1999), *The Pastoral Epistles*, ICC, London: T&T Clark.

—— (2007), *Aspects of the Atonement: Cross and Resurrection in the Reconciling of God and Humanity*, London: Paternoster.

Martin, R. P. (1959), *The Epistle of Paul to the Philippians*, TNTC, Grand Rapids: Eerdmans.

—— (1973), *Colossians and Philemon*, NCBC, Grand Rapids: Eerdmans.

—— (1983), *Carmen Christi: Phil. ii.5–11*, rev. edn, SNTSMS 4, Grand Rapids: Eerdmans.

—— (1989), *Reconciliation: A Study of Paul's Theology*, rev. edn, Grand Rapids: Zondervan.

—— (2014), *2 Corinthians*, 2nd edn, WBC, Grand Rapids: Zondervan.

Martin, R. P., and B. J. Dodd (eds.) (1998), *Where Christology Began: Essays on Philippians 2*, Louisville: Westminster.

Melick, R. R. (2010), 'The Glory of God in the Synoptic Gospels, Acts, and the General Epistles', in C. W. Morgan and R. A. Peterson (eds.), *The Glory of God*, TIC 2, Wheaton: Crossway, 79–106.

Metzger, B. M. (1968), *A Textual Commentary on the Greek New Testament*, New York: UBS.

Meyer, N. A. (2016), *Adam's Dust and Adam's Glory: Rethinking Anthropogony and Theology in the Hodayot and the Letters of Paul*, NovTSup 168, Leiden: Brill.

Milne, B. (2002), *The Message of Heaven and Hell: Grace and Destiny*, BST, Downers Grove: InterVarsity Press; Leicester: Inter-Varsity Press.

Moo, D. J. (1996), *The Epistle to the Romans*, NICNT, Grand Rapids: Eerdmans.

—— (2008), *The Letters to the Colossians and to Philemon*, PNTC, Grand Rapids: Eerdmans.

—— (2013), *Galatians*, BECNT, Grand Rapids: Baker.

Morgan, C. W. (2009), 'The Glory of God as a Church Ethic', Annual Meeting of the Evangelical Theological Society.

—— (2010), *A Theology of James*, EBT, Phillipsburg: P&R.

—— (2013), 'The Church and God's Glory', in K. H. Easley and C. W. Morgan (eds.), *The Community of Jesus: A Theology of the Church*, Nashville: B&H Academic, 213–235.

Morgan, C. W. (ed.) (2016), *The Love of God*, TIC 7, Wheaton: Crossway.

—— (2019), *Biblical Spirituality*, TIC 8, Wheaton: Crossway.

Morgan, C. W., and R. A. Peterson (eds.) (2004), *Hell Under Fire: Modern Scholarship Reinvents Eternal Punishment*, Grand Rapids: Zondervan.

—— (2008a), *Faith Comes by Hearing: A Response to Inclusivism*, Downers Grove: InterVarsity Press; Nottingham: Apollos.

—— (2008b), *Suffering and the Goodness of God*, TIC 1, Wheaton: Crossway.

—— (2010), *The Glory of God*, TIC 2, Wheaton: Crossway.

—— (2011), *The Deity of Christ*, TIC 3, Wheaton: Crossway.

—— (2012), *The Kingdom of God*, TIC 4, Wheaton: Crossway.

—— (2013), *Fallen: A Theology of Sin*, TIC 5, Wheaton: Crossway.

—— (2014), *Heaven*, TIC 6, Wheaton: Crossway.

Morgan, C. W., with R. A. Peterson (2020), *Christian Theology: The Biblical Story and Our Faith*, Nashville: B&H Academic.

Morgenstern, J. (1911), 'Biblical Theophanies', *ZA* 25: 139–140.

Morris, L. (1959), *The First and Second Epistles to the Thessalonians*, NICNT, Grand Rapids: Eerdmans.

—— (1960), *Spirit of the Living God*, Downers Grove: InterVarsity Press.

—— (1965a), *The Apostolic Preaching of the Cross*, 3rd edn, Grand Rapids: Eerdmans.

—— (1965b), *The Cross in the New Testament*, Grand Rapids: Eerdmans.

—— (1985), *1 Corinthians: An Introduction and Commentary*, TNTC, Downers Grove: InterVarsity Press; Leicester: Inter-Varsity Press.

—— (1988), *The Epistle to the Romans*, PNTC, Grand Rapids: Eerdmans.

Mounce, W. D. (2000), *Pastoral Epistles*, WBC, Nashville: Nelson.

Naselli, A. D. (2012), *From Typology to Doxology: Paul's Use of Isaiah and Job in Romans 11:34–35*, Eugene: Pickwick.

Nash, R. H. (1983), *The Concept of God: An Exploration of Contemporary Difficulties with the Attributes of God*, Grand Rapids: Zondervan.

Nebeker, G. L. (2000), 'Christ as Somatic Transformer (Phil. 3:20–21): Christology in an Eschatological Perspective', *TrinJ* 21.2: 165–187.

Newman, C. C. (1992), *Paul's Glory-Christology: Tradition and Rhetoric*, New York: Brill.

—— (1993), 'Benedictions, Blessings, Doxology, Thanksgiving', in *DPL*, 68–71.

—— (1997), 'Glory', in *DLNTD*, 394–400.

—— (2007), 'Glory, Glorify', in *NIDB* 2.577–580.

Nichols, S. J. (2010), 'The Glory of God Present and Past', in C. W. Morgan and R. A. Peterson (eds.), *The Glory of God*, TIC 2, Wheaton: Crossway, 23–36.

Ortlund, D. C. (2014), 'Inaugurated Glorification: Revisiting Romans 8:30', *JETS* 57.1: 111–133.

Ortlund, R. C. (2005), *Isaiah: God Saves Sinners*, PTW, Wheaton: Crossway.

Oswalt, J. N. (1980), 'כָּבוֹד', in *TWOT* 1.246–247.

—— (1986), *The Book of Isaiah, Chapters 1–39*, NICOT, Grand Rapids: Eerdmans.

—— (1998), *The Book of Isaiah, Chapters 40–66*, NICOT, Grand Rapids: Eerdmans.

Owen, J. (1684), *The Glory of Christ: His Office and Grace*, repr., Fearn, UK: Christian Focus.

Packer, J. I. (1961), *Evangelism and the Sovereignty of God*, Chicago: InterVarsity Press; London: Inter-Varsity Fellowship..

—— (1988), 'The Glory of God', in *NDT*, 271–272.

—— (1993), *Knowing God*, Downers Grove: InterVarsity Press.

—— (2004), 'Universalism: Will Everyone Ultimately Be Saved?', in C. W. Morgan and R. A. Peterson (eds.), *Hell Under Fire*, Grand Rapids: Zondervan, 169–194.

—— (2005), *Keep in Step with the Spirit*, 2nd edn, Grand Rapids: Baker; Leicester: Inter-Varsity Press.

Pate, C. M. (1991), *Adam Christology as the Exegetical and Theological Substructure of 2 Corinthians 4.7–5:21*, Lanham: University Press of America.

—— (1993), *The Glory of Adam and the Afflictions of the Righteous: Pauline Suffering in Context*, Lewiston: Mellen Biblical Press.

Peterman, G. W. (1997), *Paul's Gift from Philippi: Conventions of Gift Exchange and Christian Giving*, SNTSMS 92, Cambridge: Cambridge University Press.

Peterson, D. (1995), *Possessed by God: A New Testament Theology of Sanctification and Holiness*, NSBT, Downers Grove: InterVarsity Press; Leicester: Apollos.

Peterson, D. (ed.) (2001), *Where Wrath and Mercy Meet: Proclaiming the Atonement Today*, Carlisle: Paternoster.

Peterson, R. A. (1995), *Hell on Trial*, Phillipsburg: P&R.

—— (2001), *Adopted by God: From Wayward Sinners to Cherished Children*, Phillipsburg: P&R.

—— (2007), *Election and Free Will: God's Gracious Choice and Our Responsibility*, EBT, Phillipsburg: P&R.

—— (2009), *Our Secure Salvation: Preservation and Apostasy*, EBT, Phillipsburg: P&R.

—— (2012), *Salvation Accomplished by the Son: The Work of Christ*, Wheaton: Crossway.

—— (2014a), 'Pictures of Heaven', in C. W. Morgan and R. A. Peterson (eds.), *Heaven*, TIC 6, Wheaton: Crossway, 159–184.

—— (2014b), *Salvation Applied by the Spirit: Union with Christ*, Wheaton: Crossway.

—— (2019), *The Assurance of Salvation: Biblical Hope for Our Struggles*, Grand Rapids: Zondervan.

Piper, J. (1983), *The Justification of God: An Exegetical and Theological Study of Romans 9:1–23*, Grand Rapids: Baker.

—— (1991), *The Pleasures of God: Meditations on God's Delight in Being God*, Portland: Multnomah.

—— (1998), *God's Passion for His Glory: Living the Vision of Jonathan Edwards, With the Complete Text of The End for Which God Created the World*, Wheaton: Crossway.

—— (2003a), *Desiring God: Meditations of a Christian Hedonist*, rev. and exp. edn, Portland: Multnomah.

—— (2003b), *Let the Nations Be Glad! The Supremacy of God in Missions*, 2nd edn, Grand Rapids: Baker.

Plantinga, C. (1995), *Not the Way It's Supposed to Be: A Breviary of Sin*, Grand Rapids: Eerdmans.

Poythress, V. S. (2000), *The Returning King: A Guide to the Book of Revelation*, Phillipsburg: P&R.

—— (2016), *The Lordship of Christ: Serving Our Savior All of the Time, in All of Life, with All of Our Heart*, Wheaton: Crossway.

Preuss, H. D. (1995), *Old Testament Theology*, Louisville: Westminster John Knox.

Rad, G. von (1962), *Old Testament Theology*, tr. D. M. G. Stalker, repr., Peabody: Hendrickson/Prince.

Räisänen, H. (1983), *Paul and the Law*, WUNT 29, Tübingen: Mohr Siebeck.

Ramm, B. L. (1963), *Them He Glorified: A Systematic Study of the Doctrine of Glorification*, Grand Rapids: Eerdmans.

Ridderbos, H. N. (1953), *The Epistle of Paul to the Churches of Galatia*, NICNT, Grand Rapids: Eerdmans.

—— (1975), *Paul: An Outline of His Theology*, Grand Rapids: Eerdmans.

Ross, A. P. (1997), *Creation and Blessing: A Guide to the Study and Exposition of Genesis*, Grand Rapids: Baker Academic.

—— (2006), *Recalling the Hope of Glory: Biblical Worship from the Garden to the New Creation*, Grand Rapids: Kregel Academic and Professional.

Ryrie, C. C. (1990), *Transformed by His Glory*, Wheaton: Victor.

Sanders, E. P. (1977), *Paul and Palestinian Judaism: A Comparison of Religions*, Philadelphia: Fortress.

Sanders, F. (2017), *The Deep Things of God: How the Trinity Changes Everything*, 2nd edn, Wheaton: Crossway.

Savage, T. B. (1996), *Power Through Weakness: Paul's Understanding of the Christian Ministry in 2 Corinthians*, Cambridge: Cambridge University Press.

Schmisek, B. (2013), 'The Body of His Glory: Resurrection Imagery in Philippians 3:20–21', *BTB* 44: 23–28.

Schnelle, U. (2005), *Apostle Paul: His Life and Theology*, tr. M. E. Boring, Grand Rapids: Baker Academic.

Schreiner, T. R. (1998), *Romans*, BECNT, Grand Rapids: Baker.

—— (2001), *Paul, Apostle of God's Glory in Christ: A Pauline Theology*, Downers Grove: InterVarsity Press; Leicester: Apollos.

—— (2008), *New Testament Theology: Magnifying God in Christ*, Grand Rapids: Baker; Nottingham: Apollos.

Seifrid, M. A. (2004), 'Unrighteous by Faith: Apostolic Proclamation

in Romans 1:18–3:20', in D. A. Carson, P. T. O'Brien and
M. A. Seifrid (eds.), *The Paradoxes of Paul*, vol. 2 of *Justification
and Variegated Nomism*, Grand Rapids: Baker, 105–146.

—— (2014), *The Second Letter to the Corinthians*, PNTC, Grand Rapids,
Eerdmans.

Shedd, W. G. T. (2003), *Dogmatic Theology*, 3rd edn, ed. A. W. Gomes,
Phillipsburg: P&R.

Sherlock, C. (1997), *The Doctrine of Humanity*, CCT, Downers Grove:
InterVarsity Press; Leicester: Inter-Varsity Press.

Shogren, G. S. (2012), *1 & 2 Thessalonians*, ZECNT, Grand Rapids:
Zondervan.

Silva, M. (2005), *Philippians*, 2nd edn, BECNT, Grand Rapids: Baker.

Sivonen, M. (2005), 'The Hermeneutical and Theological Significance
of *to mysterion* in Ephesians', ThM thesis, Golden Gate Baptist
Theological Seminary.

—— (2008), 'The *Doxa* Motif in Paul: A Narrative Approach to the
Vindication of the Glory of God Through Christ', PhD diss.,
University of Helsinki.

Skaug, B. M. (2020a), 'The Doctrine of Hell as It Functions as a Means
of Comfort for the People of God in the New Testament', PhD diss.,
Gateway Seminary.

—— (2020b), *Why Would a Loving God Send Anyone to Hell?*, The Big
Ten, Fearn, UK: Christian Focus.

Sprinkle, P. (2008), 'The Afterlife in Romans: Understanding Paul's
Glory Motif in Light of the Apocalypse of Moses and 2 Baruch',
in M. Labahn and M. Lang (eds.), *Lebende Hoffnung – Ewiger Tod?!
Jenseitsvorstellungen im Hellenismus, Judentum und Christentum*,
ABG, Leipzig: Evangelische Verlagsanstalt, 201–233.

Stott, J. R. W. (1979), *The Message of Ephesians: God's New Society*, BST,
Downers Grove: InterVarsity Press; Leicester: Inter-Varsity Press.

—— (1986), *The Cross of Christ*, Downers Grove: InterVarsity Press;
Leicester: Inter-Varsity Press.

—— (1994), *The Message of Thessalonians: The Gospel and the End
of Time*, BST, Downers Grove: InterVarsity Press; Leicester: Inter-
Varsity Press.

—— (1995), *The Message of Romans: God's Good News for the World*,
BST, Downers Grove: InterVarsity Press; Leicester: Inter-Varsity
Press.

Stott, J. R. W., and D. L. Edwards (1989), *Evangelical Essentials: A Liberal-Evangelical Dialogue*, Downers Grove: InterVarsity Press; Leicester: Inter-Varsity Press.

Stuart, D. K. (2006), *Exodus*, NAC, Nashville: B&H.

Tasker, R. V. G. (1958), *The Second Epistle of Paul to the Corinthians*, TNTC, Grand Rapids: Eerdmans.

Thielman, F. (2005), *Theology of the New Testament*, Grand Rapids: Zondervan.

—— (2010), *Ephesians*, BECNT, Grand Rapids: Baker Academic.

Thiselton, A. C. (1977), 'Semantics and New Testament Interpretation', in I. H. Marshall (ed.), *New Testament Interpretation: Essays on Principles and Methods*, Grand Rapids: Eerdmans, 75–104.

—— (1978), 'Realized Eschatology at Corinth', *NTS* 24: 510–526.

—— (2000), *The First Epistle to the Corinthians*, NIGTC, Grand Rapids: Eerdmans.

—— (2004), 'The Origin of Paul's Doctrine of the Two Adams in 1 Corinthians 15.45–49', *JSNT* 25: 343–370.

—— (2009), *The Living Paul: An Introduction to the Apostle's Life and Thought*, Downers Grove: InterVarsity Press.

—— (2013), *The Holy Spirit: In Biblical Teaching, Through the Centuries, and Today*, Grand Rapids: Eerdmans.

Thrall, M. E. (1994), *A Critical and Exegetical Commentary on the Second Epistle to the Corinthians*, ICC, London: T&T Clark.

Tidball, D. (2010), *The Message of Holiness*, BST, Downers Grove: InterVarsity Press; Nottingham: Inter-Varsity Press.

Towner, P. H. (2006), *The Letters to Timothy and Titus*, NICNT, Grand Rapids: Eerdmans.

VanDrunen, D. (2015), *God's Glory Alone: The Majestic Heart of Christian Faith and Life: What the Reformers Taught . . . and Why It Still Matters*, The 5 Solas Series, Grand Rapids: Zondervan.

VanGemeren, W. A. (1991), *Psalms*, EBC, Grand Rapids: Zondervan.

Vanhoozer, K. J. (2005), *The Drama of Doctrine: A Canonical Linguistic Approach to Christian Theology*, Louisville: Westminster John Knox.

Vos, G. (1994), *The Pauline Eschatology*, Phillipsburg: P&R.

Vriezen, C. (1966), *An Outline of Old Testament Theology*, Newton: C. T. Branford.

Waltke, B. K., with C. Yu (2007), *An Old Testament Theology*, Grand Rapids: Zondervan.

Wanamaker, C. A. (1990), *The Epistles to the Thessalonians*, NIGTC, Grand Rapids: Eerdmans.

Weinfeld, M. (1995), 'Kābôd', in *TDOT* 7.22–38.

Wells, D. F. (1984), *The Person of Christ: A Biblical and Historical Analysis of the Incarnation*, Westchester: Crossway.

Wellum, S. J. (2016), *God the Son Incarnate: The Doctrine of Christ*, FOET, Wheaton: Crossway.

Wenham, J. (1985), *The Enigma of Evil: Can We Believe in the Goodness of God?*, Grand Rapids: Zondervan.

Wink, W. (1984), *Naming the Powers: The Language of Power in the New Testament*, Philadelphia: Fortress.

Witherington, B. (1992), *Jesus, Paul and the End of the World*, Downers Grove: InterVarsity Press.

Wright, C. J. H. (2004), *Old Testament Ethics for the People of God*, Downers Grove: InterVarsity Press; Leicester: Inter-Varsity Press.

—— (2006), *The Mission of God: Unlocking the Bible's Grand Narrative*, Downers Grove: InterVarsity Press; Nottingham: Inter-Varsity Press.

Wright, N. T. (1987), 'Reflected Glory: 2 Corinthians 3:18', in L. D. Hurst and N. T. Wright (eds.), *The Glory of Christ in the New Testament: Studies in Christology in Memory of George Bradford Caird*, Oxford: Clarendon, 139–150.

—— (2003), *The Resurrection of the Son of God*, Minneapolis: Fortress.

—— (2013), *Paul and the Faithfulness of God*, Minneapolis: Fortress.

Yarbrough, R. W. (2018), *The Letters to Timothy and Titus*, PNTC, Grand Rapids: Eerdmans.

Index of authors

Index of Scripture references

Romans (cont.)
5 – 8 *54*
5:1 *48, 58, 147*
5:1–11 *48, 49, 54*
5:2 *22n53, 38, 54,*
58, 60, 90, 193,
194, 199, 217,
226, 242, 250
5:2–4 *58*
5:3 *250*
5:3–4 *217*
5:5 *220*
5:6–11 *48*
5:8 *149, 214*
5:8–9 *220*
5:9–10 *58*
5:10 *48, 146, 147,*
207
5:10–11 *49*
5:11 *67, 148, 208,*
209, 249
5:12 *35, 79*
5:12–19 *205*
5:12–21 *23, 34,*
49, 78, 79
5:15–17 *79*
5:17 *79*
5:18–19 *49, 79,*
207
5:19 *82*
5:20 *55*
6 *56*
6 – 7 *55*
6:1 *56*
6:1–4 *50*
6:1–14 *56*
6:3–11 *56*
6:4 *4, 7, 12, 27,*
37, 38, 50, 90,
203
6:8 *195*
6:12–23 *56*
6:15–23 *56*

6:17 *208*
6:17–18 *56, 216*
6:19 *56*
6:20 *208*
6:22 *203*
6:23 *228, 229*
7:7–25 *57*
7:10–11 *104*
7:12 *57, 104*
7:23 *55, 216*
7:25 *216*
8 *53, 218*
8:1 *151, 218, 228*
8:2 *104*
8:7–8 *57*
8:9–11 *6*
8:10 *246*
8:11 *246*
8:14 *54*
8:14–16 *59*
8:15 *215*
8:16 *54, 217, 220*
8:16–17 *59, 188*
8:17 *38, 59, 60,*
61, 176, 193,
215, 217, 227
8:17–18 *199*
8:18 *38, 54, 55,*
59, 60, 91, 180,
193, 194, 195,
208, 215, 217,
227
8:18–19 *243*
8:18–23 *42, 199*
8:18–27 *4, 39*
8:18–30 *23*
8:18–39 *54*
8:19 *180, 195,*
244
8:19–21 *208*
8:19–22 *61*
8:20–21 *162, 226*
8:20–22 *35*

8:21 *38, 60, 195,*
215, 220
8:23 *59, 61, 208,*
215, 220
8:24 *42*
8:26 *220*
8:28 *26*
8:29 *25, 155*
8:29–30 *46, 218*
8:30 *38, 54, 55,*
60, 227
8:31 *218*
8:32 *219*
8:33 *219*
8:33–34 *144*
8:34 *219*
8:35 *219*
8:37 *219*
8:38–39 *54*
8:39 *219*
9 – 11 *62*
9:2 *62*
9:2–3 *222*
9:3 *114*
9:3–5 *136n27*
9:4 *18, 62, 63*
9:4–5 *62, 222*
9:5 *67, 251, 252*
9:11–13 *135*
9:14–24 *64*
9:17 *63, 212*
9:18 *63*
9:20–23 *6, 13, 22,*
23, 26
9:22 *64, 203*
9:23 *7, 38, 60, 64,*
203, 212, 227
9:25 *154n69*
10:1 *114*
10:2–3 *62, 222*
10:9 *120*
10:16 *182, 183*
10:17 *120*

11:13 *231*
11:13–14 *231*
11:17 *248*
11:26 *62, 222*
11:26–29 *62*
11:28 *62*
11:28–29 *62, 222*
11:30–32 *182*
11:32 *69, 252*
11:33–35 *69, 252*
11:33–36 *16, 23,*
25, 26
11:36 *7, 11, 69,*
202, 251, 252
12:1–2 *57, 85n22*
12:17–21 *179*
14 *52, 67*
14 – 15 *8*
14:1–2 *65*
14:1 – 15:6 *68*
14:1 – 15:13 *65*
14:6 *68, 252*
14:8–9 *68, 252*
14:13–23 *65*
14:17 *198*
14:22–23 *53*
14:23 *53*
15:1–6 *65*
15:2–3 *65*
15:5–7 *66*
15:6 *43, 66, 68,*
252
15:6–7 *8*
15:6–9 *17n43, 24*
15:7 *29, 43, 65,*
66, 68, 252
15:7–13 *65, 69*
15:8–9 *7*
15:9 *43, 69*
15:10 *69*
15:11 *69*
15:17 *250*
16:1–2 *101n9*

Index of Scripture references

Titles in this series:

An index of Scripture references for all the volumes may be found at http://www.thegospelcoalition.org/resources/nsbt.